VIOLENCE OF DEMOCRACY

VIOLENCE OF DEMOCRACY

Interparty Conflict in South India

RUCHI CHATURVEDI

DUKE UNIVERSITY PRESS
Durham and London
2023

Designed by A. Mattson Gallagher
Typeset in Garamond Premier Pro by Westchester
Publishing Services

Library of Congress Cataloging-in-Publication Data
Names: Chaturvedi, Ruchi, [date] author.
Title: Violence of democracy : interparty conflict in South India /
Ruchi Chaturvedi.
Description: Durham : Duke University Press, 2023. | Includes
bibliographical references and index.
Identifiers: LCCN 2022045985 (print)
LCCN 2022045986 (ebook)
ISBN 9781478020776 (paperback)
ISBN 9781478020011 (hardcover)
ISBN 9781478024606 (ebook)
Subjects: LCSH: Communist Party of India (Marxist) |
Rashtriya Swayam Sevak Sangh. | Bharatiya Janata Party. |
Political parties—India—Kerala. | Political violence—India—
Cannanore (District) | Right and left (Political science)—India—
Kerala. | Democracy—India, South. | Kerala (India)—Politics and
government—21st century. | BISAC: HISTORY / Asia / South /
India | POLITICAL SCIENCE / World / Asian
Classification: LCC JQ620.K477 C44 2023 (print) | LCC JQ620.
K477 (ebook) | DDC 306.20954/83—dc23/eng/20230213
LC record available at https://lccn.loc.gov/2022045985
LC ebook record available at https://lccn.loc.gov/2022045986

Cover art: Sasikumar Kathiroor and Natasha Vally, *Of Fear
and Peace*. Illustration courtesy of the artists.

For my parents,
Neelam and Gopal Chaturvedi

Contents

At the heart of this book is an enduring violent conflict between members of the party left and the Hindu right in the Kannur district of Kerala, South India. Green and picturesque, Kannur has a strong history of peasant and working-class struggles as well as interparty conflict dating back to the 1940s, when electoral democracy began taking root in the country. I use the term *party left* across the book to refer to members of the Communist Party of India (Marxist), CPI (M); the term *Hindu right* denotes affiliates of the Rashtriya Swayam Sevak Sangh (RSS), also known as the *Sangh*, and the Bharatiya Janata Party (BJP). Together I refer to the latter as the RSS-BJP.

I first began studying the violence between CPI (M) and RSS-BJP workers in Kannur in the early 2000s. The passage of time revealed how the violence between the two groups holds up a telling mirror to the ways in which political life and relations have been organized not only in India but also, more generally, in modern democracies. In this time, Indian democracy has taken a particularly violent majoritarian and authoritarian turn. Analysis of the decades-long violent conflict between the party left and the Hindu right helps us grasp some of the pervasive political factors underlying that turn. Political violence, in this work, refers to physically injurious acts associated with collective efforts to protect and perpetuate group interests or a shared understanding of good through engagement with instruments of rule. Post-colonial India, like large parts of the contemporary world, mobilizes tools of representative democracy to institute state rule and distribute power. This study of the violent conflict between the party left and the Hindu right in Kannur shows how features of democratic life have helped condition and indeed intensify various forms of group violence.

The last few years have been especially alarming in this regard. The year 2021 ended with Sangh-affiliated Hindu religious leaders calling for genocide of the Muslim population. In June 2019, when I began drafting this preface, the killing of twenty-four-year-old Tabrez Ansari in a small village in the eastern state of Jharkhand was staring me in the face. The details of Ansari's killing, like those of many others like it, are heartbreaking. I recount them here so as not to turn my face away from the violence surrounding us and the difficult questions it poses for Indian democracy. Here are, therefore, some terrible particulars of the incident: Residents of Dhatkidih village that young Ansari was passing through suspected him of stealing a motorcycle and subsequently beat him for twelve hours; during this ordeal bystanders jeered at and mocked Ansari while cheering on the assailants. They forced him to shout slogans such as "Jai Shree Ram! Jai Hanuman!" (Hail Lord Ram! Hail Hanuman!) associated with assertions of Hindutva identity.[1] In all this time, police failed to come to Ansari's assistance and continued to fail him by deriding him and mistreating his family when the incident was reported.

This incident is one of 902 reported hate crimes that took place in the country between September 2015 and June 2019, the first four years of Narendra Modi and the BJP-led National Democratic Alliance's rule. Attacks, assaults, and killing of Muslims by vigilante Hindu crowds have seen a particularly sharp increase.[2] Such attacks have, dare I say, become a normal part of life in the country: routine, commonplace, and appearing with predictable regularity. The details of each act of collective violence against members of the minority Muslim or Dalit community that have taken place since 2015 are disturbing due to the extraordinary cruelty, as well as the callousness, on display; at the same time, the cruelty and the callousness have started to seem very familiar, normal, and expected. I find myself, like many others, worrying and wondering if the normalcy of the exceptional violence India has witnessed in the last five years implies that our polity has been programmed to hurt, to be cruel, and to be callous. If indeed such programming has been at work, it has been happening for de-cades and we are now witnessing the outcomes. In order to explain what I mean by this programming and conditioning for violence, I move between the regional and the national, between Kannur, Kerala, and the country as a whole. I also move between the present and the past, going back to the years that make up the prehistory of the partition of the subcontinent in 1947, as well as the practices that make up the prehistory of the violent conflict between the party left and the Hindu right in Kannur.

The decades preceding the Indian partition saw intensification of competition for public visibility and electoral victories among elites who sought the backing of their respective local Hindu or Muslim communities in order to obtain a place in legislative councils and state offices.[3] Partition prehistory is hence, among other things, one of elite efforts to infuse local-level religious communities with new cohesiveness, and of competition between these communities as strong moral unities. When the drive to obtain regional and state power via elections (albeit with a limited franchise) escalated in the early twentieth century, the need for local-level Hindu and Muslim communities to graduate from their regional affinities and achieve broader unity became more pronounced. At the time, the Indian National Congress was ascending on the national scene not only as a popular anticolonial force but also as a contender for state power. Votes of the franchised Hindu electorate that now emerged as a clearly measurable majority supported this rise. Against this backdrop and in order to be nationally competitive, Muslim unity also sought to express itself in electoral victory for a single party. The Muslim League under Muhammad Ali Jinnah's leadership took on that mantle. This meant obtaining cohesion through public performances, while subsuming some local differences and accentuating others for the sake of a larger political collective that could dominate the national stage. Particularistic affiliations, kinship, and patronage networks now came to be mitigated as well as tapped and drawn into larger organized and sharply divided majority and minority—Hindu and Muslim—identities. These homogenized and polarized communities became important agents of the violence that accompanied India's partition. Since then, the push to homogenize and polarize has translated into repeated acts of communal violence. It has been iterating itself lately through terrible attacks against members of minority groups, especially Muslims.

Local-level CPI (M) and RSS-BJP workers in Kannur are not divided along religious, caste, linguistic, or cultural lines; occupationally and, in terms of their economic status, they share many similarities. And yet, the conflict between them resembles communal and ethnicized conflagrations that India as well as other parts of the world have repeatedly witnessed. I find this discrepancy analytically productive. My book studies the violence between socially similar workers of the party left and the Hindu right as an exceptional phenomenon that sheds light on the more typical antagonisms between religious and ethnically distinct communities. To explain my reasons for so reading the exceptional political conflict in Kannur alongside more normal forms of communalized conflict in the country, I proceed from the present moment we are in—in Kannur and in the country—while evoking the violence(s) of decades gone by.

The pattern of attacks and counterattacks, killings, and counterkillings between members of the CPI (M) and the RSS-BJP has not stopped in Kannur. Recently, in February 2022, workers from these two groups traded deadly assaults against each other, just as they have done in preceding years.[4] In May 2018, for instance, two local leaders—one belonging to the CPI (M) and another to the RSS—were killed within an hour of one another. The news headline, akin to those published in previous decades, announced: "CPM worker hacked to death in Kerala's Kannur, RSS activist killed in retaliatory attack."[5] Statements from the spokesperson of each group, carried in the rest of the news story, had them pointing fingers at each other. According to the first information report (FIR), filed at the local police station, both murders were considered to be "politically motivated."[6] The phrase *politically motivated* recurs prominently in police and court records that document violent acts by members of the two groups against each other. In many others, "political enmity" is cited as the impulse behind the acts of violence performed by the Communist Party and the Hindu right. The loaded phrase *political enmity* is layered with suggestions of antipathy and antagonism.

This book examines the nature of the antagonistic relations underlying political violence between members of the party left and the Hindu right in Kannur. Like hostility between religiously defined groups in other parts of the country, the clock of interparty conflict and antipathy in Kannur goes all the way to the first decades of the twentieth century that saw the coalescing of the anticolonial movement. In this heavy political atmosphere, parties of various ideological shades and social makeup were formed and came into their own. Struggles for social, economic, and political equality of the 1920s, 1930s, and 1940s revolved around the unjust nature of the caste and gender systems, in addition to peasant and industrial workers' rights. Simultaneously, aspirations for national and popular sovereignty were taking shape through both small and large collective efforts. In the midst of these struggles, the colonial government introduced a limited political franchise, as well as elected councils with restricted powers, that Indian elites could hope to join. Thus, Indian public life began to see the emergence of new political blocs across the spectrum of political thought competing for influence, legitimacy, and ascendancy.

It is important to understand the history of political life in Kannur in the beginning of the twentieth century in order to understand the subsequent interparty conflict and political violence in Kannur. To recount its details in this book, I wade through the autobiographies of emerging local politicos and leaders that reveal the collectives they forged, political practices and subjectivities they fostered, and contests that they were a part of at the time. I then turn to each decade between 1950 and 1990, finally ending my account of political violence in Kannur in the mid-2000s, when the political careers of some of my interlocutors who engaged in interparty violence in different ways started to wane. In this analysis, the production of enmity or antagonism between members of the Communist Party and the Hindu right in Kannur does not stand alone as a unique or peculiar phenomenon. Instead, as I noted previously, there are strong similarities between paradigms, practices, and processes that have generated other divisions, hostilities, and violent polarities in the country including those that preceded the partition of the subcontinent into the two states of India and Pakistan (India as a Hindu-majority state and Pakistan as a Muslim-majority nation).

Many factors contributed to the violence between Hindus, Sikhs, and Muslims in 1946–1947, when one to two million people from minority communities in different regions were brutally killed and nearly 75,000 women were raped. One crucial factor among them was the imperative to, in David Gilmartin's words, "cleanse" local realms of relationships with members of other communities.[7] And hence identification of Hindus and Sikhs on the one hand, and Muslims on the other, with their respective larger moral communities, could be more complete and purer. Purer majorities over the determined territories called India and Pakistan were thus instituted. Once the two states were founded with Hindu and Muslim communities as the numerically dominant groups in India and Pakistan, respectively, their unquestioned preeminence as the majority group in those territories was secured. That history informs the analytical thrust of this book. As we know, the tale of competing constituencies, competing *for* constituencies and competitive moral unities carries on. The search for cohesive political identities, assured electoral backing, and the consequent containment and cleansing away of dissenting and opposing groups has not ceased. This book argues that practices that propitiate this aggressive process are a normal aspect of representative democracies.

Representatives are chosen in constituency-based electoral democracies such as India on the basis of the majority vote. In its "first past the post" system, the party that commands the greatest number of votes in the greatest number of constituencies obtains greater legislative powers, ascends to the seats of executive authority, and becomes a major force. Systems of proportional representation also revolve around the drive to win as many votes as possible, albeit across constituencies. The practice of maximizing legislative majorities in both systems has very often proceeded via attempts to forge strongly tied local and translocal[8] communities that pitch themselves for a party or leader against an adversary. This book reveals how such a quotidian aspect of the democratic system has the propensity to divide, polarize, hurt, and generate long-term conflicts. I show how in Kannur representative democracy has, for many decades, helped to generate antagonisms between local-level members of political parties who are not otherwise separated along religious, caste, or ethnic lines.

Aggressive polarizing postures have not only been the hallmark of Hindu nationalist groups but have also shaped the lives and work of many in the Communist Party and, to a varied extent, other formations ranging from the Indian National Congress (INC) to the Trinamool Congress. This is what makes the violence between different groups in Kannur exceptional and yet so normal: different political parties and their cadres across the ideological spectrum live out the relentless drive to command a majority and become major, while rendering the opposition small or minor. To so minoritize, to make small the social and political capital of those who oppose and/or bear another dissenting identity, and to also injure them in the process, is an aspect of democratic life that has been playing out in Kannur just as it has been in various parts of the country for many decades.

Nationally, the tremendous rise of the extreme right is a testimony to the long and hard efforts that the RSS, the BJP, and their many affiliates have been making since the early 1920s to create the demographic majority that is the Hindu community into a permanent electoral and political majority.[9] Their work of tightening communal bonds and cultural identity as Hindus has gone hand in hand with opposing purported enemies of Hindutva, especially members of the Muslim community. The violence of the extreme right and the figures of its victims like Tabrez Ansari that we behold today is a legacy of these endeavors and of a political system that divides populations into majority and minority groups and provides grounds for practices of majoritarianism and minoritization.

India, however, is hardly alone in enacting such hurtful majoritarian politics. Independent India's ascent on the world stage in 1947 as a democratic republic heralded a new age of hope and optimism among colonized states across the world. Many followed in its footsteps and embraced multiparty democracy in the years to come. Four decades later, in the late 1980s, the end of the Cold War and the fall of the Berlin Wall provoked widespread euphoria about the rise of new democracies that would accommodate multiple identities, protect individual and group rights, and end totalitarianism. Since then, however, a range of organizations that develop indexes of democracy and score countries on the basis of variables such as political culture, pluralism, civil liberties, freedom of expression, and association have been raising alarm bells about the rise of ethnonationalism, "illiberal democracies," and "electoral autocracies."[10]

I suggest that such concerns may be raised not only about postcolonial states such as India or other "new democracies" like Hungary or Turkey, but also the older democratic polities of Europe and North America. There too, much like India, hostility against minorities, immigrants, and purported outsiders is a forceful part of political life. This hostility is not new; neither is it a sign of the degradation of older Western democracies. Indeed, to use Partha Chatterjee's words, "postcolonial democracies like India are today revealing features that were always a constitutive, even if concealed, part of Western democracy."[11] Substantiating this statement, Chatterjee recounts how authoritarianism and fascism arrived on the back of popular sovereignty and democracy in Europe. He reminds us of the annihilatory violence that Native Americans suffered in North America in the instituting instance of the American nation-state and democracy, and the structural, carceral, and police violence that Black, Latinx, and Muslim minority groups continue to face there. Violent minoritization hence emerges as part of a shared legacy that bedevils India as well as many other democracies across the world.

In this book I study interparty conflict in South India to highlight the ways in which representative democracies have facilitated the emergence of violent majoritarianism and minoritization. The young men of Kannur closely associated with the party left and the Hindu right, whom I write about, have aspired to the forms of equality and sovereignty that democracies promise. At the same time, I show how these local-level political workers, on the left and the right, have become entangled in the drive to obtain majority support, become major, and make minor those who oppose their respective parties. Biographies of party leaders and workers help me plot the ways in which competitive democratic politics in the region generated antagonistic violence. The violence of democracy, as workers of the party left and the Hindu right in Kannur have lived it, is central to this book.

Acknowledgments

This book was written over several years and in many places. It germinated in Kerala, found life as a doctoral thesis in New York, and was worked and reworked in Delhi and Cape Town. My friends in Thalassery and Kannur made the research possible. Baby, Suju, Premnath, and their extended family made Kabani a beautiful sheltering home. Premnath, Manoharan, Govindraj, P. P. Sasindaran, Pradeep, Neelima, Sasi, and Asha became supportive guides at different times helping me understand and navigate Kannur's fraught social and political terrain. Many others, linked to party networks, offered inroads and insights into those worlds. The Center for Development Studies campus, Trivandrum was my second base in Kerala. Sowjanya, Anne, Suresh Babu, K. Veeramani, Aziz, Arasu, and Sarmishtha brought camaraderie and laughter in the early years of the project. Praveena Kodoth, Beena, and K. Gilbert were trusted members of an encouraging network. Over the years, I have especially treasured J. Devika's friendship. I am inspired by the depth of her engagement with the world around her, her warmth, and her incisiveness. Devika also read an earlier version of the book manuscript. I have not necessarily answered the questions she posed but hope that its concerns and arguments will speak to her own.

Janaki Abraham and Dilip Menon belong to the small network of people whose research lives have revolved around North Kerala. Both of them in their different ways have supported this project for many years. Sharing the ups and downs of this book's journey with Janaki, a dear friend from my University of Delhi days, has been particularly meaningful. Deepak Mehta, Susan Visvanathan, Suranjan Sinha, J. P. S. Uberoi, Veena Das, Roma Chatterji, and Pratiksha Baxi were my formative teachers and seniors there. I have learned from their edifying voices and writings. I would also like to thank E. Valentine Daniel, whose generous spirit sustained me during my graduate career at Columbia University. His lessons about what it means to have an ethnographic eye, how to write, and how not to write about violence have guided me for many years. I was fortunate to have Partha Chatterjee as a co-supervisor. Chatterjee's large corpus of work on Indian polity and democracy has strongly shaped my analytical orientations and standpoints. A gentle and percipient interlocutor, his recent interventions have helped me hold together two disparate parts of the postcolonial world—India and South Africa—that I am invested in. They have hence enabled me to craft the intellectual and political location from which I revised and finalized this book.

Considerable work of revising and finalizing this book has taken place in Cape Town. Here I met Anaïs Nony, a formidable media studies scholar, who became my developmental editor. Anaïs steadily steered the project through the pandemic and lockdowns. She helped me obtain writerly nuance, clarity, and a voice in ways that I am deeply indebted for. Some friends and interlocutors know the multiple places, Kerala, Delhi, and Cape Town, where this book has come to life. Conversations with G. Arunima, Udaya Kumar, Sanil V., and Simona Sawhney have helped bridge analytical, political, and affective distances between these contexts; their scholarship and insights have enriched my own. Leslie Witz, Patricia Hayes, and Shaheed Tyob extended invitations to present in rich provocative forums at the University of the Western Cape and Stellenbosch University. Paolo Israel, Riedwaan Moosage, Nicky Rousseau, Brian Raftoplous, and William Ellis offered comments and posed questions that have stayed with me through the revision process. At other stages of the project, Karuna Mantena thoughtfully weighed in. Her observations allowed me to see its affinity with branches of political theory that I was previously unaware of. I would like to thank her for her consistent support for this project. Feedback I received at the Yale South Asia Council Conference, and the seminar at Center for Indian Studies, University of Gottingen has helped to hone my arguments. I would like to thank Srirupa

Roy, Rupa Viswanath, Nathaniel Roberts, Gajendaran Ayyathurai, Radhika Gupta, Razak Khan, and Shahana Bhattacharya among others for their close engagement with arguments of the book and their warm hospitality.

Lebohang Mojapelo and Emma Daitz put in valuable editorial labor. Smitha B. and Nirmala Nair assisted with final translations of two key autobiographical texts that have enabled me to access confusing parts of Kerala's complicated political history. Sunilkumar Karintha and I reconnected recently; I look forward to his own book on interparty conflict in North Kerala and am thankful for his assistance with translation of key parts of M. V. Raghavan's autobiography.

Grants from The Wenner-Gren Foundation, Harry Frank Guggenheim Foundation, support from Hunter College (City University of New York), University of Cape Town, and the Mellon Foundation–funded Other Universals Consortium made research and writing for this book possible. Sections of chapters 2 and 3 have been published in *Contributions to Indian Sociology* and *Cultural Anthropology*, respectively. Most of chapter 4 appeared in *The Tumultuous Politics of Scale*, edited by Don Nonnini and Ida Susser (Routledge, 2020). Ida Susser was a warm and attentive mentor at Hunter College. Jackie Brown, Francis Cody, Marc Edelman, and Sanjay Krishnan offered helpful advice as I was embarking on the book project.

In all the years that I have worked on it, I have been fortunate to have nourishing friendships. Jessica Rothman and Ignasi Clemente were fellow junior faculty at Hunter who became my buddies in the best sense of the word. Treasured friends, Jasmine Boparai, Sofian Merabet, Sonali Pahwa, Yukiko Koga, Jonathan Bach, Arudra Burra, Krista Hegburg, Dipti Khera, and Puneet Bhasin helped to make New York home. Uma Bhrughubhanda, Ravi Sriramachandran, Nauman Naqvi, Karin Zitzewitz, Anuj Bhuwania, and Trisha Gupta were links to so many things South Asian—from politics, to music, films, food, and art. Friends and comrades at early avatars of the South Asia Solidarity Initiative, Sangay Mishra, Balmurali Natarajan, Rupal Oza, Vidya, Biju Mathew, Prachi Patankar, Sangeeta Kamat, Ahilan Kadirgamar, and Sadia Toor showed me how to grapple with and strive for a better South Asia, from afar. My old and dear friends Jinee Lokaneeta and Bhavani Raman were also part of that formation. I have learned from the rigor and commitment they bring to their work on state power, law, and violence, and I have been enriched by their affection and my years-long bonds with them. Paula Chakravartty is that fierce, faithful, caring, and courageous friend who is a "must have." I thank her for being my "must have," always invested in my life, work, and well-being.

I am also thankful to my Cape Town peeps and "sistas." The list is admittedly long: Amrita Pande, Asanda Benya, Ari Sitas, Bianca Tame, Shari Daya, Jonathan Grossman, and Elena Moore. Natasha Vally, Blanche Hoskins, Adi Kumar, and Astrid von Kotze. Annachiara Forte, Koni Benson, Shekesh Sirkar, Kelly Gillespie, Leigh-Ann Naidoo, Lameez Lalkhen, Ciraj Rassool, Thiven Reddy, and Mark Hoskins. Together with the Makerere friends and colleagues, they made the move to a new continent and city a rich and rewarding experience. Nina Sylvanus and Antina von Schintzler are not based in South Africa, but they are cherished friends who helped me navigate and settle in its complex social and academic worlds. Jasmina Brankovic and Victoria Collis-Buthelezi have been steadfast mates who have helped me swim through challenging waters to arrive at calmer, happier places.

Some friendships defy time and space. I frequently find myself in conversation with the late Kavita Datla. Her ability to think across scales and to outline a more redemptive horizon through history writing was, I believe, exemplary. Her appreciation for this book project was a valued gift that propelled me along at an important time. I hope it has lived up to her rigorous standards. Rajyasri Rao, Shirin Khanmohamadi, Aparna Balachandran, and Teena Purohit are the kind of friends who I can only refer to as sisters from other mothers. I struggle to describe the importance of these besties in words and shall not try except to say that I would be bereft without them.

In his work and life, my brother Deepak is the epitome of sincerity, virtue, and passion. I am overawed by the ways in which he puts his heart and soul into the world around him. Deepak and my sis-in-law Rinchen Yolmo are our familial backbone. I cannot thank them enough for all they do to hold us up and together. The Khannas were my familial support in New York, and I am extremely grateful to them. Florence Pillay, Arvind Vasson, Aurelia, Anita, and the Narshis have helped recreate a new loving family. The late Nathan Pillay is dearly missed. He would have been proud and happy to see this book become a reality. I dedicate the book to the memory of my grandparents, my uncle Ashok Chaturvedi, and my parents, Neelam and Gopal Chaturvedi. They have not only been wellsprings of generosity, affirmation, and affection but also live a form of pluralism that I hope transcends the threats it is currently facing in India.

Suren is everything: the one who I share every idea with, who I iterate all my worries with, and who brings music, humor, care, and harmony into my life. Naledi has made our cup of life brim with joy, dance, and song. She has also made her parents slog more at their respective books. I look forward to celebrating them all.

Introduction

Kannur and India, Past and Present

This book studies a long-standing violent conflict between members of the party left and the Hindu right in the Kannur district of Kerala, South India. The term *party left* refers to members of the Communist Party of India (Marxist) (CPI (M)); the term *Hindu right* denotes affiliates of Rashtriya Swayam Sevak Sangh (RSS, or the Sangh as it is commonly known) and the Bharatiya Janata Party (BJP). The history of both the party left and the Hindu right's formation goes back to the late nineteenth and early twentieth centuries. Both the CPI (M) and the BJP have been part of provincial and national governments in independent India. When I initiated my research on the conflict between the two groups in 2001–2002, few people outside Kerala were aware of the political violence between CPI (M) and RSS-BJP workers that had been playing out in Kannur since the late 1960s. In the recent past however, particularly since 2014, Kannur has repeatedly grabbed national headlines. The year 2014 was an important turning point in India's contemporary political history. In the May 2014 national elections (and then subsequently in 2019), the BJP obtained a large parliamentary majority to become the reigning party of the country. Its rule has taken the country down a particularly violent majoritarian path. Kerala on the other hand, especially its northern district of Kannur, is seen as a bastion of the CPI (M). The Hindu right began making concerted efforts to generate popular and electoral support in Kerala from the late 1960s and 1970s onward. Since then, the Kannur district in the northern part of the province has witnessed intermittent but often dramatic violent confrontations, attacks, and counterattacks between local-level workers of the party left and the Hindu right.

I use the phrase "local-level workers" to refer to those on the left and the Hindu right who have been involved in a range of mobilization activities at the village, peri-urban, and urban neighborhood branches of the two groups. Attempts to gather popular and electoral support for their parties have often culminated in group or individuated clashes and attacks between left- and right-wing workers in Kannur. These clashes, attacks, and counterattacks have involved the use of fists, sticks, and homemade bombs as well as swords, daggers, and iron rods. Some violent acts have resulted in spectacular murders that have been memorialized, lingering in the memories of residents for decades. In various instances, the *rashtriya sangharsham* (political conflict) between local-level workers of the party left and the Hindu right simply produced a sense of foreboding and apprehension that something terribly violent might happen. At other times it led to numerous murders of CPI (M) and RSS-BJP workers in a matter of a few hours and days.[1] This has been the nature of political conflict between the party left and the Hindu right in Kannur.

These incidents, while significant for the persons involved and for the residents of the region, have fortunately not taken as severe a toll on individual and collective lives as several other conflicts across the country.[2] Nevertheless, in March 2017 the student branch of the Hindu right brought the conflict in distant Kannur to the national capital Delhi by pasting gruesome pictures of slain RSS-BJP workers across Delhi University's campus and adjoining neighborhoods. The posters accused the CPI (M) of sponsoring the murders of these RSS-BJP workers. Such accusations were part of a wider campaign to corner left-wing student collectives and undermine their credibility. Around the same time, in a vitriolic speech, an RSS *pracharak* (publicist) in Madhya Pradesh offered a bounty for anyone who would avenge the killings of right-wing Hindu workers in the southern state of Kerala.

In all these displays and statements, members of the Sangh sought to position themselves as innocent and abject victims of the dark and menacing "antinational" hand of the left, which they alleged had destroyed Hindu lives. These and other such actions set the stage for the BJP's month-long *Jan*

Raksha Yatra, or people's protection rally, that took place in October 2017 and moved through most major towns and cities of Kerala. All eminent RSS-BJP leaders participated in this rally where, once again, they erased their complicity in the Kannur conflict. They sought to not only paint the CPI (M) as an embodiment of so-called red terror but also conjoin it with what they referred to as Islamic terror. The Hindu right leaders asserted that the Muslims of Kerala, together with the left, were able and ready to violate the lives and well-being of the majority Hindu population. In the course of this rally and at several other junctures, members of the Hindu right reverted to its typical mobilization techniques—of creating schisms between different communities against each other, particularly the Muslim minority against the Hindu majority, and the secular left against so-called Hindu patriots—constantly positing RSS-BJP as the true representatives of the latter.

The Sangh's practice of creating rifts within the body politic has found a legislative expression with the introduction of a new citizenship law and national registry. These measures expose socially marginal groups, especially the Muslim minority, to the danger of being deemed noncitizens. Introduced in 2019, the new citizenship law contravenes the promise of equality that the constitution offers.[3] It transforms Muslims into a vulnerable underclass who must prove their place in the country. Members of minority communities, students, and others who protested new discriminatory citizenship laws have been targeted by state agencies as well as by the Hindu right's vigilante violence.[4] With this one law, the BJP-led state has legislated its majoritarian agenda and taken concrete steps to legally minoritize the demographically smaller and socially weaker Muslim community.[5] In this instance, I use the term *minoritize* to refer to practices that disempower a group in the course of establishing the hegemony of another. I recount these details of Muslim minoritization because I believe that the story of political violence in Kannur and the challenges that Indian democracy is facing today are linked. Essentially, while this book is about the recent political past, namely political violence in North Kerala, violent practices of minoritization that are currently unfolding in India offer sharp cues to understanding decades of violence in Kannur. In turn, Kannur's violent history illuminates structural conditions that have led India to its majoritarian present.

I define majoritarianism as a mode of rule that asserts and sustains the political, social, and cultural primacy of a numerically predominant group pitching itself against rights and claims of minorities. In his comparative account of the production of Jews and Muslims as vulnerable minorities in

Europe and late colonial India, Aamir Mufti situates the binary between major and minor in the history of liberal citizenship and secular nationalism.[6] He outlines the relationship between the legacies of European liberal enlightenment and the rise of majoritarian culture in a postcolonial state such as India. Secular liberal nationalism has historically upheld abstract equality and universality while propping up particular cultural, linguistic, and racialized groups as national subjects. Minorities have been offered putative equality and "protection," while national character has been equated with specific identities. The ground has hence been laid for the emergence of exclusionary polities. I suggest that in order to grasp the character and formation of these exclusionary states, we need to look not only at the contradictory priorities of liberal citizenship but also at the mechanisms of instituting rule and distributing power in modern democracies.

The principle of majority rule has a crucial place in modern democracies.[7] In the course of the twentieth century, it became the self-evident albeit imperfect route to realize aspirations for justice especially for those who were bearing the brunt of minority colonial rule. In the last two decades, scholars such as Qadri Ismail and David Scott, grappling with violent effects of Sinhala majoritarianism in neighboring Sri Lanka, have enjoined us to critically reflect on that equation between democracy and majority rule.[8] As Scott notes in a 1999 essay, "We instinctively recoil from those who appear to resist this transparent principle of political arithmetic." Such resistance suggests that we prefer rule of the lesser number or minority. "If not one, then the other: majority rule or minority rule. The binary is fixed."[9] Most modern democracies make accommodations and adjustments to protect minorities,[10] but they also continue to uphold rule of the majority as the source of their legitimacy.

The Kannur conflict compels us to come to grips with critical aspects of representative democracies that have fostered aggressive assertion of group identities, especially majority against minorities. Building on my study of interparty conflict in Kannur, I argue that violent majoritarianism of the kind that India has witnessed in recent times is not simply driven by an ideological agenda but activated and accommodated by the workings of representative democracy. Underlying majoritarianism are an assemblage of competitive practices through which various groups try to get the upper hand and become the winning force. In the next few sections of this introduction, I describe how and why I have come to identify the modern democratic system with the competitive struggle to gain ascendance, become major, and make minor. In order to do so, I outline the history of democratic models that postcolonial democracies such as India inherited from the Euro-American West. To use Sudipta Kaviraj's words, I consider democracy "unromantically" and "nonideologically"[11] as a phenomenon with particular beginnings, changing form and shape across time and space, as a bearer of liberatory hopes but also a political system capable of fostering homogeneity, divisions, and violence.

A Paradoxical Bequest

In Kannur, the drive to gain ascendancy translated into sharp antagonisms and political violence between the party left and the Hindu right. My account of its emergence seeks to illuminate modern democracy's violent propensities, revealing how democratic competition can cultivate violent modes of obtaining power. As I analyze the ways in which this propensity has iterated itself in North Kerala, I am guided by scholarship that grapples with concrete lived political histories in postcolonial societies with the aim of developing a "critical theory of modern democratic forms."[12] Partha Chatterjee and Sudipta Kaviraj's work has been particularly formative in this regard.[13] They remind us to not consign research located in the non-West to area studies or mere case study, but to take up the opportunities such research affords to arrive at generalizable incisive understandings of democratic life.[14] Both Chatterjee and Kaviraj have attended to the "real emancipatory force" of modern democracies.[15] They have described how democracy in India created prospects for equality, sovereignty, and popular claim-making on the developmental state. At the same time, both of them have observed how various forms of political violence have haunted democratic life in India. In his writings on popular politics, Chatterjee notes ways in which violence, criminality, and communitarian scripts have often accompanied collective assertions of marginalized groups.[16] Kaviraj discusses the presence of "untreated violence" that frequently accompanies elections but gets ignored in the din of party parleys, victories, and defeats.[17] The question of violence has not been central to Chatterjee and Kaviraj's work, but each one in his different way prompted by its prevalence calls for attention to the multiple paradoxes of democratic states such as India where "deep social exclusions, forms of fundamental economic injustice and great deal of violence"[18] continue to prevail and indeed intensify.

Alongside Chatterjee, I suggest that paradoxes are not only an aspect of life in postcolonial democracies; they have been built into the structure of the democratic order that postcolonial states across the globe have inherited.

Chatterjee's published lectures on populism exemplify a comparative approach, which attends to the history of postcolonial democracies like India in ways that shed sharp analytical light on the contradictions that have also dogged Western democracies.[19] In this work Chatterjee is especially concerned with the career of popular sovereignty, its disciplining in the liberal welfare states of Europe, and current passionate populist iterations that the turn to neoliberal governmentality laid the groundwork for. Chatterjee's analyses help the reader plot connections between insider–outsider divisions that have accompanied the rise of populism in contemporary Europe and North America, the emergence of charismatic authoritarian voices, and the role of melodrama and visual media in the workings of popular sovereignty as they have played out in India as well as the West. A close look at the career of political violence in Western democracies is outside my scope and capacity. But as I turn to understand the relationship between violence and democracy in Kerala and offer it as a lens to apprehend the role that democratic competition has performed in the production of polarized communities, I too turn to the history of popular sovereignty and the contradictory shapes that it has acquired in democracy's long career. The genealogical understanding of democracy and its various implementations across time and space helps us grasp the pitfalls of democratic power, its paradoxes, and its subterfuges. It especially enables us to relate the emergence of violent antagonistic political communities and the kind of interparty violence I study in this book to popular sovereignty's ambivalent bequest.

The longer history of popular sovereignty reveals the sharp disjuncture between forms of self-rule that the earliest democracies promised and the rule by representatives that has come to be accepted across the world in the name of democracy. Chatterjee maps this disjunction through Richard Tuck's history of political thought and the intellectual and institutional distinction that emerged, particularly from the sixteenth and seventeenth centuries onward, between sovereignty as rule by the people and sovereignty as rule by representative government in the name of the people.[20] The late Nigerian political scientist Claude Ake outlined this disjuncture in the mid-1990s at a time when his own country was reeling from military rule and struggling to obtain meaningful democracy.[21]

Ake traced democracy's long history and returned his readers to the Athenian instance when citizen assemblies sought to secure popular participation in the work of rule.[22] The decline of Athenian democracy was also mirrored several centuries later in the overshadowing of French revolutionary ideals of radical egalitarianism and its theory of popular sovereignty and participation. These were overtaken by the American model of representative democracy, which equates political equality with the equal right to compete and invokes popular sovereignty as a mode of legitimating government of those who compete successfully. Representative democracy, notes Ake, "repudiated" the meaning of democracy as direct participation and popular power.[23] To paraphrase Chatterjee, the democracy that emerged at the end of the American Civil War was, in principle, a government *of* the people; it also had the capacity to be a government *for* the people, but nowhere has its legacy translated into a government *by* the people.[24]

American founding fathers, including James Madison, advanced it not because they saw direct democracy as inexpedient but because they regarded representation as a desirable good in itself.[25] A republic in which the ratio of representatives to the represented could be limited was deemed more appropriate than local autonomy and comprehensive self-government. Since then, democracy has come to approximate a political form where people "cannot . . . actually rule . . . Democracy means only that the people have the opportunity of accepting or refusing the men who are to rule them."[26]

This "trivialized"[27] form of democracy was conferred on most of the postcolonial world, including India, in the late colonial period when colonial governments sought to placate increasingly effective liberation movements by introducing executive and legislative councils and granting some forms of native representation. They hence initiated a "new game of politics," opening the door for rule based on electoral competition and the majority principle to emerge as the most desirable and legitimate form of government.[28] Democratic legitimacy became equated with electoral victories and democratic politics with their pursuit. Democracy no longer offered equal right to participate in the work of ruling but equal right to choose rulers, and the equal right to compete in order to become rulers. One set of postcolonial elites after another accepted this model of democracy and entered into the fray to compete with and defeat one another.[29] In India, that included members of the party left and the Hindu right.

In some parts of the world, democracy as mere multiparty competition to become representatives and obtain state power paved the road for deployment of authoritarian measures to win the competition and ultimately the institution of single-party rule.[30] In others, this competition intensified the appeal to vectors such as ethnicity, race, language, caste, and religion. Political movements and parties have activated "divisive 'substance codes' of blood and soil" in the course of elections.[31] They have hence ignited and reignited conflicts and intense violence between communities in several electoral democracies across the world.[32] Writing about various parts of the African continent, Achille Mbembe describes how democratization and the vying for access to resources through state structures "clearly contributed to the resurgence of conflicts over autochthony and heightened tensions between a locality's autochthonous peoples and migrants and outsiders."[33] In Kenya, violence during electioneering over consecutive electoral cycles in the 1990s and 2000s became gravely gendered and sexualized.[34] These histories of violence pose critical questions for strands of political theory and discourse that see democracy as an essentially pacifying political system. Repeated elections and routine competition, scholars and public intellectuals maintain, makes losses bearable.[35] Given the ways in which various spheres of life are differentiated in modern times, losing political office does not have to mean economic and social losses. Property, honor, and status can continue to be maintained even in the face of political loss. Representative democracy, several political theorists argue, thus fosters peace.[36]

I agree that the "dramaturgy of democracy" makes violence and killing notionally unnecessary in the struggle to obtain power. But many democracies have routinely seen reinterpretation and relaunching of solidarities based on genealogy and territory.[37] This includes not only countries of the non-West, such as Kenya, Nigeria, Sri Lanka, or India where representative democracy was instituted relatively recently, but also Europe and North America, where the growth of anti-immigrant and white supremacist parties and leaders has brought back memories of dark interwar years.[38] How do we then account for this relationship between the formation of violently polarized communities and democratic life? So far, I have situated the answers that this book offers by reviewing the history of democracy and the center stage that competitive politics has acquired in it. In the next section, I further take up the question of competition by critically appraising the arguments of poststructuralist theorists of democracy who hail it. In the course of doing so, I also articulate my understanding of terms such as agonism and antagonism that I mobilize in this book to grasp the nature of interparty conflict in Kannur as it evolved through the decades.

Competitive Politics, Majority Rule, and Its Critics

The term *agonism* has acquired an important place in the work of theorists such as Chantal Mouffe, Bonnie Honig, and William Connolly. Animated by interpretations of the ancient Greek concept of the *agon*,[39] they have come to consider competitive struggles as the means for ensuring not just peace but also pluralism and freedom in diverse democracies.[40] Their focus however is not so much on the world of electoral gains and losses and forms of economic and social capital that might be retained in the face of defeat, but the act of competing and the subjective life of groups contesting one another.[41] Mouffe, Honig, and Connolly acknowledge that differences between various groups bearing a range of identities can be dogged. Institutions and ideologies, they rightfully remind us, are never so well-ordered that they fit all selves and subjects; resistances are constantly engendered, and new issues are always there to be settled. But contest, they maintain, is good for democracies; a shared sense of contestability of problems, they argue, can engender respect among competing identities. The possibility for what Connolly calls "agonistic respect," a form of respect steeped in and born of conflicts and contests between opponents, thus emerges in democracies where the seat of power, notes Mouffe (following Claude Lefort), is an "empty place."[42] Disruption, subversion, destabilization, relativization, and denaturalization of identities become desirable actions and practices in this normative universe.[43]

Agonistic respect, relativization, and denaturalization are indeed highly desirable practices that can help foster pluralism. However, I believe that theories of democracy that hail the possibilities of agonism fail to adequately engage with the workings of power that mark modern polities. Power in modern democracies may not be located in a person, substance, or place, and it may not always seize upon bodies to directly extract obedience or surplus from them, but it still structures the conditions of subject and community formation and shapes their inner lives.[44] This power is pastoral and governmental, addressing entire communities and populations as well as the individuals who constitute them. It is concerned with the health, security, and well-being of groups as well as appeals to individual minds, dispositions, and inner selves. Such power can, to quote Foucault, "make live and let die."[45]

The forms of social, political, and procedural equality that democracy offers in the face of this power, and the ways in which it promises to shield citizens from power's capriciousness, have historically been lopsided. Most democracies of the world are a site of a range of inequalities distributed along class, caste, race, gender, religious, or ethnic lines. Conditions of life and vulnerability to death remain unequally distributed. Democracies allow disadvantaged groups to claim rights, install their representatives, and seek access to state power. And while it is true that in a democracy power is not embodied in the person of a prince imbued with traditional authority, democracy still demands the appearance of "the people" as a vivid force. Such popular force may be enacted by people who are socially marginalized and/or mobilized by members of dominant groups. In order to claim rights, "the people" must iterate themselves as a strong unity; and, to influence elections and state power they must translate into a numerical majority even though theoretically they are expected to act as unmarked individual agents.

Plurality is possible here, but the persistent search to become a/the people and a calculable majority or measurably significant group is also pervasive. Even when collectives are forged on the basis of shared nonascriptive class or occupational status, they vest themselves with the moral qualities of community complete with real or fictive kinship bonds and symbols, rituals, and other collective representations.[46] A "politics of similitude"[47] and what Blanchot has called a "valorized relation of Same with Same"[48] crystallizes as these communities posit themselves in "us and them" terms while becoming purposive public actors.

Theorists of agonism suggest that competition can "contain" their adversarial postures; it can keep it (antagonism) at bay.[49] Their critics remind us that competition might also "entrench divisions" and polemicize them in ways that generate "hostility and aggression."[50] This book narrates how such hostility and aggression were produced among mostly "lower-caste," blue-collar members of the party left and the Hindu right in North Kerala. Elsewhere in the world, agents of this hostility and aggression have variously been ground-level supporters and members of a political group, as well as their representatives elected to highest state offices. As I noted earlier, a number of persons and parties in the present day and in contexts of the recent past come to mind. These range from Mwai Kibaki's Kikuyu and Riala Odinga's Luo supporters in Kenya's ethnicized polity; working-class, non-elite Justice and Development party voters in Turkey; plebian cadres of the Shiv Sena in Mumbai and the RSS-BJP in many other parts of India; and, of course, anti-immigrant white supremacist allies of Marine Le Pen and Eric Zemmour in France and Donald Trump in the United States. Symbolic, structural, and actual physical violence has been enacted by all of them and/or in their name in all these democracies. That violence, I argue, not only reflects the paradoxes of democratic life, but democratic competitive politics has also helped to condition and produce it.

I associate the term *politics* with "expressive, performative and instrumental" acts and practices mobilized in the collective pursuit of shared interests and good that appeal to or seek to subvert, channel, or occupy seats of state power and institutions of rule.[51] Such acts and practices include everything from a public rally to demand better land redistribution policies or access to education to maneuvers to obtain ministerial positions and violent attacks on groups or individuals. In modern representative democracies underwritten by the principles of competition and majority rule, the questions of winning and losing, obtaining ascendance, and containing or minoritizing opponents haunt all such actions. Actions that seek to transform this democratic order and obtain another system not hinged on the game of winning and losing, becoming major and making minor, also count as political. In part II of the book I associate such attempts with the quest for political justice rather than criminal justice.

Each political pursuit produces contests and schisms but also helps to transcend divisions.[52] Divisions and unities, the possibility of generating friendships and enmities, are an ever-present part of political life so understood. Such an understanding of political communities has considerable affinity with Carl Schmitt's writings on the topic. In Schmitt's scheme, the distinction between friend and enemy is posited as a defining character of political groupings.[53] Like his concept of sovereignty (identified with decision on the state of exception), Schmitt's concept of the political (identified with the friend–enemy binary) has an ontological always-already-given character that serves as its own explanation. In the first instance, it stands apart from acts and practices that make up politics.

The distinction between the political and politics became academically popular in the 1970s through Lefort's work.[54] Prathama Banerjee reminds us of the distinction he posited at the time between the political (*le politique*) as a formatively prior instance that shapes the order of things from the everyday work of doing politics (*la politique*)—mobilizing support, organizing collectives, rallies, and movements. Banerjee has incisively problematized this distinction between the political and politics that not only Schmitt and Lefort but a number of other theorists have also posited.[55] Each one, she notes in her recent book, conceives the political as a field accessible only to philosophy, which disciplines such as sociology, history, economics, and political science, preoccupied with the empirics of politics, cannot adequately grasp.

Like Banerjee, I do not proceed from the assumption that there is a "force, an essence, an orientation, a subjectivity, a site—that is a priori or ontologically political."[56] I do not seek to excavate an original ordering principle and trace its workings over time and space. Hence my analysis does not take off, for instance, from sovereignty as decisionism or a given ubiquitous life force that iterates through "self-born, excessive, and violent will to rule."[57] I also do not posit the friend–enemy distinction as a founding feature of political communities in order to explain interparty conflict in Kannur. Instead, I seek to wade through the details of North Kerala's recent history and examine murders and counter murders between workers of the party left and the Hindu right in Kerala to delineate how particular political modalities accentuated differences and hostilities, and conditioned violence in Kannur. Drawing on the formulation I offered earlier, politics here stands for collective pursuits, expressive and instrumental acts and practices of networks that grapple with or seek to occupy institutions of rule. By "coursing" through Kannur's recent past and pursuits of parties, their leaders, and workers, this book seeks to illuminate how competitive democratic politics encourages and accommodates violence as a mode of obtaining popular and state power.[58]

Competition and the imperative to become a major force are crucial pivots of modern democracy. We might even (after Banerjee) describe them as "elementary aspects" of representative democracy that are not simple, stable, or singular but "complex," "coded," and historically tied to each other in a paradoxical way.[59] Hence, while multiparty competition and majoritarianism are meant to cancel each other out, competition also serves as the condition for the emergence and cover for the persistence of majoritarianism. A review of Indian history shows that concerns about their effects on political life in India go as far back as the early twentieth century. Critics of the majority principle include the late nineteenth-century modernizing figure Sir Syed Ahmad Khan and Dalit leader B. R. Ambedkar who, alongside leaders of other minority groups, proposed measures to undo the tyranny of the majority at several critical junctures in the early and mid-twentieth century.[60] The anticolonial luminary, Mahatma Gandhi, also expressed deep skepticism about the workings of competitive politics and dangers of majoritarianism.

Gandhi questioned the emergent consensus that republican democracy anchored in competition to obtain majority rule was the most desirable way of organizing the postcolonial polity. Ajay Skaria highlights how Gandhi discerned a continuity between majority as a numerical category and major as a term that signifies the bearer of power who can prevail over others. The former in Gandhi's reading can be the agent of domination in the same way as the latter. The power of the majority and/or the major could exert itself through the show of hands, votes, or sheer "brute force."[61] A political system anchored in the rule of the majority would therefore always be prone to its forceful command. Furthermore, achieving and instituting a majority in modern democracies implies competing for it. The project of obtaining a majority might then entail not only holding sway and obtaining extensive influence but also containing, undermining, and reducing competitors, dissent, and opposition to a minor position. This book describes how the practice of containing political opponents transformed into brutal antagonistic violence in North Kerala.

For his part, Gandhi not only critiqued the practice of competition and the principle of majority rule but also another key feature of modern democracies, namely rule of law. According to Gandhi, like democracy, the modern-day legal system is also designed to become an instrument of immoral force.[62] It extends quarrels and mobilizes legal shrewdness as well as rhetorical and money power to obtain victories and inflict defeats.[63] In Kannur too, as I show in chapters 4 and 5, the courts became sites for extending domination of one group over another. The forms of justice on offer treated a number of local-level party workers unjustly. They also allowed interparty conflict and acts of violent domination to perpetuate by failing to interrogate the political system that conditioned this violence. This study of a more than five decades long conflict between members of the party left and the Hindu right in Kerala thus highlights the ways in which the modern democratic and criminal justice system produced and sustained interparty violence.

Political Violence in Kannur: An Exceptional-Normal Phenomenon

Violence—both routine and spectacular—between members of the party left and the Hindu right has occurred in Kannur since the 1960s in the course of competition over displaying party colors and symbols on walls and trees as well as altercations at polling booths and counting centers. Some incidents were hardly noticed while others that I call spectacular impacted the public domain with terrible force. I use the term *spectacular* to signify the latter.[64] Significantly adding to this violence was the keeping of equal scores of those attacked or killed, and then more terribly, seeking vengeance. It is important to note that workers of the party left and the Hindu right who have been involved in this violence as assailants and victims largely belong to the same social background. Assailants and victims from both sides have tended to be unemployed or semi-employed youth working as construction or headload workers, bus or auto drivers, cleaners, conductors, weavers, painters, and carpenters, or simply described in court records as "ryot" or agriculturists.[65] Many of them are members of the *Thiyya* community, a onetime untouchable group now deemed lower caste. Hence it is not their own or their potential supporters' caste or religious affiliation per se but competition *over* communities of potential supporters—ranging from members of various unions to residents of fishing villages—which impelled the conflict between CPI (M) and RSS-BJP workers.

In other words, unlike competitive group violence in many other democracies, political communities of the left and right in Kannur cannot be easily mapped on to divisive ethno-religious categories. Members of the two groups do not belong to ethnic, racial, linguistic, or religious groups that have been historically pitched against other. Nevertheless, competition over supporters has both polarized members of the two groups and created greater internal cohesion, feelings of oneness, and internal unity. The fact that workers of the two groups share similar backgrounds and are not divided along religious, caste, ethnic, or class lines makes this conflict between members of the party left and the Hindu right in Kannur exceptional. At the same time, this apparently anomalous phenomenon draws attention to what is general and typical: the ways in which competitive democratic practices influence the drive for creating cohesive but adversarial communities among the rank and file, or the so-called plebeian members of various political parties, and condition antagonism and violence between different groups. I note the exceptional nature of the political violence between the party left and the Hindu right that has prevailed for nearly five decades. It has frequently taken heinous dimensions, which members of the same religious, caste, and class background have inflicted and suffered on one another. At the same time, I seek to avoid exoticizing the region or mark Kannur as deviant; instead, I regard the political violence it has witnessed as that telling phenomenon that stands out like a clue revealing aspects of the surrounding world.

Read via the work of microhistorians like Carlo Ginzburg and Giovanni Levi, the exceptional is not the exoticized, deviant other to be explained only through its own "microdimensions" but that especially expressive entity that stands out and is discontinuous from the world around it.[66] At the same time, it is continuous and connected to it. Matti Peltonen is instructive when he describes this micro-macro link via the "method of clues" that Ginzburg and Levi proposed. He writes, "Take for instance the concept of the clue as a macro-micro relation. On the one hand a clue is something that does not quite fit with its surroundings, something that seems odd or out of place. It is in certain respects discontinuous with its environment. On the other hand, a clue leads thought to somewhere else, reveals connections, exposes some secret or crime. So there is continuity, too, which is equally important."[67] Edoardo Grendi describes such phenomena that are both continuous and discontinuous from the world around them, and that seem out of place but also explain the dynamics of a place as "exceptional normal" or "exceptional typical."[68]

Drawing on this concept of the exceptional normal, I closely examine the long-standing conflict between CPI (M) and RSS-BJP cadres in North Kerala and situate it in regional and national history. As I do so, I describe the conflict between the two groups as that phenomenon whose extremeness makes it stand out, but which also holds clues for understanding crucial typical aspects of modern democratic life. Other scholars of South Asia, such as Amrita Basu and Srirupa Roy, have also found the exceptional normal a productive framework for understanding political violence. They particularly mobilized it to analyze the Gujarat pogrom of 2002, when members of the Hindu nationalist Modi government in Gujarat actively commissioned a genocide. Electoral politics, a thriving civil society, as well as social and political movements anchored in the spirit of equality and popular sovereignty all contributed to the rise of the Modi government where crucial "usual" aspects of democratic politics did not just "countenance" extreme violence but "facilitated" it.[69] Basu and Roy thus describe Gujarat 2002 as an exceptional instance of state-sponsored majoritarian violence but one whose origins lay in democratic "politics-as-usual."[70] Its bases and effects, they write, can be traced "within the everyday, banal, often invisible configurations of politics and power in contemporary India."[71] The scale and nature of violence in Kannur has not been genocidal as it was in Gujarat 2002, but aspects that stand out as exceptional are its long-standing, intergenerational character spread over several decades, its often brutally vengeful character, and the fact that its victims and protagonists share similar social backgrounds.

Public discourse about the violence in Kannur has frequently focused on this intergenerational vengeful character. It has however done so in terms that not only draw attention to the exceptional character of the violence between the two groups but in fact pathologize the whole region and its people. Reductive writings that describe political violence in Kannur as the function of a cultural inheritance have contributed to this discourse.[72] They invoke descriptions of unbridled rage and belligerence that have characterized political contests in Kannur as evidence of a traditional martial culture of physical confrontations.[73] Other commentaries offer essentializing and racialized explanations of that inheritance.[74]

I take issue with these racialized accounts of Kannur's martial history and plot another genealogy that compels us to investigate the entailments of modern democratic life. I emphasize the latter not because I believe that an older martial culture has no resonance in current times but because I am wary of analyses that examine political experiences of the present only to describe them as residues of an archaic, apparently traditional past. The quest to upstage, or what I call the project of becoming a major force, is not peculiar to Kerala or India or the new democracies of the postcolonial world. The biographies and narratives of local-level political workers of Kannur that I draw on recount acts of aggression, rage, and the pain and agony of victory and defeat in the wake of party formation and competition for civic recognition and popular support. These affective strains have accompanied instances of interparty violence in Kannur since the early twentieth century. In my renditions of these instances, I have desisted from an interpretive mode that might make Kannur and its political and cultural ethos appear especially exotic or unique or reduce the violence to deterministic essentializing variables.[75] I address the exceptional character of conflict between the party left and the Hindu right in Kannur and paint vivid pictures of Kannur and its political life building on it to forge generalizable critical insights about modern democracies.

Going hand in hand with my skepticism about essentializing explanations of the political violence in Kannur are my concerns about evolutionary and historicist perspectives that tend to frame the violence as a sign of Indian democracy's immaturity and deviation from desirable norms. Norm deviation models posit postcolonial politics as a historical latecomer, a bearer of old cultural residues, and considered pathological or deviant because it does not approximate appropriate forms of the modern present.[76] One notable academic response to such exoticization and deficit-based paradigms has been to take the opposite route and insist on the unexceptional nature of sociopolitical life in the postcolony. Such responses have, for instance, come from scholars of contemporary African politics who have swung from one end to the other—from exotic to banal.[77] In these writings, Africa is not seen as apart from the rest of the world, but its history is "dissolved" in a "general flow" and described as an expression of the same modern forces, dispositions, and affects as anywhere else.[78] What stands out, however, are the ways in which Africa and more broadly the postcolony is described as the site of heightened contradictions and afflictions of modern life. Multiplicity of identities, violence, corruption, occult, and "excess and disproportion" in the ways in which power iterates are said to characterize the postcolony.[79] Offering "speculative interpretations"[80] of these excesses without a detailed account of the institutions that have produced them, such scholarship flattens the histories of different postcolonial contexts, blending and merging them with one another. In the end, flattened postcolonial locations are often rendered as little more than grotesque expressions of the dysfunctional aspects of modern life; their excesses in turn appear as an aspect of the postcolony's primordial character.[81]

In this book I have sought to avoid the pitfalls of a particularism that essentializes and often even racializes without giving in to a generality that effaces all specificity. In other words, I attend to forms of acting and feeling, exerting, and obtaining power that have accompanied interparty conflict in North Kerala while situating them across different spatial and temporal scales. I review various local, regional, and national circumstances that conjoined to produce the exceptional violence of the party left and the Hindu right in North Kerala; at the same time, I try to relate them to typical modes of social, political, and judicial power that prevail in different parts of the country and the world since the late nineteenth and early twentieth century.

Some specific aspects of Kerala's contemporary history are well known. It was the first place in the world to elect a communist government through the electoral ballot in 1957. That victory came on the back of intense peasant struggles under the Communist Party banner, which reached their zenith in the 1930s and 1940s. Together with the social and educational reforms of the early twentieth century, these agitations made Kerala and Kannur the site of dramatic iterations of egalitarianism and self-determination in a deeply hierarchical caste-ridden society. Here Kerala followed the lead of other parts of the country such as Bengal and Telengana, and parts of the world where assertions of social and political equality became more frequent particularly in the wake of anticolonial struggles. In early and mid-twentieth-century Kerala, calls for commonality, ideas of "one caste," parity, fairness, and the accompanying thrusts to appear and be acknowledged on the larger sociopolitical stage became increasingly vivid.[82] This was a time when large diverse collectives took to the streets of its towns and cities in *jathas* (political processions) demanding a fair price for their produce or work and an end to caste discrimination, police repression, and British rule.

In Kannur, members of the lower-caste Thiyyas formed a key part of this new egalitarian public seeking better living conditions but also striving to become more visible in everyday political life.[83] One section of this large caste group managed to rise up the social ladder through educational and occupational opportunities that missionary education and offices of the Madras presidency provided during the colonial period. Over the decades, others, who followed the "traditional occupation" of toddy tapping,[84] who became "beedi workers," who did blue-collar work such as masonry or carpentry, who did daily wage work in the construction or transport industry, or who had been unemployed and semi-employed, joined the Communist Party in large numbers. Many remained indebted to the party's land redistribution reforms and welfare-based public policies and continue to occupy its lower echelons. From the late 1970s onward, Thiyya youth and their families residing in different parts of Kannur were also drawn to the Hindu right as it intensified its mobilization among them.

In the 1970s, 1980s, and 1990s, Kerala's model of development gained exceptional global fame when it came to be exalted as a state that had provided its citizens with high levels of well-being (a high literacy rate, low infant and adult mortality, and low levels of poverty) without the stimulus of an industrial revolution. Nationally and regionally, the party left frequently claimed credit for its developmental success that can also be attributed to other factors ranging from state intervention in the early twentieth century to the Gulf migration of the post-independence era. In the meantime, the Hindu right pushed its own ethnonationalist discourse as well as welfare-based *sewa* (service) strategies to obtain greater influence in several parts of the country, including Kerala. On the ground, local-level members of both groups sought to mobilize support for their parties and leaders by forging networks of care and assistance, helping people access educational and health services, a place in a school, a bank loan, or a hospital bed for residents of small neighborhoods, towns, and villages. They became conduits of pastoral power[85] on behalf of their groups competing to obtain popular legitimacy, electoral success, and state control. Pastoral power and hegemonic forms of masculinity, as I map in part I of the book, have played an important role in the production of interparty contests in North Kerala.

Part I: Pastoral Power, Masculinity, and Interparty Conflict

Pastoral practices of power seek to shepherd entire groups and populations, attending to their welfare while shaping subjectivities and molding everyday practices. In her critical account of Kerala's development model, Jayakumari Devika describes how the exercise of this pastoral power allowed Kerala's "upper-caste" communist leaders to reinscribe hierarchical relations with members of Dalit and marginal groups at the receiving end of their largesse. Such "secularization of caste," as she notes, is not entirely peculiar to Kerala but part of a general trend seen across the country where "egalitarian developmentalism" remade caste relations even as it attacked caste.[86] Marginal groups became beholden to those who dispersed welfare and care, leading to the formation of political communities that reciprocated care with votes and other expressions of support. In time, members of caste groups such as the Thiyyas also took up local and regional leadership positions among political communities allied particularly with the Communist Party but also the Hindu right. These new leaders were not upper-caste patriarchs and overlords of yore but big-brotherly figures from relatively underprivileged backgrounds who were equal to but also more equal than some others.[87] These leaders (some of whom are protagonists of the chapters that follow) extended practices of disbursing welfare and care but also embodied a form of political masculinity that has become hegemonic in contemporary Kerala[88] and modern life more generally.

Devika's work on early and mid-twentieth-century Kerala helps us situate the emergence of this hegemonic political masculinity. She describes how even as caste hierarchies came to be enforced less rigorously, presumed gender differences, and beliefs about the inherent capacities of women and men, became a major organizing principle of life in Kerala.[89] Cultivating distinct gendered capacities and enacting them in civic and domestic domains became a sign of growth and freedom for both women and men. If women were associated with the power of "tears, prayers and gentle advice," which they could mobilize to foster sympathetic family life, men were respected for the public influence they could gather, the intellectual reflections they could offer, and the economic stature they enjoyed.[90] These capacities were especially celebrated in Kerala's political sphere. The protester, the mass mobilizer, the skillful administrator, and the shrewd manipulator who could forge and sever pacts and deals became the idealized masculine political figure by the 1950s.[91] Women who pursued political careers had to mimic these figures and gain their badge of "honorary masculinity" in order to succeed.[92]

These historical developments form the backdrop of the opening chapter. Biographies and self-narratives of several male political figures of Kannur who rose to prominence as well as those who remained on the ground are central to the first three chapters that make up part I of this book. Coupled with police and news reports, and secondary literature on regional and national events, their narratives help me plot the political structure, context, and affective landscape that conditioned decades of interparty violence in North Kerala. In tracking the formation of adversarial and antagonistic political communities of the left and the right through the lives and careers of these political figures active in the region, this book sheds light on two related hegemonic masculine scripts: first, of righteous rage as a form of ethical agency that the literary scholar Udaya Kumar also writes about in his study of political stalwarts of early and mid-twentieth-century Kerala.[93] And, second, a script that marks life in several democracies characterized by the sheer drive to expand influence. Acts that iterate the first script include ardent outbursts reminiscent of Fanonian modes of masculinist anticolonial resistance that several postcolonial scholars have drawn attention to.[94] Such acts that recur in many modern democracies also mobilize the "narcissistic ego" through the competitive imperative to become ascendant and come out on top.[95] The play of this ego, the "elder brother's seizure of the father's place" in modern democracy, writes Juliet MacCannell, undermines hopes for justice, equality, and freedom.[96] Fraternity in this order of things, as Carole Pateman famously noted, becomes a "brotherhood of men."[97]

The emergence of young party leaders embodying a hegemonic political masculinity in pre-and post-independence democratic Kerala is central to chapter 1. Autobiographies of such leaders form a key part of the prehistory of the violent conflict between the party left and the Hindu right that I go on to analyze further in chapters 2 and 3. These chapters describe how feelings of love and care, as well as hate, circulated among the close-knit fraternal communities that workers of the party left and the Hindu right forged particularly from the late 1960s to the early 2000s. This period coincided with the new more populist phase of the Hindu right and its intensified attempts to become a stronger presence in Kerala and other parts of the country. I elaborate how a mimetic power struggle between the CPI (M) and the Sangh drew in young men from the two groups through the 1980s, 1990s, and early 2000s, generating feedback loops of aggression and violence, as well as tying them together into vengeful affectively charged kin-like communities strongly opposed to each other. While my analysis of these political communities is guided by insights about the masculine character of modern democracy that feminist theorists such as MacCannell and Pateman have offered, the analytical terms that I mobilize to articulate its character are reflective of my own intellectual biography and owe more to the history of India's struggle with majoritarianism, and agonistic theories of democracy and their critiques, which I have outlined in previous sections. The two sets of analytical frameworks are however aligned. Each one helps parse out how representative democracy compels greater homogenization and polarization to the point of producing competitive communities of vengeful men ready to enact terrible violence.

Part II: Judicial Responsibility and Subterfuge

Over the years, several young men—local-level workers of the left and right in Kannur suspected of various violent acts—have tried to run fast and far from the police and other state-juridical apparatuses. However, as members of legitimate political parties bound by law, a large majority of workers of the two groups have also submitted to the law's instruments and penal processes. Simultaneously, both groups have mobilized judicial processes against their adversaries, subjecting members of the opposing party to long and grueling criminal trials. Part II of the book revolves around these criminal trials.

According to my computations, more than four thousand workers of various parties have been tried for acts ranging from criminal intimidation to murder and attempted murder of members of the opposing party in Kannur in the last five decades. In each of these prosecutions, lawyers have imputed an intent to murder, or attempt to murder, intimidate, or enact other forms of violence on individual workers. The actions of these alleged perpetrators have been adjudicated in micro sequences and set up as a question of individual guilt or innocence. In the courts, justice has meant, first and foremost, prosecuting and punishing individuals who struck the violent blows.

Thus, even though the conviction rate has been extremely low, suspected persons from both groups have been named, identified, described, and tried as sources and agents of violence. In many instances, particular members of the two groups have been prosecuted at the behest of the opposing party. Trials in district and appeals courts have stretched for years and sometimes for more than a decade. Often prosecutors and judges have described the workers as "dangerous," "depraved," and pathological beings,[98] and on some occasions have called for capital punishment. In a few instances, district court judges have awarded the death penalty.[99]

Revolving around themes of rights and attributes, law in modern democracies regards individuals as bearers of specific capacities and as possessing particular properties. Actions and their consequences are believed to emanate from these capacities and properties, which can be abstracted from the contexts in which they surfaced and imputed back to individuals to hold them responsible for their deeds. In the midst of doubts and anxieties about such reasoning, judges seek to implement the individualizing judicial logic. At the same time, the fixing of judicial responsibility has been collectivized. Since the institution of modern criminal law in India, individuals have not only been judged on the basis of their concrete action but have also been acquitted or punished depending on their social and political identity. In chapters 4 and 5, I discuss the more recent and long history of that individuation and collectivization of responsibility.

Scholarship on the ways in which the Hindu right's violence in Gujarat has been adjudicated in recent years, along with the ways in which religious minorities, members of lower-caste groups, and left-wing collectives who have challenged state hegemony have been persecuted, shows that while culpable members of the Hindu majority community have often escaped punishment, a punishing legal system has beleaguered the former. In postcolonial India, due process, evidentiary requirements, and provisions around detention without trial have been fashioned and bent depending on the identity of those under scrutiny and the community—majority or minority, hegemonic or dissenting—that they belong to. The criminal justice system's methodological individualism has thus persisted side by side with impunity for majoritarian collectives and unjust imputation of responsibility for minorities and minoritized communities.

In light of this legal history, chapter 4 analyzes the ways in which trial courts have adjudicated the conflict between the CPI (M) and the RSS-BJP in Kannur. I argue that while trials of those who, for instance, carried out the 2002 pogrom of Muslims in Gujarat can be cited as extraordinary examples of the role that the law has come to play in majoritarian assertions, courts in Kannur have become everyday examples of the ways in which the battle to become a major force and minoritize the opposition has been fought through the criminal justice system. Since the ascension of the Hindu right to state power in 2014 and the BJP's election victory in 2019, majoritarianism in India has revealed its most aggressive face. In tandem, the legal system is playing an active role in promoting it. Legal impunity for the dominant and their violence and judicial persecution of minorities, and those who dissent against the hegemony of the Hindu right is pervasive. Chapter 4 analyzes the judicial face of the determined drive to become major and minoritize the opposition in which the lives of local-level workers of the CPI (M) and the RSS-BJP in Kannur have been caught up for decades.

In chapter 5, I step back into the annals of Indian legal history to give an account of how individualization and collectivization of responsibility were instituted in late nineteenth-century colonial India. Individuation, as I document, has been offering a cover for persecution of particular marginal collectives. Since 2014 that violence, exacted through widespread use of exceptional laws, has taken a heavy toll on social and political activists opposed to Sangh ideology and rule. In the backdrop of multiple arrests and cases against them, I critically examine judicial understandings of action and agency that on the one hand impugn individuals and on the other hand allow law to become a tool for repressing and minoritizing designated groups. I describe the impact of these twin strands of individualization and collectivization of punishment on the lives of workers of the party left and the Hindu right in Kerala and outline what an alternative form of justice in the context of political violence might look like.

Processes, rules, and judicial ideologies that focus largely on particular individuals as culpable antidemocratic agents of political violence produce a double subterfuge. They help mask the ways in which responsibility is collectivized and justice itself becomes majoritarian. Furthermore, judicial individuation of political violence allows us to forget how modern democratic principles and processes condition it; it obscures the ways in which exceptional violence of the kind we have seen in North Kerala is indeed typical—facilitated by well-instituted and accepted modern democratic principles, processes, and propensities. Rules of criminal law, penal processes, calls for retribution, deterrence, and the many rationales underlying individuation of responsibility hence perpetuate institutional forgetfulness about the role that modern democratic systems themselves play in producing political violence.

This book presents a genealogy of democracy and violence in Kannur through the lived encounters of party workers with principles of equality, popular sovereignty, majority rule, competition for popular and electoral power, and criminal law. These encounters bear the specific marks of Kannur and Kerala's history, which in turn conditioned particular kinds of political subjectivities, communities, dispositions, and propensities to action and violence. If we don't consign these subjectivities, communities, and Indian democracy to a lower rank or the category of a radical other in a normatively defined hierarchy of persons and polities, then we may regard this book as a means of understanding a shared contemporary political condition.

I

Pastoral Power, Masculinity,
and Interparty Conflict

Containment and Cretinism

THE EARLY DEMOCRATIC DECADES

Over the years, various media commentators and vocal members of the regional and national public sphere, as well as lawyers and judges, have characterized political violence in Kannur as the work of depraved and diabolical individuals.[1] These members of the legal and media fraternity, including lay people whose pronouncements contribute to local popular understanding, have described Kannur as an exceptional place filled with citizenry with an almost pathological proclivity for aggression and conflict.[2] I acknowledge the extraordinary nature of the political violence between members of the party left and the Hindu right in Kannur. However, I do not concur with the manner in which it has been pathologized. Instead, I maintain that the violence between the two groups is an exceptional-normal phenomenon whose extraordinarily long-running career, the terrible forms that it has taken, and the ways in which it has pitched members of the same social backgrounds against each other illuminate preexisting dynamics of competition for influence and support that are typically found in electoral democracies.

In this chapter, I track the constitution of democratic life in Kerala as a field of forces wherein the competition to be victorious, obtain electoral majorities, become a major political actor, and form governments, in time, became violently abrasive. I posit, additionally, that Kannur's violent politics is best understood through the quotidian need to contain the influence and reach of one's competitors and opponents. Contrary to arguments put forward by a range of theorists of agonistic democracy and others,[3] I plot a distinct trajectory of contests where political competition has not led to the noncombative flourishing of multiple standpoints, parties, and their passions. Instead, competition set parties on a course of violent confrontation with one another from an early period in the history of democratic Kerala. That violent course panned out over several decades and generations, affecting local-level party workers' ways of thinking about and doing politics. These violent confrontations began taking shape with another phenomenon that has come to mark the political landscape of the country: namely what Marx, Engels, and the communist leader K. Damodaran called parliamentary cretinism, or the tendency to equate purposive political action with the drive to obtain parliamentary power by gaining more seats in representative institutions.[4]

Present-day India reminds us of the important role that containment and cretinism can perform in electoral democracies. In recent years, the calculated and resolute attempts by the leaders of the BJP to obtain a parliamentary majority has enabled the Hindu right to initiate violent majoritarian rule. Currently unfolding is an exceptionally aggressive politics of not just containing but also reducing minority groups to the status of social and political minors under the Hindu right's rule.[5] The Hindu right has been a key protagonist in the political conflict in North Kerala since the late 1960s and 1970s. However, the story of containment and cretinism in Kannur that I tell in this chapter features members of other political parties such as the Indian National Congress (INC), the Congress Socialist Party (CSP), the CPI, and the Praja Socialist Party (PSP).

The history of the participation of these parties in the politics of containment and cretinism reminds us that these phenomena are not peculiar to any one left- or right-wing formation but make up crucial aspects of democracy itself. Furthermore, in India as in many other electoral democracies, containment politics and parliamentary cretinism have emerged alongside the democratic desire to realize an egalitarian society and popular sovereignty. Ideas of a more egalitarian society and polity often found an important place in the ideological makeup and practical actions adapted by the parties that I write about in this book. I argue that while a modern democratic ethos centers the search for equality and popular sovereignty, the nature of equality and society on offer in electoral democracies has been distorted. Historically, as discussed in the introduction, rather than substantive social equality, electoral democracies have only offered political equality. Furthermore, instead of effective popular participation in decision-making and executive institutions, it is only the equal right to compete that modern representative democracies have extended to their citizens. India is akin to other representative democracies where popular sovereignty does not imply people's actual rule, but rule in the name of the people. Here too, trivialized democracy[6] was instituted as rule in the name of the people through the elected representatives of the people.

Claims of representation and political legitimacy in North Kerala were underwritten by two other phenomena that I elaborate in this chapter. I am referring to the workings of what Foucault has called pastoral power and a masculine script of collective action that equates freedom and sovereignty with the assertive overthrow of a dominating force. In North Kerala, practices and pronouncements of pastoral and masculine power in the name of group freedom combined to enable young upper-caste men to emerge as notable party leaders and create conditions ripe for the formation of an intensely competitive political field. In the 1940s and 1950s, this competitive political field was made up of INC, socialist, and Communist Party members. By providing an account of the formation of this contested field, and the ways in which the accompanying democratic drive to become a majority involved members of various groups in the region, I seek to track continuities and discontinuities between interparty confrontations of an earlier era and the more recent CPI (M)–RSS-BJP conflict.

I thus lay the groundwork for my analysis of political violence in North Kerala and its relationship to the history and life of democracy, its egalitarian promises, its modes of generating collectives and communities, and the competitive and conflictual paths it sets them on. Anchoring my historicization of violent containment politics and cretinism in Kannur are the self-narratives of two leading political figures from the region. I locate their narratives in the provincial and national context of the 1940s, 1950s, and 1960s but also turn the clock back further—to the 1920s and 1930s—the decades when the socialist and communist parties were formed.

The two autobiographies that I turn to are the well-known communist leader A. K. Gopalan's English language memoir *In the Cause of the People: Reminiscences*, published in 1979, and of PSP leader P. R. Kurup's *Ente Nadinte Katha, Enteyum*, published in 1985.[7] Born a little more than a decade apart—in 1904 and 1915, respectively—both Gopalan and Kurup lived through critical periods of pre- and post-independence India when new publics began forming. It is at this time that large agitations espousing the cause of groups—ranging from lower castes, labor, peasants, youth, and teachers—became pervasive in Kerala and other parts of the country as political parties were constituted and various principles and apparatuses of an electoral democracy were inaugurated. Gopalan and Kurup participated in political life of the time as young recruits of the Kerala Congress, and then the CSP.[8] Gopalan emerged as a prominent Communist Party leader and Kurup rose through the Congress and later the socialist ranks.

Writings from various historians assist me in outlining the agrarian and caste relations crucial to understanding the emergence of socialist and communist parties in Malabar and its world of mass action and competitive electoral politics. Set against this backdrop, I draw on Gopalan's and Kurup's memoirs to describe the ways in which upper-caste men like them mobilized support for political parties as they sought to forge close ties with the local populace lower down the caste and class hierarchy, particularly those who belonged to the large Thiyya community. Important insights are also gained into their daily modes of interacting with fellow party members, along with vivid snapshots of the milieu in which competition for support between various political formations gradually transformed into violent contests. Both autobiographies thus aid in discerning the contours of political subjectivities and networks that began emerging in Malabar in the early twentieth century as a new political ethos anchored in ideas of equality, popular sovereignty, and representative institutions started taking shape.

Agrarian Relations and the Caste Question

An erstwhile district of the Madras presidency, Malabar, came under direct colonial rule in 1792. The British colonial government ruled the other two provinces of Travancore and Cochin, which make up the present-day Kerala, indirectly through a series of treaties reached with their princely authorities in the course of the nineteenth century. Direct rule in Malabar reinforced landlord domination over sharecroppers and tenants.[9] Upon identifying various landholding castes or *jenmis*, colonial authorities granted them private proprietorship rights over land, and thereby reduced all tenants to the status of insecure tenants-at-will.[10] As the population grew and the occupant-to-land ratio shrank in the early 1900s, tenants and sharecroppers found themselves at a considerable disadvantage, while the lack of corresponding industrial growth exacerbated their precarious economic situation. In a context where most landlords were the upper-caste Nairs and some

Namboodri families, and tenant cultivators and agricultural laborers were the purportedly inferior Thiyyas, Pulayas, and Cherumas, caste hierarchies and practices continued to be maintained on unequal terms.

In the ritual hierarchy, Thiyyas, the largest subgroup of those classified as Hindus in North Kerala while placed below the Namboodris, Nairs, and other artisan castes, were placed above marginalized groups such as Cherumas, Pulayas, and Nayadis.[11] In the early 1900s, the Thiyyas also made up the largest proportion of agricultural tenants in Malabar. Indeed, sharecropping was an agrarian practice found in Malabar to a far greater extent than in other parts of the country.[12] The position of the sharecroppers was made precarious, not only due to the new property rights granted to jenmis under colonial rule but even more so by the economic depression of the 1930s.[13] Consequently, small landholders had to increasingly turn to agricultural labor to supplement their incomes. In the meantime, insecure tenancies, growing depredations by landlords, the rising population, and the shrinking occupant-to-land ratio contributed to a growing agrarian crisis in Kerala. These trends toward proleterianization led to a series of fierce rebellions among the Muslim tenants of North Kerala against British officials and Hindu landlords in the early twentieth century.[14] Other tenants, particularly from lower Hindu castes, took to another form of radical politics—the one promulgated by the newly formed CSP.[15]

The CSP in Kerala became the breeding ground for the cadres and leaders of the CPI. In Kerala, leaders like P. Krishna Pillai, E. M. S. Namboodripad, and Gopalan were, by the mid-1930s, simultaneously rebuilding a Congress organization shattered by police repression during the civil disobedience movement, forming the local unit of the CSP, and laying the foundations of the Communist Party in Kerala.[16] While doing so, these young rising leaders sought to replicate the practices adapted by CSP activists in places such as Andhra and Bihar. In both Andhra and Bihar, CSP activists had developed close connections with the emerging peasant movement, helping to organize and train them as well as articulate demands for abolition of zamindari (the exacting system by which landlords collected revenue on behalf of the colonial administration).[17] Against this backdrop of developing peasant struggles, the Kerala Communist Party (KCP), a branch of the CPI, was officially formed in May 1939.

The KCP joined forces with the peasant unions that had stepped up their activities in Malabar. In well-documented accounts, various sociologists and historians have described the KCP's relationship with peasant unions, the latter's practices and methods, confrontations with the Malabar Special

Police, and how these contributed to greater support for communists in Kerala in the 1940s.[18] The 1940s was also the decade in which the peasant struggles for rent reduction, also known as the *Tebhaga* agitations, took place in Bengal. In nearby Telengana, the Communist Party took over administration of four thousand villages and established "soviets," which seized land and distributed it among agricultural laborers.[19] In Kerala, too, land redistribution and peasant radicalism played an extremely important part in the success of the communist movement.

Simultaneously, other factors have to be taken into account to understand the ways in which the social and political landscape of Kerala changed in the first half of the 1900s, particularly between the late 1920s to the 1950s. Key among these factors is the question of caste. Caste reform movements had become exceptionally strong in Kerala by the late nineteenth and early twentieth centuries. The agricultural workers union, the CSP, and the CPI both drew on existing anticaste campaigns and contributed toward radicalizing caste-based movements in their own ways.[20] At times, CSP and Communist Party–led movements became almost indistinguishable from the movements for caste equality, especially in Travancore and Cochin where they became closely identified with civic campaigns against upper-caste landlords.[21]

In North Kerala, conflation of demands for caste and class equality went hand in hand with internal differentiation within the larger population of lower-caste groups such as the Thiyyas. The relatively better-off economic position of several landed Thiyya families did not correspond to their lower rank in the status and ritual structure of the late nineteenth and early twentieth century.[22] Additionally, while the percentage of landowning Thiyyas was relatively small, by the early twentieth century an elite class had emerged among them, deriving their position from education, employment as lawyers and civil servants, involvement with trade and commerce, and setting up of factories. What the emergent Thiyya elite brought with them were new ideas and practices of caste equality, which in turn played a significant role in the emergence and consolidation of the communist movement in North Kerala and what has been described as Kerala modernity more broadly.[23]

Dilip Menon elaborates on the crucial contribution that evolving understandings of caste equality made to the creation and expansion of a "community of worshippers" around lower-caste shrines. Many landed Thiyya families sponsored an increasing number of festivals, alongside other lower-caste groups such as Vannans and Malayans. They were also key participants in rituals that deified not just local deities and spirits worshipped by members of lower castes and tribal groups, but also lower-caste victims of upper-caste authority.[24] These rituals, practiced at various shrines, were often marked by the transgression of rules governing interaction between lower and upper castes. The transgression of caste rules did not however transform ritual events into vividly egalitarian phenomena. Nevertheless, according to Menon, the ways in which shrine festivals, and the accompanying rituals, undermined caste practices led to gradual albeit relative displacement of hierarchies and practices that enforced inequality in the social sphere.[25]

Interestingly, this displacement and the emergent community of caste equals met with resistance from Thiyyas themselves. Several Thiyya groups sought to restrict the benefits of such displacement to fellow Thiyyas only. One such form of restriction and resistance was their opposition to temple entry for untouchable caste groups considered lower than them. Indeed, it was not until the late 1930s and 1940s that the growth of peasant unions and widespread agitations for land reform gave rise to new class-based unities that could undo the hold of existing caste hierarchies. Menon gives us a detailed history of this period when the collective action of peasant unions became the grounds for challenging caste-based practices of deference.

Across the countryside old hierarchies were being challenged, further contributing to the tensions between peasant unions and the police force that was brewing at the time.[26] Conflicts between peasant unions and police in the 1940s came on the back of a severe food crisis, which lent extreme urgency to the collective actions of peasant unions against landlords. A tense, confrontational atmosphere, combined with the state's willingness to use violence in support of the landlords, laid the grounds for the emergence of what Menon has described as a contingent "community of peasants as against landlords."[27] Slogans such as "land to the tiller" also appealed to a range of groups.[28] The affiliations, which peasant unions established across castes, in turn weakened practices of caste subservience and authority. These alliances were further buttressed when, drawn toward socialism, younger members of upper-caste families increasingly opted to support cultivators and tenants in their demands against their landowning households.

Gopalan and Kurup were two upper-caste young men who identified as supporters and leaders of poor peasants and agriculturalists and whose autobiographies, comparable and divergent, are important for this study. Additionally, Gopalan and Kurup are, as I noted earlier, the key protagonists of this chapter in which I mobilize their autobiographies to map the social landscape and contested political field of Kerala in the early to mid-twentieth century. To commence my account of the contested political field they were a part of and helped create, I begin with Gopalan's self-narratives.

Peasants, Pastoral Power, and Equality, or the Making of Political Work

Gopalan's portrait is a consistent presence on the walls of the CPI (M) offices across Kannur. His smiling visage is proudly prominent on party posters for everyone to see. His widespread visual presence is a testimony to the crucial place Gopalan occupies in the pantheon of leaders of the party left in Kerala, and the country as a whole. Frequently evoked in conversations about the party's glorious past, the CPI (M) Kerala state committee's social media page describes A. K. Gopalan or "AKG" as "a great revolutionary ... a great Communist who lived with the people, learned from them and led them in ... many inspiring struggles."[29] The page continues to recount the leadership role he played in social reform movements, in the CSP and the Communist Party, and the ways in which this "general" of the poor deployed parliamentary democracy to advance "the cause of the people."[30]

Gopalan's own account of his life and career from the late 1920s to early 1970s tells a similar heroic tale and is part of a long tradition of teleological histories of political movements and the figures who led them. At the same time, Gopalan's self-narrative is a lot more than a description of greatness: his autobiography brings alive forms of collective action, association, and negotiation that have produced both emancipatory and unjust scripts associated with modern democratic life in pre- and post-independence India. It reveals modes of thinking and acting that have conditioned lives of many local-level political workers of Kannur who have been involved in violent conflicts over the years. His biographical account allows us to grasp what an egalitarian public personality looked like in early twentieth-century North Kerala, and the kinds of relationships that such personalities forged with peasants and so-called ordinary people of the region.

This category of ordinary-ness, together with other adjectives that suggest deprivation and helplessness, dominate Gopalan's self-narrative, and give us an insight into the evolution of the relationships between local socialist and communist leaders, on the one hand, and residents of the region lower on the caste and class hierarchy on the other. While subsuming groups lower on the caste order in homogenizing terms for the poor, Gopalan plots his transformation into an exemplary anticolonial, socialist, and eventually communist leader. That transformation, according to Gopalan, occurred as a result of assertive collective action, emphatic instantiations of popular sovereignty, and the CPI's turn to electoral democracy and victories that the party strived for, especially from the early 1950s. His discussion of political work from the 1950s onward contains many references to intense electoral campaigns and big electoral successes alongside tensions, rivalries, and tugging and shoving between various dominant political groups. Gopalan unpacks these issues in his autobiography that predictably begins with the familial but soon shifts to the broader neighborhood, village, and community that his family was a part of.

Like some of his leading contemporaries in the KCP, Gopalan belonged to a prominent landed Nair *tharavadu* or household of North Malabar. The power and influence that such families enjoyed was usually anchored on their caste status, affluence, and traditional right to rule.[31] However, the slowly creeping economic depression of the late 1920s and the reduction in the prices of cash crops such as pepper and coconut began affecting most major households of the region. In the meantime, changing notions of family, marriage, and property led many tharavadus to partition into smaller fragments.[32]

Gopalan grew up in a nuclear section of his family, and this nuclear setting is central to his descriptions in the opening pages of his biography. Here, Gopalan pointedly foregrounds the life and activities of his reformist father, a public figure in his own right. A prominent member of the local Nair society, Gopalan's father edited a weekly publication about his community, and started an English medium primary school in the early 1900s. Gopalan tells us that his father was interested "in the public needs of the sub-district" like diversification of agriculture, construction of bridges and drainage, as well as equal education for girls.[33] Rendering his father as a man of his times, Gopalan highlights how the new forms of education, movements for social reform, lower-caste struggles, missionary activities, and colonial governmentality were producing rapid social transformation. With these descriptions of the activities that his father engaged in, Gopalan recounts the social world of the early twentieth-century Malabar that influenced and stimulated his own evolution as a modernizer deeply invested in the well-being of his local community.

The trope of public and social work is perennial in Gopalan's narrative, as he gradually links it to his transformation from an energetic schoolboy to a responsible schoolteacher. School became a setting in which Gopalan could live out his own nascent egalitarian public-minded consciousness and start enacting forms of pastoral power, which became a key characteristic of celebrated masculine political figures by the 1950s. Devika describes pastoral power as the hallmark of reformist upper-caste men and progressive leaders of the time.[34] Relevant here are two sets of practices that Foucault associated with nonecclesiastical modern expressions of pastoral power:

efforts and claims to care for the welfare of the flock, and an address to the community as a totality while also appealing to the inner dispositions of the individual selves who make it up.[35]

Schoolteachers were especially well placed to embody and enact early forms of pastoral power and emerge as leaders who allocated to themselves the "moral right" and agency for uplifting the "hapless" poor.[36] The transformation of schoolteachers as young enlightened leaders occurred in a context where, with the coming of missionaries, many schools began opening their doors to members of lower castes as well as girls.[37] Subsequently, several upper- and lower-caste associations also started schools across the region. Lower-caste associations increasingly equated literacy with freedom from poverty and inequality, and thus education became a source of affirmation for groups relegated down the social and economic ladder.[38] By 1931, Malabar became the district with the highest school-going population in the Madras presidency, and schools emerged as key sites for the production of new political actors—students and educators.[39] We encounter Gopalan's descriptions of his work as a schoolteacher, and a public/social and political worker, against this backdrop. He writes:

> A teacher's life is wholly a kind of public service. Just as a reactionary teacher can turn his pupils into puppets of the present ruinous educational system, a revolutionary teacher can instill patriotism, a sense of freedom and the courage and stamina to fight against oppression and social vices in the minds of boys who are to become citizens of the future. A teacher can of course turn his wards into bureaucrats by insisting on blind loyalty to superiors. He can also make them soldiers of war in the battle to salvage the country from the present educational, economic and political morass. The greatest service that I rendered as a teacher was to instill political consciousness in my students.[40]

As the preceding passage suggests, in Gopalan's view the work of inculcating political consciousness was closely linked to the opportunities for performing public or social service that Gopalan obtained as a teacher. He describes how he frequently visited students and their families at home, spent extra time with students who were flagging, and played games with them during free time. And, like other young emerging leaders in the area, he also undertook public works that included repairing roads and cleaning tanks for the families and households that made up the local community.[41]

Descriptions of acts of service, care, and consciousness raising thus recur in Gopalan's autobiography just as they do in accounts of many modern political leaders who have sought democratic legitimacy through popular support. He builds on this account in ways that further sharpen our insights about what was understood as political work in early twentieth-century North Kerala, what mobilization entailed for an upper-caste, progressive leader like him, the emerging forms of hegemonic political masculinity, and the pastoral underpinnings of the relationships that budding leaders cultivated with the wider populace.

Gopalan's reflections on his work during the 1940s agrarian movement are particularly telling. While writing about activities in the movement, Gopalan mentions a "special trait" that peasants lower down the social ladder possessed: "If there is somebody to guide them," he notes, "they are ready for anything."[42] Elaborating in that vein, Gopalan describes himself as one of the key people in North Malabar who would guide peasants lower down the caste and class order, rid them of their "childish" fears of the police and other elites, "arouse" the poor, and impel them to action.[43] Underlying his political work, Gopalan maintains, were the ways in which he attended to the community as a whole, as well as to particular individuals and their families; his efforts were meant to benefit one and all but were also apparently extended one act of care and consideration at a time.

In a deeply hierarchical society, pursuits and acts of care intimated the need to address the issue of caste prejudice and discriminatory practices. Like many upper-caste leaders of the time, Gopalan describes instances when he apparently transcended caste prejudices. In his young days, Gopalan tells us, he braved many beatings to attend Thiyya weddings, eat there, and publicly defy norms of purity and pollution.[44] Subsequently, he became an active participant in the temple-entry movement for those considered lower caste and went on to marry Susheela Panicker, who was from an Ezhava family (albeit a well-established one). At each juncture in his narrative, Gopalan links his egalitarian disposition to his public works and mobilization activities; simultaneously, he plots a transformation in himself and the world he mirrored, and upon which he acted as a political agent.

Freedom and the Masculine Subject

Nationally this period—in the late 1920s, when Gopalan began his political life—was a time when the anticolonial movement and the INC were advancing fast under the qualified hegemony of dominant peasant groups and urban upper classes. Subaltern mass actions often found themselves absorbed into and appropriated by this flow. At the same time, an independent left challenge was also emerging with the growth of trade unions, radical student and peasant organizations, and the formal inauguration of the CPI in Kanpur in 1925.[45] Soon after, in 1928, massive demonstrations took place in several large cities against the all-white Simon Commission that the British government appointed to institute constitutional changes in India. Consolidation of trade unions in this period also encouraged unemployed youth, industrial, railway, jute, and textile workers in cities such as Calcutta and Bombay to make much louder demands for radical social and economic transformation through large-scale prolonged strikes.[46]

However, toward the end of 1928, leaders of the CPI chose to shift the attention of the mass movements they were leading. On the advice of the Soviet Communist International (Comintern), they decided to stop aligning with INC nationalists as part of a united anti-imperial front and instead focus the party's attack on exploitative Indian capital and the "middle-of-the-road" Congress politicians who represented it.[47] In Kerala though, sharp schisms between socialists, communists, and the INC did not emerge until the late 1930s. Till that time, the anticolonial struggle under the aegis of the Congress continued to be the rearing ground for a number of important left-inclined figures like Gopalan.

In his self-narrative, Gopalan describes this period as one when he was becoming deeply aware of the slave-like cudgels of colonialism, drawn to the anticolonial struggle led by Gandhi, Nehru, and the INC, as well as excited by the events in Europe and the Russian Revolution.[48] The civil disobedience movement of 1930 and the mass actions that took place in North Kerala have a particularly important place in his account, for it is in the course of these events that Gopalan experienced the pinnacle of popular collective action, sovereignty, and the associated affects. Describing one of the first *jathas* (political processions) that he was part of during the civil disobedience movement, Gopalan writes: "Somebody was walking in front drenched in sweat in the scorching sun. A short man had turned grey. Behind him were some followers brimming with patriotism. A very dark-complexioned youth was singing excitedly, and the others were singing in chorus. A jatha that would thrill anyone. Unknown to myself, it stirred me, and a flash passed through my heart."[49] The flash that passed through Gopalan's heart might have been signaling a range of things. Gopalan frames that moment and the jatha as an equalizing space of collective action, which produced a sense of "we" subsuming the diverse "I," "him," and "her." His account testifies to the ways in which, over the years, incorporation of the individual in the collective, or the "I" in the "we," became a key pivot of twentieth-century

Kerala's political sensibility.[50] Eight years after this jatha, in the midst of the struggle against the Travancore ruler's policies of restricting suffrage and the agitation for "responsible government," the upsurge of this "we" became even more compelling and overwhelming for Gopalan.[51] The police apparatus was at work, and violence was in the air, but Gopalan was enthused. He wished to embrace the violence and become a martyr. In detailed, vivid, and celebratory prose, he notes:

What enthusiasm! What ardour! What courage! Firings were a daily event. People were dying like flies. The army was out in the streets. I was thrilled by the courage of the vast populace.... Completely unconcerned about the guns and *lathis* [batons] of the army and the reserve police, they seemed to say, "Your firing is like grass, grass to us, to be trampled underfoot." Forgetting myself for a moment, I shouted "State Congress *ki jai*," "Travancore people *ki jai*" [victory to State Congress, victory to people of Travancore]. That was the chant of these youthful agitators. A spectacle that would have electrified anybody with a human heart or a pulsating body.... I yearned for an opportunity to die a victim to the police firing. I believed that my death in this vast stir—in this upsurge of the brave Travancore people fighting for responsible government—would serve a purpose. I felt an urge to die.[52]

With these words, Gopalan outlines and hails a political subject who disrupts old hierarchies and loudly proclaims an impulse to sovereignty and equality. He describes himself and others around him as emboldened agents of resistance who undermined the feudal pater's authority,[53] were drawn to mass action, and experienced the excitement of merging with a collective, taking on an oppressive force, and embracing death. Often cast in a quintessentially masculine form, such a subject lends himself to what David Scott has termed the "alienation-realization" script of liberation.[54] Especially associated with anticolonial forms of struggle, this Fanonian narrative posits a "hydraulic" tension between power and freedom, suggesting that if the yoke of repression is lifted the oppressed self would be free.[55] The possibility of self-realization and freedom, as per this paradigm, proceeds from that instance when the violence performed by the colonized undoes the colonizer's authority.

Violent encounters between the colonized, particularly masses of small peasants and tenants, and the colonial constabulary were to come to North Kerala very soon. On their part, socialist and communist leaders like Gopalan decried what they described as individual acts of terror but upheld the rebellious energy of collective action over Gandhian methods of *satyagraha* (firmness bestowed by truth)[56] and nonviolence.[57] A number of other noted political figures of Kerala also participated in the hydraulic model of freedom and action. Udaya Kumar's discussion of the life narratives of the Ezhava leader C. Kesavan (1891–1969) and Kumbalathu Sanku Pillai (1898–1969) of the Travancore State Congress, together with Gopalan's Malayalam memoir, gives us a sense of the place that aggressive expressions of righteous indignation had in their worlds.[58] Kumar notes: "Rather than a disciplined and reflective apprehension of the world, their [Kesavan, Pillai, and Gopalan's] life narratives privilege spontaneous moral reactions marked by a good deal of physical courage and a strong sense of masculinity.... A spontaneous masculinity, which is unable to hide or control its just outrage and turbulent emotions, underlies the conception of ethical agency in these narratives."[59]

Gandhi appears as an important reference point and even an inspiration in the autobiographies of all three political stalwarts of Kerala—Kesavan, Pillai, and Gopalan—that Kumar has written about. At the same time, like many others, all three also engaged in modes of political action that Gandhi often denounced. In the course of his career Gandhi had categorically criticized expressions of popular sovereignty that, according to him, lacked premeditation and reflection. Associating frenetic agitations with communists and communism, he had decried unreflexive collective actions in 1920;[60] in the same vein, Gandhi warned against the heady character of a general strike while censuring the call by socialist leader Acharya Narendra Dev for one in 1934.[61]

This was the same year that the CSP, critical of more indigenous capital-friendly sections of the Congress, was constituted as a distinct wing within the party. Gandhi maintained his critique of the forms of political action that the socialists supported while also sharing a close rapport with some of them.[62] And, while they shared a tense relationship with parts of the Congress leadership, socialists continued to grow in strength in different parts of the country, generating popular sentiment against colonial authorities as Congress members. During this phase, Gopalan too was an important socialist leader of Malabar as well as a Congress member. Indeed, his mobilization efforts contributed to the constitution of a Congress committee office in almost every village. These offices were run together with reading rooms where socialist and communist texts were disseminated and discussed on a regular basis. Circulation of this literature went hand in hand with the formation of eighty local unions, two district unions, and a Kerala-wide trade union congress.[63] At the same time, more conservative sections of the leadership sought to resist the socialist and communist penetration of the INC. Congress was now said to be divided between "Congress of the rich and Congress of the poor."[64] While the former successfully linked the anticolonial movement with struggles against exploitation by landlords and questions of caste discrimination, fights for control of the internal working committee as well as newly constituted representative institutions followed. In the wake of those clashes, Gopalan went on to join the Communist Party of India while Kurup remained in various other incarnations of the Socialist Party for a long time.

The Coming Government and the Fights to Represent

The 1939 elections for the Malabar District Board occupy an important place in the contentious history of the Congress in Kerala and Gopalan's biography. During this period, District Boards administered schools and hospitals and were responsible for the running of charitable endowments, and for tasks such as construction and maintenance of roads.[65] They were, therefore, well placed to carry out the kind of functions that are often identified as public works, which Gopalan and his peers referred to as social work and which I have associated with exertions of pastoral power. Increasingly, endeavors to facilitate and improve the conditions of people's lives, assisting them with school and hospital admissions, constructing and maintaining the roads around their homes, and ensuring sanitation, and other infrastructures of well-being, had a reciprocal dimension. In other words, those who performed and delivered these public works increased their chances of winning popular and electoral support.

The District Board elections of 1939, therefore, were taking place in a new emergent political field in which governmentality, political legitimacy, and the chances of electoral success were increasingly entwined. However, while public or social work may have expanded support for a particular leader or party, in order to effectively carry out that work, parties and their leaders needed to be elected to seats of government offices and boards. Organizations contending for greater influence thus found themselves competing at elections, trying to gain the upper hand while simultaneously seeking to contain and neutralize the opposition.

This was also true of the Congress and the socialist and nonsocialist wings that had emerged within it. Each wing of the INC hoped to obtain representation on the board, and concurrently, all wings were increasingly finding themselves at loggerheads with each other. According to Gopalan, "intense rivalry and bad blood" between the socialist and nonsocialist wings of the INC soon followed during the 1939 District Board elections.[66] The air was filled with condemnations, recriminations, and aggressive efforts that each wing directed against the other to restrict the influence of the other. "Disturbances" were organized to "upset" the elections, and "ballot boxes were cordoned off" to impede electoral victories for the socialists and communists within the INC.[67] Nevertheless, socialist-sponsored candidates in alliance with the Muslim League won at the polls,[68] and soon after, Gopalan together with ninety other Congress colleagues broke away to form the Kerala unit of the CPI.

The CPI's close cooperation with the Krashaka Sangham saw the beginning of the heightened phase of agrarian unrest that I briefly recounted earlier. As is well documented, agitations in Mattanur, Morazha, and Kayyur led to clashes with the police, the deaths of three policemen and two beedi workers, and the eventual execution of three young protesters.[69]

The late 1930s and 1940s were eventful years in the life of the Communist Party for additional reasons: A long-standing ban on the CPI was lifted in the wake of its support for Britain's war against fascist forces. This support led to charges of collusion with the colonial state. At the same time, the lifting of the ban also enabled the party to carry out mobilization activities and draw more and more support for its advocacy of economic causes.[70] The party hence grew as an important pro-peasant and working-class force, especially in places such as Malabar, other parts of present-day Kerala, Bengal, and Andhra, and many urban centers in central and North India.

The winter of 1945–1946 brought elections for provincial assemblies via limited franchise and separate electorates. With the end of colonial rule and an imminently independent government in sight, Congress chose to focus all of its energies on the elections. Separate electorates and communal voting patterns introduced a new phase of majority-minority politics in the country, characterized by extreme polarization and the subsequent violence between members of the Hindu and Muslim communities. Leaders of the CPI had misgivings about the elections to come, the intentions of the colonial government, and the polarizing ways in which the British were instituting electoral politics in the country. Nevertheless, the party chose to join the "last battle" against colonial rule.[71]

Only 13 percent of the total population was eligible to vote in these elections. The CPI emphasized the need for universal suffrage; at the same time, it "embraced" the idea of representative government and put up 108 candidates across the country.[72] In constituencies where Congress and CPI candidates opposed each other, the competition between them was frequently intense.[73] Gopalan reports a "bizarre incident" that took place in the course of his election campaign, when a man under the influence of alcohol "set up by some Congress friends" drew a knife and dashed toward him.[74] Gopalan escaped the attack and describes it as part of a plan to distract him with security concerns and legal matters. He lost the 1945 elections but writes that he remained unfazed.[75] The travails of the period serve in his narrative as the backdrop of his statements about the party's electoral victories to come.

The first set of major electoral victories for the CPI came in 1951 with universal suffrage in the now independent India.[76] Just prior to that, however—between 1948 and 1951—the CPI went through a particularly challenging and complicated period that many analysts and party members, including Gopalan, refer to as its "adventurist"[77] or "ultra-left" phase.[78] Encouraged by the mass action in Telengana, Malabar, and other parts of the country, this difficult period was initiated when, on advice from Moscow, the CPI's new leaders promulgated a single-stage struggle for people's democracy as democracy and socialism to be waged from below. While B. T. Ranadive emphasized large-scale urban strikes, Rajeshwara Rao called for peasant guerilla action.[79] However, this rebellious line did not have widespread public support, and their hopes for such insurrections were thwarted. Furthermore, the party lacked organizational strength to sustain the insurrectionary approach through long-term armed activities and underground work. Key leaders of the party were arrested, and prison became the place where the detained leaders debated the insurrectionary line.[80] In the wake of the failure of the "insurrectionary thesis," and after many deliberations and discussions with members across the country and the Soviet allies, the party developed a different "tactical line" to achieve its political goals.[81]

The CPI's newly forged tactical path integrated parliamentary methods into the program of attaining people's democracy. In other words, the CPI gave up the call for a single-stage transition to socialism in favor of bloc by bloc, "step-by-step dislodging of the bourgeois from their honorable position."[82] There to lead and persuade party comrades about parliamentary methods as more than just a tactic but part of the party's key strategies, was well-known communist leader from Kerala, E. M. S. Namboodripad.[83] Gopalan described the crises of that era and the attempts to overcome it in these words:

Towards the end of 1951 a new experiment was initiated. The Communist Party decided to give parliamentary democracy a trial. The Party had made mistakes. It had over-involved itself in heroic and adventurist activities. But these were all undertaken with the welfare and interest of the people as the overwhelming aim. Members of the Party had been willing to suffer any hardships for this. Their selfless living had helped to forge a bond between themselves and the people. It was because of this that the people welcomed the Party wholeheartedly when it emerged after correcting its mistakes. The 1951 election was a proof of this.[84]

The CPI and CPI-led fronts won the majority of seats in Madras, Hyderabad, and Travancore-Cochin provinces with popular candidates such as Gopalan elected by huge margins. In 1957, Gopalan won again in the reconfigured constituency of Kasargod. The INC-led opposition campaign against him that year was especially strong and even featured public meetings by Prime Minister Nehru. The opposition, Gopalan tells us, was all set to celebrate his defeat by erecting effigies of him, his wife, and daughter to set alight in anticipation of his election defeat. But, in his words, "the awakened people of Kerala frustrated them [the opposition]. The enemies who were waiting to celebrate my defeat and thus to demoralize the comrades and sway the election in other constituencies slunk away as my victory was officially announced. My victory was to be the harbinger of a long series of victories."[85]

Both the party and Gopalan exalted in these new successes. Communist Party members had disavowed the parliamentary process between 1948 and 1951, but they were no strangers to polls and campaigns that sought to translate popular support into electoral triumphs. While the restricted electorate and its conservative character meant that the CPI and Gopalan did not fare well in the 1945–1946 elections, a new era of electoral competitions had risen.[86] At the same time, a comparison between the 1939 and 1951 moments helps to illuminate certain things that remained the same.

In 1939, the competition for the Malabar District Board had become the occasion for a contentious unraveling of the relationship between socialists and communists such as Gopalan and Namboodripad (who were, at the time, still members of the INC) and the more conservative wings of the INC. Twelve years later, as the country became an autonomous parliamentary democracy with universal suffrage, the Communist Party reentered the electoral fray as an independent formation together with the INC, socialists, and the League, among others. This signaled the beginning of another phase of interparty strife, the politics of containment, and alliances in Malabar.

In an interview with Tariq Ali in 1975, Gopalan's long-time colleague, K. Damodaran, offered an insightful critical assessment of these early years in the life of the CPI. According to Damodaran, the electoral successes in the 1950s, the institution of the first elected communist government of the world in Kerala, and the redoubled efforts of the Congress, Muslim League, and other institutions to bring the communist government down in the late 1950s "left within the CPI leaders an overwhelming desire to win power and form ministries through electoral means."[87]

Between 1948 and 1951, parliamentary majority and the acquisition of allies to form governments became the party's major aims as it switched from "ultra-leftism" to "parliamentary cretinism."[88] At the same time, electoral wrangling after 1951 resembled that period in 1939 when, during the Malabar District Board elections, sharp conflicts emerged between different sections of the Congress leadership. The 1951 moment, viewed reflexively, mirrored the 1939 contest for governmental power. From 1951 onward, as Damodaran sees it, the institution of the supposed people's democratic government became the party's official goal, and class struggle was conveniently reframed as a battle against parties hindering the achievement of that goal.[89] Some passages in Gopalan's self-narrative suggest that he would have concurred with Damodaran's critique of the party's approach and practices. Writing about the years that led up to the 1964 split in the CPI and the formation of the CPI (M), Gopalan notes in a disapproving lamenting tone: "One factor that weakened the Party was the failure to handle the 1952 election and the Parliamentary program with the vigilance that should characterise a revolutionary party. The entire Party organisation was turned into election machinery, from *panchayat* [village council] level to parliamentary. Opportunist policies were adopted in order to capture votes. It was not possible to build up a well-organised party on the basis of policies and programs alone. Alliances and tie-ups aimed at getting a majority of the votes were forged."[90]

On his part, Damodaran categorically blames the preoccupation with coalitions and alliances for the split in the Communist Party. According to Damodaran, a widespread agreement emerged by the early 1960s that electoral victories were the road to realizing communism in India; the only difference of opinion was about the nature of alignments between parties that could facilitate those victories. The pitfalls of parliamentary cretinism meant that the CPI was no longer an insurrectionary exception but had begun resembling other parties normally seen in representative democracies: each one seeking to obtain the majority of votes in order to ascend to the major rungs of government.

Democratic Life and Ascendant Leaders

In Kannur, the list of other prominent mainstream parties at the time included the Congress, the PSP, and, to a lesser extent, the Muslim League. Gopalan's and Kurup's self-narratives enable a closer look at interactions between their local leaders and workers that highlight how the desire for victories and the imperative to come out on top infiltrated the political life of the region. Gopalan had witnessed the transformation of a competitive political spirit into disruptive and aggressive acts in 1939; with the advent of independence and the promise of democracy, the equal right to compete came alive with new vigor.

Kurup's memoir supplements Gopalan's rendition of this competitive political spirit at play. Several chapters of Kurup's self-narrative are dedicated to violent containment politics that he, and his party members, became involved in even before independence. These chapters are also closely tied to the political history of Panur town and villages such as Dharmadam, Pattiam, and Puthur that were sites of frequent interparty strife in the early 1960s. In other sections of the biography, Kurup gives exhaustive evidence of what Damodaran and others identify as parliamentary cretinism: agreements, disagreements, and negotiations between local leaders of various groups as they bonded and sought to align with, maneuver, and outmaneuver each other in their efforts to secure electoral victories and a place for themselves and their parties in various state governments.

Such alliances won Kurup a place in two CPI (M)-led Kerala governments in spite of a long history of conflicts with its members at the local level. These ministerial positions came on the back of significant electoral successes: Kurup's electoral record shows that he won the Kuthuparamba and Peringalam assembly elections six times by large margins.[91] In his self-narrative, Kurup also explains these successes through a familiar teleological script that begins with his family history, a description of his youthful days, initiation into the INC and socialism, and the work he did over the years to earn popular support. At each step, both Kurup's memoir and Gopalan's autobiography illuminate important aspects of the sociopolitical history of the region from their respective vantage points. Furthermore, each work allows us to gain insights into the political scripts, subjectivities, practices, and networks that were coalescing at the time that Gopalan and Kurup's lives and careers were coming into their own.

Kurup's political biography mirrored and intersected with Gopalan's in various ways. However, unlike Gopalan who gained national eminence,

Kurup remained a regional socialist leader known more for a "big man" persona, strong-arm tactics, and the local networks of political support he nurtured over the years to maintain his party's presence in Kerala in spite of its national decline. His biography highlights how egalitarianism, collective action, social work, and pastoral power came together in Kurup's mobilization practices just as they did in the lives of his contemporaries. At the same time, its vivid personalized details, and the occasional affective charge of his writing, spill out of established frames to enliven aspects of Kannur's political history that might have otherwise remained obscure.

The opening pages that launch with an account of his family are telling as Kurup recounts life in his prominent Nair tharavadu. Incidentally, his family was related to Gopalan's by marriage, but unlike Gopalan who provides a barebones sketch of his matrilineal household, Kurup takes his readers into the inner life of a family that enforced caste and gender hierarchies but was also engulfed by winds of change. The injustices of this social setup inscribed themselves on the walls of Kurup's family house and, apparently, in the crevices of his mind. In Kurup's words, "Father's ancestors were landlords. They had the right to unleash violence, slaughter and murder.... Once upon a time, they used to rule over an entire region."[92]

After penning these early lines, Kurup proceeds to create the dramatic image of a dark, cave-like room in his father's matrilineal home where those who transgressed against the family's decrees were imprisoned and punished. He writes: "Only the walls of the *pukayara* [smoke-room] know how many people died there coughing and breathless. The characters of the stories of that region are the people who died this way. They were helpless, unable to even clench their teeth against the authorities and destined to stew in the fire."[93]

This stinging pain was not in vain. At a time when "untouchability and caste rivalries were widely prevalent,"[94] Kurup claims that the pain he felt upon hearing his grandmother's tales about his family's oppressive acts signaled and facilitated the development of his egalitarian consciousness. In a characteristic self-congratulatory mode, he describes how over the years he "tried to go above it all," how he defied prohibitions against commensality, never "reluctant to take a meal in the houses of those who were called untouchables," but always behaved as if he was "one of them."[95]

"Lexicons of modernity" and enactments of equality thus make their presence felt strongly in Kurup's narrative.[96] We gather that in the new community of equals that was being formed at the time, the principle and performances of egalitarianism paved the way for figures such as Kurup to exercise influence and become more equal than others. For Kurup, this modernist turn implied acquiring "a mature mind" that would enable him to "regard everyone equally."[97] The friendships he forged by treating people equally enabled him to, in Kurup's words, "have a hold amongst people."[98] The language of equality also helped Kurup, just as it enabled Gopalan, to assume the moral right and agency to help members of lower classes and castes.

Kurup informs his readers that he was "always a refuge" for those who put their trust in him and "never hesitated to be a part of their hurt and loss, joys and unhappiness," for "each time there was some trouble they would come running to me in the hope that I would help them and I never let them down."[99] Through statements like these, Kurup seeks to institute himself as a key figure around which a new political community emerged. Here we not only see the dimensions of pastoral power but are also pushed to interrogate the sense of self at play. To elaborate on the singular self that emerged together with exercise of pastoral power in the life of young emergent public figures like Kurup, it is important to remind ourselves of the deeply gendered nature of the political modernity that we inhabit. Modern political communities, like the one Kurup describes, hail the principle of equality and liberty, but come to be anchored in the narcissistic figure of an overbearing male who is not like the traditional pater of former times. Instead, the domineering figure assumes the character of the older brother who protects, saves, and facilitates the well-being of a populace while claiming to treat everyone equally. In the process, he also generates a fraternity of men—friends and/or putative younger brothers—who help him pursue his public vocation and ambition.

Kurup tells his readers that he especially attended to the concerns of people he designates as Thiyya coolie laborers: they became the objects of his care and members of the fraternity he fostered. "This section of the oppressed," he writes, "was ignorant of their abilities to organise (themselves). The Thiyyas were not free of the traditional beliefs that they were slaves."[100] With these words Kurup sets the stage for his detailed description of occasions when he championed the Thiyya cause together with a band of young Thiyya men who he also describes as his friends. He narrates incidents when, in tandem with the young friends, he confronted, intimidated and even beat up the elites who discriminated against them or hurt and offended Thiyya women in various ways.[101]

Descriptions of these "strong-willed masculine assertions"[102] are in keeping with other instances when Kurup describes brimming with rage and righteous anger at various injustices that he witnessed, taking them on with bravery and sovereign abandon. The hydraulic model of freedom, resistance, and agency[103] and a "political culture of virile contestation"[104] that Gopalan extoled also underpin the subjectivity that Kurup celebrates in himself and his associates. One early incident that Kurup recounts especially highlights the nature of the masculine subject in formation. This incident occurred at the training school where Kurup was enrolled to obtain his qualifications to be an educator. The rage in this instance was directed against the elder brother of a fellow student who had offended a respected and well-liked teacher. Kurup writes:

> I could not bear to stand there and watch my teacher being insulted without getting involved. I grabbed and beat him [the offender] up. . . . He [the offender] left quietly. He used to live in Anjarakkandy. Next day he was at the gates of the school with the strong burly men of Anjarakkandy. I was expecting a counterattack. I gathered some students and came towards the gate. We were about twelve of us. Seeing us come towards them, they too got ready.
>
> There was a good fight at the school gates between the people from Anjarakkandy and the students of the school. We packed them off at the gates itself. Nevertheless, the *velluvili* [mutual challenges] did not end. Anticipating that the troubles might intensify the teachers and the tehsildar living nearby mediated between and pacified the two sets of people. After this incident, the teachers of the school began to call me "*mallan* Kurup" [strongman/wrestler Kurup]. Initially I found this alias annoying but as the days went by, I prided myself on this name.[105]

A few more years and such incidents later, mallan Kurup came to be known as "rowdy Kurup"; Kurup's associates who participated in such confrontations with him became notorious as "Kurup's rowdies." But such branding also did not bother Kurup. In his words, "Later my political enemies began calling me a rowdy. I did not feel offended when I heard it because I do what I feel is right. I have used physical force only where it has been necessary. Going my own way, I have never been shaken by the abuses handed out by my enemies."[106] Kurup does not always explain what necessitated the use of physical force. In some instances, he acknowledges that he and his associates were provoked to aggressively confront an opponent, while at other junctures, he claims that he or his sympathizers were attacked first. Nevertheless, each statement and account points to the emergence of a field of action that upheld unfettered and righteous masculine rage as an expression of the desire to be free, equal, and autonomous. Importantly, this field was being constituted at a time when competition for influence and the desire to win electoral support, gain majority, become major, and form a government were also becoming crucial aspects of Indian political life. This period in the early 1940s was one in which an emergent democratic political life generated the use of force in vivid ways. Against this backdrop, emerging leaders like Kurup also expressed their skepticism toward Gandhian nonviolence or disavowed it altogether.

Repudiating Nonviolence

Kurup's accounts of the aggressive episodes of the 1940s especially relate to his encounters with members of the Communist Party as well as the Congress. Moved by the protest actions during the civil disobedience movement, Kurup had joined the INC in 1933. While he gradually veered toward the socialist wing of the Congress, Kurup was not among those who also turned to communism and joined the CPI in 1939. But even as he remained in the Congress, Kurup positioned himself strongly against the "Congress bourgeoisie" in various local committees in the Panoor region and the 1943 panchayath board elections where he and his close associates came on top. All along he was also ready to contest and confront communists of the CPI.

Kurup claimed ideological proximity with the Communist Party but he could not, he maintained, make peace with the arrogance of its members. There was, his memoir suggests, only room for one ascendant figure and party in the area. In 1943, "a series of clashes and conflicts" with CPI members occurred as tensions emerged between CPI members and Kurup's associates around the organization of Theyyam festivities in a local temple.[107] Subsequently, in a series of events whose sequence is uncertain, a CPI jatha was disrupted, one of Kurup's "followers" was attacked, and tussles and fist fights between members of the two groups in Puthur and Maakulpeediya followed, leading to criminal charges and counter charges. Kurup was the first accused in this case, but eventually the charge sheet against him was not filed.[108]

Kurup remained a Congress member until 1948 when the socialists finally broke away from the INC. For many years prior to that, national-level CSP leaders like Narendra Dev and Jayprakash Narayan sought to push the Congress in a leftward direction. They tried to persuade the party to be more sympathetic to trade unions, labor, and small peasant interests, and obtain leadership positions in its central committees commensurate with the popular support that they had gained in the wake of the Quit India movement. Gandhi played a mediating role between the socialist and conservative wings of the Congress for a long time; with his assassination, the relationship between them came undone and the Socialist Party became an independent entity. In 1952, it merged with the Kisan Mazdoor Praja Party to form the PSP.

While the Congress was the leading protagonist of the anticolonial struggle and enjoyed the maximum mass support, the PSP became the second largest political party in North India. In parts of South India including Malabar, it emerged as the third largest formation after the Communists and the Congress.[109] In Kannur, Kurup was a key agent of the Socialist Party's consolidation efforts as he mobilized his networks among various unions, local-level voluntary associations, old Congress sympathizers, landed and poor Nair and Thiyya families, as well as the Muslim elite. In public and private meetings, he pressed them to support his new party.[110] At this stage in the life of the Socialist Party, its efforts to gain majority support and become a major force in the region triggered intimidatory and violent encounters, especially with Congress workers. Kurup's description of one such clash in 1948 between Socialist Party and Congress workers is particularly vivid.

Kurup informs us that this conflict came up at a time when prominent socialist leaders were touring Malabar and also publicly criticizing INC leadership.[111] Congress members, Kurup tells us, had recently disrupted Socialist Party meetings in Taliparamba, Mattanur, and Muzhappilangad. Kurup and his associates were determined that the next gathering would be a success. During the meeting, he launched a vehement verbal attack on Congress *goondas* (goons), and, according to Kurup, the hundreds of people gathered there received his speech very well. The next day, however, a violent clash ensued between Kurup, his associates, and a group of men affiliated with the Congress.

Kurup's description of the clash is akin to many other accounts, which position his opponents as the key assailants. Who sparred with whom has been hard to verify, while it is also a judicial question that is outside my scope. But if autobiographies are a "means of tracking the manifestation of the social in the self,"[112] then the political actor and formations that we encounter through Kurup's description of events are ones that are embedded in the thick of efforts to mobilize support, spread and contain influences, gain a foothold, become major, compete, win, or face defeat. In other words, the political self appears caught up in contests that lend themselves to the play of aggression and gendered masculine enactments.

Thus, for instance, we learn that in the course of the confrontation with Congress people, Kurup charged toward one person "like an enraged wild animal," and "grabbed" another one and "beat him up."[113] What followed, he writes, "was a really strong fight. I used all my physical abilities. A few attackers fell down due to my blows; and some ran away."[114] As he describes his own actions, Kurup also weighs in on questions of violence and nonviolence, having spent nearly fifteen years in Congress with Gandhi as its most widely respected leader. Now he was in the Socialist Party, many of whose key national figures also espoused Gandhian principles. Kurup, however, was clear about their inefficacy and his lack of belief in the tenets of nonviolence. He writes that those who had attacked him and his colleagues professed *ahimsa* (nonviolence). "I do not have much faith in ahimsa. I regarded it as cowardice to be non-violent towards those who come to attack you."[115]

Kurup's dismissal of the principles and practice of non-violence, the role he played in the clash with Congress members, his emphasis on physical strength and righteous anger, and his penchant for aggressive reaction lend themselves to interpretations that see this group violence in North Kerala as a vestige of its archaic martial culture.[116] On the other hand, I draw attention to these details of his biography to highlight the emergence of a modern political field that organizes itself around masculine affirmations of freedom, popular action, and sovereignty and cultivates what Hannah Arendt calls a "fiercely agonal spirit."[117] Adversarial forms of public display and narcissistic expression have been a normal part of democratic life since Athenian city-states and figure prominently in many present-day polities across the world. In a number of postcolonial settings where modern democratic practices have been instituted, the hydraulic model of resistance and liberation has strongly imprinted on performances of collective action. Kurup embodied the agonistic and adversarial energy of competitive democratic life, its machismo, and a political script that equates freedom with the forceful overthrow of oppressive rule. He could thus disdainfully reject ideas of ahimsa and nonviolence, position himself as a popular socialist leader, and embrace the electoral process, being repeatedly elected as the representative of his panchayath and constituency. Kurup's case implicitly makes clear how the democratic imperative to defeat an opponent and render them to a minor position aligned well with the violence needed to contain or react against a difficult adversary. Furthermore, as I discuss in the latter half of the book, rules of criminal law did not mitigate this violence; instead, they created conditions that perpetuated it and continue to do so.

Kurup and his associates in Kannur lived out this relationship between democracy and violence over the next few years. It was a time of frenetic electoral parleys, negotiations, coalitions, the institution of new constitutions in new governments, and their subsequent dissolution in the wake of what its partisans referred to as another liberation struggle. This professed new liberation struggle that unfolded in the late 1950s brought its own share of mass action, violent clashes, and police firings—this time to South Kerala.

The Liberation Years

In 1954, the PSP formed a government in Travancore-Cochin on the back of different interparty alliances after winning only nineteen seats in a legislature made up of 117 members.[118] The PSP-led government was dissolved eleven months later due to mishandling of labor disputes and judicial indictment in the wake of police firing on protesters seeking separation of Tamil-speaking areas from the rest of the province.[119] This made way for the Congress, and subsequently the CPI, to the helm of state government. Leaders of the CPI spent most of the 1950s strengthening their organizational machinery and popular base, as well as entering into a number of alliances to secure electoral victories.[120] While some leading members continued to harbor reservations about the parliamentary path, the party's efforts proved to be a spectacular success in 1957 when it won sixty out of the 126 assembly seats (albeit getting only 35.28 percent of the polled votes) and allied with various independent candidates to form the first elected communist government in the world.[121] Here was the chance for the pragmatists in the party to demonstrate all that could be achieved through an elected People's Democratic Government. The newly elected CPI ministry braced themselves to fulfill the promises made in its manifesto, ranging from a substantial increase in state spending on new industries, cooperatives, wage increases, and house building to educational and comprehensive agrarian reform. These last two measures, however, became the source for the fall of the communist ministry in Kerala.

The government's efforts to reform private school management, intervene on behalf of schoolteachers, and standardize school curriculums, in particular, incensed Christian religious leaders who described the education bill as an antiminority totalitarian act.[122] Once again there was call for mass action, but this time it was to free the state from the hold of the Communist Party. Similar to the socialist- and communist-led actions of the 1930s and 1940s, this alleged liberation struggle or *vimochana samaram* was also anchored in a hydraulic understanding of freedom, and its leaders often espoused the overthrow of the communist government through collective acts of aggressive resistance, much like the ones that Gopalan had participated in.

Massive demonstrations took place in South Kerala in which members of landed upper-caste groups and Christians of different denominations and class backgrounds participated. These protests followed virulent exhortations by Church leaders against the communist government. Landowning members of the Nair community opposed to the proposed agrarian relations bill, and opposition parties such as the Congress and the PSP, joined in the protests.[123] Amid calls for the CPI to marshal its own militant members to counter the mobilizations against it, several violent encounters between Communist Party workers and anticommunists ensued. In one of the worst incidents in Trichur district, six congressmen were killed,[124] and the following year, seventeen people were killed in police firings.[125]

Violence thus became closely entwined with the institution of democracy in Kerala. If the pursuit of popular sovereignty generated acts of collective violence, then defense of elected parties and governments produced violence by party workers and police. Strong communitarian response from Church groups, which wrongly or rightly felt minoritized especially characterized this period. Matters came to a head as the conflict between Communist Party members and the anticommunists led to more spectacular public and police violence. Eventually, in July 1959, Nehru dismissed the elected communist government citing its incapacity to rule according to constitutional provisions.

Some authors, including the economist and ex-finance minister of Kerala, Thomas Isaac, have sought to establish American complicity in this chain of events. These commentators describe the vimochana samaram and the ouster of the communist government as aspects of American policy to, in their words, "contain" communism in Asia.[126] But the CPI was unlike other major communist parties in Asia, and the vimochana samaram became one dramatic episode in its long career. The party had taken to representative democracy and was on its way to becoming a key electoral force. Attempts to preserve its position as the duly elected representative of "the people" yielded its workers' and police violence. In the next elections, the CPI increased its vote share by a fair amount even though it failed to form a government,[127] and once again, PSP leader Pattam Thanu Pillai became the chief minister when his party entered into a coalition with the Congress.

North Kerala did not experience the vagaries of the vimochana samaram with the same intensity as some parts of South Kerala. Writing about it several years later in his memoir, with the benefit of hindsight and in the wake of critiques of the Church and Nair leaders of the movement as communal defenders of bourgeois interests, Kurup expressed his disapproval of several aspects of the movement.[128] Nevertheless, he recounted his participation in vimochana samaram, the jatha he led, how he broke the law against large gatherings that had been imposed at the time, the short speech he gave at the public meeting in Jawaharghat, and his subsequent arrest. Supporters of the PSP and Kurup were especially active in the anti-CPI government rallies that were organized at the time. In the 1960 polls that followed, Kurup defeated his Communist Party rival by twenty-nine thousand votes, which was the largest margin of victory that anyone had against a communist candidate in those elections.

Turn from Agonism to Enmity

The CPI began recovering the ground it had lost in the 1957–1959 period and further extended its popular support and vote share. The Panur area however proved to be a challenging place for the party's mobilization activities, as Kurup and the PSP enjoyed considerable support in this area. But the CPI was not alone: according to various accounts, Congress and Muslim League members similarly encountered indignant PSP workers when they ventured into parts of Thalassery taluk where Kurup was influential.[129] A number of these young PSP workers belonged to Thiyya peasant families, and others came from more modest Nair households, including some Muslim share-croppers. When Kurup writes about his supporters, he reminds us, in his own narcissistic fashion, about the alliances he had forged by attending to their and their families' everyday concerns—marriage, death, death anniversaries, house warming, managing quarrels about property, and mediating during personal altercations.[130] Members of other groups also acknowledge Kurup's ability to draw on various vectors of social power to create fraternal solidarities with young men and other male heads of households, and families who became, in his words, his "followers."[131] Among these youths were some who came to be described as Kurup's "rowdies."

Versions of the dramatic events of the early 1960s period in the Panur, Peringalam, Pattiam, and adjoining villages from Kurup's young associates when discussing the political conflicts of the region vary.[132] By early 1960, Kurup's leadership and his associates' actions had become a matter of concern and debate in the legislative assembly.[133] The CPI workers of that time, and those who became active soon after, recall how PSP workers disrupted communist fund drives and manhandled their colleagues.[134]

While Congress and the PSP were in alliance during the vimochana samaram and running the provincial government of the time together, competition for influence on the ground also led to conflicts between their members. PSP workers disrupted Congress meetings in Pathayakunnu and Panur, and viciously surrounded and beat up an important local Congress leader critical of Kurup. As a result, ten PSP workers were charged with assault. Additionally, in January 1962, a CPI activist was killed in a skirmish with PSP workers, and consequently, two PSP workers including the head of a PSP-led union were charged with murder.[135]

Soon after, CPI, Congress, and Muslim League members came together to form what they refer to as a "defense committee," which Kurup describes as an "area committee" forged to harass and hurt him and his supporters. Kurup's genealogy of the attacks and counterattacks, which took place especially between 1960 and 1964, predictably emphasizes his opponent's (that is, the committee's) aggressive postures and acts against him and other PSP workers. He names several PSP workers who were injured at the time, murder victim V. P. Kumaran, others whose houses were broken into and vandalized, and those whose crops were damaged. He describes times when members of the committee prevented agricultural produce from the villages where the PSP had a major presence from passing through and discusses police complicity in this violence and harassment. He alleges media bias against him and describes the partisan attacks in the legislative council where questions were raised about his "rule" in the Panur area.[136]

But, according to Kurup, it was not the nature of his or his party's rule that was at fault, and neither does he describe PSP workers as mere victims. "In many instances," he writes, "both sides were wrong. I would not claim that we were innocent in all respects. We took unjust and wrong decisions to win over the enemy. But we were often compelled to do so."[137] When approached to negotiate a truce, Kurup notes that he was categorical. In his words, "I did not oblige.... I would rather commit suicide than kneel before the enemy. I never felt I did something wrong. I never instigated anybody to attack anyone. We have often been compelled to retaliate, and I was compelled to help the comrades who sought revenge."[138]

Switching between "I" and "we," Kurup once again gives us a sense of a political field where not only had competition translated into violence but the imperative to become a major political force and reduce the opposition to a minor position was increasingly interlaced with calls for reprisals. I have posited that vengefulness was not an always already-given ontological or cultural trait but tracked its emergence over time. The agonal spirit evident during the District Board, panchayath, legislative assembly, and national elections in 1939, 1943, and 1951 now reverberated with feelings of and claims to enmity. In the interim occurred grave agrarian unrest, a turn to insurrectionary tactics of the late 1940s, and the short-lived but sharply virulent vimochana samaram of the 1950s. At the same time, the larger electoral field was laced with coalitions that could be forged, friends made, alliances dissolved, and allegiances that could be switched.

In different ways, the careers of both Gopalan and Kurup as well as their respective parties are a testimony to the paradoxical character of postcolonial polities that anchor themselves in popular power in their search for equality and sovereignty, but also equate democracies with electoral competition and multiparty politics. In such a context, mere engagement of various parties in periodic electoral contests and attempts to secure a numerical majority becomes a sign of a polity's democratic intentions. In the meantime, competition to occupy the place of power enfolds young members of different political parties and recruits from lower rungs of the social order. In Kerala, the competition and resultant politics of violently containing opponents began turning particularly ugly from the late 1970s with the more purposive entrance of the Hindu right into an intensely contested field.

What is important to note, however, is that the grounds for the emergence of violent political conflict were laid down beforehand. The role of particular parties and persons is crucial, but more importantly we need to consider the responsibility of modern democracies as political formations that offer inducements of popular power and sovereignty but uphold rule by selected representatives. In the competition between them to become rulers lived out over several decades and the thwarted aspirations for meaningful popular sovereignty lies the prehistory of long-running political violence in Kannur.

The CPI (M) and the Making
of an Antagonistic Political Field

Drivers of Violence and Political Workers

I concluded the last chapter with a review of intensified reprisals, attacks, and counterattacks between members of different political parties dominant in Kannur in the early 1960s. The politics of containing their competitors' influence had brought local leaders and workers of the communist and socialist parties and the Indian National Congress to a vitiated place where agonistic politics was starting to generate not just occasional clashes between members of different groups but frequent grievous attacks. Party leaders increasingly drew on righteous aggressive energies of their young cadres who had come to equate liberating political action with masculine assertions. Young local-level workers of various parties sought to contain and upstage their competitors as they forcefully countered their opponents' efforts to mobilize support in small towns and neighborhoods of Kannur. At the same time, parliamentary cretinism, or the purposive pursuit of electoral majorities and seats in representative institutions, was pervasive.

Set against the backdrop of the continued comingling of the logics of containment and cretinism in North Kerala, this chapter describes how agonistic contests transmuted into antagonistic conflicts from the late 1960s to the early 2000s—especially among members of the CPI (M) and the RSS–Jan Sangh/BJP combine. At various junctures in this period, members of the two groups enacted exceptionally grave violence against each other. Such grave acts included armed attacks on multiple sites at the same time as well as murder in front of young children. The ways in which violence between members of the CPI (M) and the Hindu right took this exceptional character, I argue, highlights a more typical process by which representative democracies and their competitive ethos have contributed to the formation of antagonistic political communities.

A competitive political milieu led workers of the CPI (M) and the Hindu right in Kannur down the road of a mimetic struggle to become the major force in the region. One act of aggression followed and looped into the other, stitching the workers of the two groups together into opposing close-knit communities—each not only seeking to outdo the other but also increasingly seeking reprisals against the other. The language of love and hate along with the ideological and discursive formulations that accompanied the violence between the two groups bear the marks of Kannur's particular social and political history. At the same time, these imitative acts of aggression and violence that accentuate divisions and intensify hostilities are present in many other political contexts. In analyzing Kannur's recent history, I show how competition for popular and electoral support, central to the workings of modern democracies, created the conditions and ground for the emergence of hate-filled and vengeful acts of violence between opposing political communities.

I map this rise of violence between the two groups through multiple sources. These sources include police and court records as well as media reports that help me outline the contours of violence between members of the party left and the Hindu right. I also pay particularly close attention to the rate of incidence and the character and social backgrounds of people involved as victims and apparent culprits. Oral interviews and biographies relating the lived experience of escalating violence, as well as the regional and national political histories of the period, help me recount the formation of hurt, hateful political agents who inflicted the violence, and those who suffered its consequences. These political agents—local-level workers of the party left and the Hindu right—came into their own in a competitive representative democracy where they not only were ideological adversaries but were caught in the play of obtaining greater visibility, as well as popular and electoral support as competitors.

This chapter especially focuses on the lives and actions, motivations, and affects that marked the biographies of select CPI (M) local leaders and workers active between the late 1960s and the early 2000s.[1] I situate their biographies in the contentious political life of the region. Additionally, I describe how the workings of competition for popular and electoral support shaped it and shed light on the nature of relationships that local-level CPI (M) workers and leaders came to share with the party and among themselves. I investigate how political competition contributed to the formation of the tight-knit, vengeful communities of young men associated with the party left and the Hindu right, and how the contests for ascendancy and one-upmanship between them transmuted into an antagonistic conflict. As I do so, I foreground the modalities that frequently accentuate polarities and generate dangerous divisions between different groups in modern democracies. These are, I suggest, the drivers of political violence in democracies lived over several years and generations.

My academic association with Kannur began in the early 2000s when I first ventured to do research on the genealogy of the conflict between the two groups. At the time, Kannur and Kerala were reeling from the December 1999 murder of a schoolteacher and BJP youth wing leader, K. T. Jaykrishnan. Jaykrishnan was attacked in front of his nine- to eleven-year-old students with weapons such as iron rods, a chopping knife, and an axe. This setting and these details drew the attention of national as well as international media. Seven CPI (M) workers were accused of the murder.[2] In the wake of this murder, several other violent attacks and counterattacks took place. According to media calculations, six men were killed in the next few weeks. Four of them were affiliated with the CPI (M), and two belonged to the RSS-BJP. Eight young men—five affiliated with the CPI (M) and three affiliated with the RSS-BJP—were killed the following year.[3]

Jaykrishnan's murder was part of a longer chain of notable attacks in the late 1990s and early 2000s on leading local figures of the CPI (M) and the Hindu right. I recount their details to outline how violence between the two groups was intensifying as well as to provide a glimpse into the milieu that local-level workers of the two groups inhabited. The attacks and counterattacks I mention here were important reference points in the history of the conflict as CPI (M) and RSS-BJP workers described it. The chain of attacks and reprisals that they described in the course of my research included the murders of the CPI (M)'s Mamman Vasu in 1995 and district BJP president Pannianur Chandran in May 1996, as well as the attack on CPI (M) leader P. Jayarajan.[4]

Like the attack on Jaykrishnan, the BJP-affiliated schoolteacher, the attack on the CPI (M) leader Jayarajan drew considerable attention. It occurred in August 1999, a few months before the attack on Jaykrishnan. Jayarajan was attacked in his home in his wife's presence with weapons such as crude bombs, axes, and cleavers. He was severely injured but survived thanks to specialist care and a thirteen-hour-long surgery. These details became part of the local discourse about the gravity of the political violence that Kannur was witnessing at the time. The district court convicted six people of the attack and sentenced them to rigorous punishment. Two of the six people convicted were well-known local-level Sangh workers, and others were said to be their associates.[5]

Outrage at these and other assaults, and indignation against those believed to be responsible, reverberated among workers of the two groups. They increasingly experienced every attack as a visceral sting and sought to hit back. In other words, a feedback loop was created as each group sought to keep up with the other, have the upper hand in the scorecard of attacks, and thereby imitate as well as escalate the other's violence. In this context, I began gathering oral accounts of the violence and biographies of local-level workers of the party left and the Hindu right involved as victims or assailants in the violence. That first core phase of my research with workers of the two groups took place in the early 2000s. It concluded as the district court trial of six CPI (M) workers accused of murdering the BJP leader and schoolteacher, Jaykrishnan, in his classroom was drawing to a close. By that time, my research assistant and I had interviewed about thirty workers from the two groups, and I draw on a small selection of those interviews as I write this chapter and the ones that follow. I especially draw on interviews of local-level political workers with whom we could forge a close rapport and who, I believe, allowed us a glimpse into aspects of their biographies and lives that help to make analytical sense of the violence that has troubled Kannur.[6]

Attacks, counterattacks, bail hearings, trials, and calls for reprisals as well as calls for peace were an overwhelming part of the milieu when I first carried out my research in Kannur in the early 2000s. In subsequent years, I chose to restrict my research with local-level workers of the CPI (M) and the Hindu right to follow up conversations with some workers who had been on trial in the early 2000s, been imprisoned, and/or been acquitted on appeal. At the same time, I continued to piece together the prehistory and the regional and national context in which the conflict between the two groups unfolded. In the course of the interviews with workers of the party left and the Hindu right, my research assistants and I gathered dramatic accounts of violence suffered and inflicted and became familiar with stories of complicity and absolution. We witnessed the precarious daily lives of the political workers anticipating revenge and/or judicial punishment, all the while depending on party beneficence for sustenance and legal defense. Vividly present in these interactions were tensions and concerns around the possibility of a vengeful attack and concerns about what workers could or could not say about their respective political parties. In addition, the workers were conscious of making themselves culpable and often spoke in ways that would lessen their burden of criminal responsibility.

Workers of the two groups who spoke to my research assistants and me at length allowed me to apprehend the texture of their private and public lives. I gained insights into the ways in which political contests contributed to their formation, how they propelled political violence in Kannur, and how they were affected by it. Built into these conversations, I believe, was an expectation of anonymity even when it was not expressly sought. I have done my best to abide by that expectation. Thus, while I present some granular details of the CPI (M) and RSS-BJP workers' contexts, biographies, and encounters with violence, I also withhold information about them. The real names, places, and times of the events I share are those present in public records. However, I obfuscate others to fulfill my obligations to the workers of the party left and the Hindu right who were drawn into the long cycle of political violence that the region has witnessed. It is under this discretion that I present the grounds on which I rest my argument about the relationship between representative democracy and political conflict in Kannur.

In particular, this chapter revolves around members of the CPI (M), with one of its key protagonists being a daily wage laborer and CPI (M) worker whom I call Preman. When I first met him in 2002, Preman was in his early thirties. Through his biography and self-narrative, I seek to understand how the world of conflict and combat between the CPI (M) and other parties drew in young men like Preman from lower-caste, poor families. His life story, descriptions of the local political milieu, and encounters with violence help me outline the nature of political agency at play in the conflict between the party left and the Hindu right in Kannur.

From Aggression to Vengeance

Like Preman, several young CPI (M) workers whose narratives I draw on came into their own in the late 1970s, 1980s, and 1990s and lived through the various phases of the conflict between the CPI (M) and the Sangh.

For many of them, membership in the Communist Party was an intergenerational heritage that had, to some extent, helped realize the promise of a more equal life as well as governmental care. In Kannur, the democratic adversarial context contributed to the formation of close-knit party networks among members of the party left and the Hindu right, with each group pitched against the other. The milieu of conflict, mimetic attacks, and counterattacks intensified their identification and attachment to these networks and transformed competitive aggression into vengeful violence. I share two excerpts from conversations with Preman about the violence to provide glimpses into its nature, which was quotidian as well as dramatic. Each account is vivid and recounts moments infused with possibilities of grave injury. At the same time, the two accounts are also different; together, however, they vivify the nature of conflict between the party left and the Hindu right. The experience of violence, along with the web of feelings and meanings surrounding it, that Preman's accounts illuminate, assist in framing my questions about the relationship between the violence and the broader political context in which it occurred.

Recounting in grave and measured tones, albeit with a degree of boastfulness, the first excerpt relates to an incident that took place in September or October 1989.[7] In those days, Preman said:

> There was usually a "power-cut" around 7:30 p.m. Our house was very small then, my financial situation was very bad at the time; there was no bed to sleep on, we used to sleep on a floor mat. The mat had started to tear, and I went to buy a new mat at a shop near Panur High School. There was a "power-cut." At the time the [party] directives were that if people like us went to Panur, we had to inform the party office [the local CPI (M) office]. I bought the mat, tied it up. On my way, a man came and taunted me. A few minutes later, another one joined him, and they threatened me. They walked ahead towards the junction just outside of town. They probably thought that if they threaten me, I would turn back. However, I decided to walk ahead. That's when I saw ten to twenty people standing near the junction. They were standing there with daggers and iron rods in their hands. Mattan Chandran, an old and well-respected bank employee I was acquainted with happened to pass by. He did not approve of attacks, clashes etc. A Neemam bus was coming by; he asked me to get into the bus and he got on as well. He dropped me off at home on the Neemam bus. That's how [I] was able to get away.

No one was hurt or injured as Preman safely got away from the crowd of RSS workers bearing daggers and iron rods. Nevertheless, the experience was significant for Preman; although it did not rupture his prevailing life, it left an imprint on him. I present Preman's account of this encounter, his apprehensions, fear, and swagger as well as his escape, to convey how the conflict between the party left and the Hindu right iterated itself in the lives of local-level political workers of the two groups. In some instances, this brush with the opposing group left party workers with an understated sense of disquiet and anxiety, whereas at other times interparty violence seized their lives in heinous ways.

The second excerpt from our conversations with Preman that I present here is a testimony to the grievous manner in which the conflict between the two groups sometimes affected local-level political workers. Reflecting on the cruelty associated with a number of attacks and counterattacks between CPI (M) and Hindu right workers, Preman said:

> To take off hands and legs.... When we are at an "action scene" then sometimes you get hands to cut, sometimes you get legs, whatever you chance upon you cut. For instance, ... if we come upon a notorious RSS worker accused of the murders of many CPI (M) activists, then all cruel things he has done to us, then all our strong (unspeakable) feelings associated with him would come to mind. When our people do something to people like that, it is with this kind of hate in their hearts. The rest ... "automatic" ... wherever you are able to you cut.... That this is cruel, I don't feel that way because the way they behaved with us, it is all in our hearts.

In this second statement, Preman's acknowledgment of hate, disavowal, and justification of cruelty all came together. It is not clear to me whether Preman was trying to grasp and articulate affective surges that he personally experienced during such an "action scene" or whether he was articulating what he believed others have felt. Perhaps he had heard his colleagues and comrades in the party speak about their violent encounters in this manner. However, in this instance I am inclined to believe that Preman was speaking as one of them. For him, active life in politics had begun at a time when agonistic competition and the need to contain the opposition was taking an increasingly violent turn in Kannur politics. The question of how interparty contests acquired this hateful antagonistic character and the conditions of its emergence are central to this chapter. Preman was a product of these conditions and a political actor who not only worked to institute the dominance of his party in his village and neighborhood but also participated in the vengeful politics that became prominent in Kannur over the years.

Vengeful violence in which political workers like Preman participated shows how containment politics and the homogenizing and polarizing force of democracies came together with masculine assertions and righteous rage in Kannur. From these conditions emerged communities and political actors who strived to make their group a major force in their region, as well as to minoritize the opposition, each action sparking a passionate reaction and turning competition into vindictive violence. But workers like Preman were minor players in the political field of Kannur as far as party strategies to institute its dominance in the region were concerned. Thus, in order to further contextualize the workings of containment politics and its transformation into antagonism riddled with hateful reprisals, I once again turn to a written self-narrative of a party leader influential in the area.

Memoirs of CPI and CPI (M) leader A. K. Gopalan and PSP leader P. R. Kurup were some of my key sources in chapter 1. In this chapter, I turn to CPI (M) and Communist Marxist Party leader M. V. Raghavan's autobiography. I draw on it to piece together slices of regional social and political history that shaped life within the CPI (M) for its young recruits and influenced interparty dynamics. Raghavan was an influential CPI (M) local leader through the 1970s and early 1980s; he was expelled from the CPI (M) in 1985 but continued to play a dominant role in the region till the early 2000s.[8] Aspects of Raghavan's career and politics illuminate forms of combative political agency and subjectivities that are often activated and rewarded in representative democracies. Political agents and leaders such as Raghavan and his associates intensified interparty conflict in Kannur, and their mirror images may be found in many other parts of India and other democratic polities.

Electoral Alliances and Volunteer Armies

As will become clear in the following paragraphs, for most of his career, Raghavan stood out as someone who both embodied and perpetuated the manipulations, cretinism, and belligerence that often characterize democratic life. Hence, his biography is a valuable resource for further examining the links between competitive democratic politics, practices of containing the opposition, masculinity, and violence. While in his self-narrative Raghavan absolves himself of moral and legal responsibility for violent confrontations with members of other parties, it nevertheless helps me plot the formation of Kannur's tense political field infused with a competitive adversarial spirit. I elaborate on events and political figures invoked in the text to elucidate the politico-economic, institutional, ideological, and discursive conditions that contributed to the formation of Kannur's conflictual political field. Issues of electoralism and campaigns to occupy seats of party and governmental power stand out just as they did in the last chapter. Additionally, I draw attention to the rise of Naxalism in North Kerala, its own violence and opposition to electoral democracy, and the CPI (M)'s response to it. Each instance helps me unpack how representative democracy was perceived and practiced in the region, the forms of violence that Indian democracy expelled, and the kinds of violence that democratic life fostered and accommodated.

The language of democratic equality and collective struggle were crucial for Raghavan's political formation just as they were for many other young men of North Kerala who grew up and came into their own in the late 1940s. Like Gopalan and Kurup, Raghavan (or MVR, as he is known in most of Kerala) belonged to an upper-caste (Nambiar) family. His family however lacked landed resources or substantial wealth. Hence, in order to supplement the family's meager income, Raghavan began working in a cloth weaving mill when he was in his early teens. He was soon caught in the thick of the mill workers' strikes that were unfolding in the area in the late 1940s. Raghavan writes in detail about those heady days when strong collective action against the old hierarchical order was underway. Some of the earliest formative strike actions that Raghavan participated in were led by CPI stalwarts like Gopalan, who emerged as an important reference point in the young man's political career. A member of the CPI's *balsangham*, or children's wing, to begin with, Raghavan formally joined the main branch of the Communist Party of India in 1949.[9]

At the time, the party had been banned for its stance against parliamentary democracy and its attempt to implement an insurrectionary line. But as I discussed in the previous chapter, the party's insurrectionary phase was short-lived, and from 1951 it was firmly on the electoral path. Raghavan was only eighteen to nineteen years old at the time when the CPI disavowed the insurrectionary paradigm and adapted the electoral route. His memoir suggests that cretinism came to have a quick and strong hold on the party and political life of the region. Sections of Raghavan's autobiography on those early years of the Indian republic are replete with details of the alliances with the PSP and the Muslim League that the party effectively forged and election victories that the CPI candidates secured. His self-narrative, as well as oral and written accounts of his rise as a regional party leader from the 1960s to the 1980s, suggest that Raghavan displayed a keen ability to mobilize electoral alliances and was, like many of his contemporaries, prone to parliamentary cretinism.

Raghavan was also adept at marshaling resources to extend governmental benefits to the local populace[10] and combined this resourcefulness with a strong zeal for electoral victories. Additionally, his capacity for competitive wrangling, lack of scruples, and masculine charisma proved useful.[11] In other words, Raghavan embodied many characteristics that can facilitate popularity and dominance in a competitive political field. Raghavan's rise as a notable local leader may thus be seen as a testimony to the ways in which representative democracies cultivate and reward those with a penchant for competition. In addition, Raghavan was associated with a community of male comrades who played an important part at various junctures in his elevation. Journalist N. P. Ullekh describes these men as the "Young Turks" who, together with Raghavan, used a range of machinations to seize leadership of the party in Kannur.[12] Through an unprecedented, well-orchestrated inner-party election, they displaced old, respected leaders associated with trade unions and peasant organizations.

This capture of the state leadership happened in 1967, three years after the split in the Communist Party and the formation of the CPI (M). Furthermore, it occurred around the same time that the CPI (M) came back to power as part of a reconfigured electoral coalition, only to see the coalition dissolve due to interparty and intraparty disputes.[13] In Kerala provincial governments were formed and collapsed in the middle of another border war (with Pakistan). Moreover, there was an intense crisis of food availability, resulting in agitations and fragmentation of electoral support across new parties.[14]

In this atmosphere, tensions prevailed on the ground between local-level workers of competing groups ranging from the CPI, the CPI (M), and the Congress to the socialist formations who were all vying to win elections and form governments.[15] While the problem of forming governments and obtaining state power preoccupied party leaders on the top, the question of their party's presence at district, block, taluk, village, and neighborhood levels concerned local leaders and workers. Competition for power in the upper echelons of political life was thus nurturing a politics of containment and contestation at the bottom. Raghavan's account gives us a sense of how this moment played itself out at the local levels and configured relations between supporters and workers of various groups in Kannur in the late 1960s and 1970s. Events that took place in 1968–1969 are especially illustrative, and I outline them below to highlight how agonistic competition became a major force and how the problem of containing the opposition aligned with righteous masculine assertiveness, molding many political careers and facilitating conflict and combat for years to come.

The CPI (M) had returned to power in 1967 as part of a united front that defeated the Congress and its partners on the back of agitations against food shortages and strikes among plantation workers and government employees. Additionally, unemployment, lack of educational infrastructure, and fraught center-state relations were some of the issues that the parties who allied with each other emphasized in their campaign against the Congress and its partners.[16] Their campaign was effective, and the CPI (M) and its allies won handsomely to form another communist-led government. However soon after, in the midst of a worsening food crisis and corruption allegations against its members,[17] the government and the Communist Party found themselves at the receiving end of public and opposition ire.

P. Sundarayya, then CPI (M) general secretary and founding member of the party, was visiting Kannur at the time when members of the Congress's student wing staged a taunting demonstration against the CPI (M)'s government's inability to procure food for Kerala's citizens. Raghavan describes his fellow CPI (M) members' reaction to the demonstrators in spare but strong terms and notes that "we sent them (Congress workers) away forcefully." The next day another Congress student's union demonstration was organized; this time too, Raghavan tells us that CPI (M) volunteers warded off the Congress demonstrators "by dint of sheer muscle."[18]

While Raghavan does not elaborate at length on the use of force and muscle in these instances, Nossiter reminds us that this was the period when both the Congress and the CPI (M) created "volunteer vigilante corps" akin to RSS cadres by bringing together youth ready to physically defend their parties against others.[19] Now translating into organized acts of physically attenuating the opposition to a minor position was the agonal spirit and the politics of containing the opposition central to democracies. In nearby Kozhikode, a sitting member of the legislative assembly and CPI (M) worker was killed in a clash between such aggressive corps of rival parties.[20] In the meantime, in Kannur, Raghavan tried to form what he describes as a "volunteer army."[21] In his words: "Party members and the party were facing many challenges and threats in those days. I thought that the party needed an arrangement to counter [the opposition]. When the new district committee was formed ... the effort to form the volunteer army was started.... [C]amps were conducted in Morazhai and Ponyattu in Thalassery to facilitate village-based training. Afterwards camps were conducted at branch level. Thus, we could form a volunteer army of 800 members for the party at the district level."[22]

Members of the press and opposition parties deemed this volunteer corps a threat to law and order. And, due to Gopalan's proximity to the party's youth formations, they reproachfully called it "Gopalan Sena" (Gopalan's army).[23] CPI (M) leaders who authorized the camps maintained that they were not designed to generate "fights and attacks" but inculcate "self-confidence and enthusiasm" among young party members.[24] However, fights and attacks were a step away from the confidence-building exercises that the camps offered in order to build an ever-ready army of combative volunteers. In the next few years, different kinds of violent strikes and confrontations came to mark the lives of some notable young men who attended the camps and became important leaders in their own right.

I am especially referring to Kerala's twelfth chief minister, CPI (M) leader Pinarayi Vijayan (reelected in 2021), and the slain Naxal activist Arrikad Varghese. Snippets from Vijayan and Varghese's biographies and the ways in which they are tied to Raghavan's career give us insights into the nature of political selves and subjectivities of the new generation of CPI (M) politicos that were being shaped in the late 1960s and early 1970s—almost two decades after the inauguration of the independent democratic Indian republic.

New Leaders and the Democratic Pact

The emergence of the Naxalite movement in Bengal and its iteration in Kerala as a Maoism-inspired armed insurrection against landlords, police, and the so-called bourgeois state has to be viewed against the backdrop of the socioeconomic conditions of the time. This was a time when the pervasiveness of deep inequalities as well as state corruption were generating protests and revolts against the political structure more broadly.[25] The first organized armed attack by the Naxalites in Kerala took place in November 1968 in the Wayanad district.[26]

At the time, both Vijayan and Varghese were part of CPI (M) youth and student formations in Kannur. They were contemporaries, and, according to Raghavan, both of them attended the highly successful camps that he organized to raise an army of volunteers for the party.[27] In the coming years, both Vijayan and Varghese were implicated in different forms of political violence—one in interparty conflict and the other in insurrection against the democratic state. Vijayan rose through the party ranks to become its current leading figure and chief minister of Kerala while Varghese became a

Naxalite and was gunned down. Their linked yet disparate trajectories and differing fates, which I elaborate on in this section, clarify the nature of the pact that modern democracy made with political violence in contemporary India. The democratic dispensation housed and rewarded violence that abided by its competitive ethos and representative structure while it eliminated agents of violence who questioned its grounding principles and practices.

Vijayan, unlike Gopalan, Kurup, and Raghavan, did not belong to the upper castes but was from a Thiyya family where he was employed as a weaver and his father as a toddy tapper. Vijayan's rise through the ranks of the party's youth wing and emergence as a local leader testify to the ideology and performances of egalitarianism that suffused the Communist Party and larger public discourse in the 1960s and 1970s. His career also reminds us of the possibilities of educational, social, and political mobility that had been opening up in the region since the early twentieth century. Vijayan drew on them as well as the opportunities that the party's youth wing offered to forge a close-knit community of supporters, and keenly positioned himself in the competition to become politically ascendant.

Like many other young men who were politically active in Kannur at this time, Vijayan was drawn into the burgeoning conflict between the CPI (M) and the Hindu right. According to Ullekh, Vijayan used to train members of the CPI (M)'s student wing in "self-defense techniques."[28] In 1969, while he was still extremely young, Vijayan was accused of the murder of a tailor, sweet-maker, and RSS–Jan Sangh supporter, Vadikkal Ramakrishnan, in an attack that is often described as one of the earliest grievous moments in the history of violence between the CPI (M) and the Hindu right.[29] According to various accounts, this attack occurred close on the heels of a clash between workers of the RSS and the CPI (M)'s student wing in which another young CPI (M) member was badly hurt. While the nature of Vijayan's involvement in these events remains hazy and he was indeed acquitted in the murder case, over the years Vijayan too has been seen as a symbol of his party's "muscular politics,"[30] its ability to physically confront opponents and contain their activities and influence. At the same time, Vijayan has successfully navigated the workings of electoral and party dynamics, occupied important government and party positions, and emerged as an influential regional leader.[31]

Varghese on the other hand disavowed electoral democracy and the parliamentary path and, in turn, met a terrible fate. After several years as a CPI (M) worker and member of the Kannur unit of its youth federation, Varghese had become deeply involved in the CPI (M)'s agricultural workers union. He was especially involved in its efforts to challenge land relations and distribution in places such as Wayanad, which were home to some of the most marginal groups in the region. Subsequently, Varghese moved away from the CPI (M), questioned the electoral route it had taken, and joined the insurgent path and the short-lived armed campaign of Naxalite groups against landlords, police, and state personnel.[32] These groups did not subscribe to electoral democracy but advocated the use of force to bring about structural change. In a short period of time, the Naxalites in Bengal and Kerala in the late 1960s and 1970s moved from espousing large-scale peasant revolts to singular acts of annihilation of class enemies.[33] The armed actions of Naxalite groups met with quick and strong state response; and while some activists were arrested or felt compelled to surrender, Varghese was found dead in Wayanad forests, killed ostensibly in an "encounter" with Kerala police in February 1970.[34] It has since become clear that the encounter was staged and Varghese's death was the result of an extrajudicial killing carried out by Kerala police personnel.[35]

Vijayan and Varghese had emerged from the same party and political milieu with Raghavan as their senior colleague. They belonged to a party that actively led peasant and working-class revolts before independence, had briefly gone down the insurrectionary path, and then turned to electoral democracy. That turn and Raghavan's own experience with it had led him to the conclusion that the path of revolutionary action and violence was unsuitable[36] and "inappropriate"[37] for independent India and that electoral democracy needed to be accepted and embraced rather than shunned on the road to achieving substantive change. But with an embrace of representative democracy came fervent competition to rule and mobilization of degrees and forms of "muscle power" and aggressive force. Raghavan recognized these conditions and contributed to them by mobilizing young men from the ranks of the CPI (M) in Kannur.

Varghese, on the other hand, broke away and joined Naxal activists and, as I noted earlier, many like him paid a heavy price for this violence and the disavowal of electoral democracy. Others like Raghavan and Vijayan who participated in democratic political life flourished in its competitive milieu and contributed to it through their own aggressive masculine postures. Their careers and those of many others like them remind us that democracy not only accommodates *some* acts of political violence but has also allowed various groups to benefit from it as long as it appears that they also maintain an allegiance to its structures. This includes, as I have described, the CPI (M) as well as other parties.[38]

The CPI and the CPI (M) engaged with the question of violence in Indian democracy in various official documents and offered their own view of its place and potential. Party statements about possibilities of violence and militant collective action give us a sense of the discursive space that local CPI (M) leaders and workers inhabited while interparty conflict accentuated in Kannur. As I have described earlier, the CPI gave up the goal of insurrection in 1951 and assimilated parliamentary methods into its program of attaining People's Democracy.[39] In the first general elections, the party had emerged as the largest opposition group in the parliament and the communists thus shifted from their demand for an "immediate overthrow" of the government to more modest assertions for "change" or "replacement" of the "government of landlords, princes, financial sharks and speculators."[40] What was hence envisaged was no longer a single-stage transition to democracy and socialism, but a bloc by bloc, "step-by-step dislodging of the bourgeois from their honorable position."[41] But that step-by-step process was a fraught one and not free from the possibility of violent encounters. A mere shift to parliamentary form did not guarantee that violence had been eliminated from the polity.

As the 1951 CPI "Statement of Policy" noted, members of the party should not harbor the idea that parliamentary methods alone would bring People's Democracy in place of bourgeois democracy. It stated: "Because insurrection and civil war do not exist, some would like to believe as if they are living in a democracy with rights and liberties and nothing need be done to protect the Party and leadership of the mass organizations from the onslaughts of the law run mad. With such an outlook, we shall get smashed and will be able to build nothing."[42]

What was then required of the party workers was that they be cognizant and always aware of the prevalence and possibilities of violence that might be committed against them. The statement adopted anew in 1964 and then in 1972, continued on: "It needs always be borne in mind that the ruling classes never relinquish their power voluntarily. They seek to defy the will of people and seek to reverse it by lawlessness and violence. It is, therefore, necessary for the revolutionary forces to be vigilant and to so orient their work that they can face up to all contingencies, to any twist and turn in the political life of the country."[43]

Furthermore, such vigilance required a special category of people who could face up to the challenges posed by the ruling classes and their violence. The party had to, in the words of the policy statement, recruit "the most militant, most conscious, most self-sacrificing elements from among the fighting masses."[44] That was the first condition for achieving "full democracy" or realizing a "people's democratic state." The party did not call upon these agents to counter the violence of the bourgeoisie. However, it did call upon the most militant, conscious, and self-sacrificing of the fighting masses to be vigilant and face up to all the contingencies and twists and turns in the political life of the country.

In my conversations with them, CPI (M) workers often described the Hindu right's attempts to expand its influence in Kannur in the late 1960s as such a twist in the political life of the region that rightfully galvanized militant party members against members of the ruling class. This interpretation might be viewed as a justification for the violence to become major, containing and minoritizing the opposition in which both groups were engaged in the years to come. At the same time, it is important to note that the first set of grave confrontations between the party left and the Hindu right did in fact grow out of a dispute around wages and welfare of workers with wealthy owners of beedi factories, which were one of the main sources of employment in the region. The details of that dispute, how it unfolded and merged with competition to secure popular support to lay the grounds for the sharply antagonistic conflict between the two groups in the years to come, are the subject of the next section.

The Early Clashes, or the Sangh Comes to Kannur

For the first two decades after independence, the RSS's party affiliate at the time, the BJS (Bharatiya Jan Sangh), had been close to business sections of the middle classes and actively opposed Nehru's attempts to introduce a redistributive socialist dispensation.[45] However, by the late 1960s, the Jan Sangh was seeking to broaden its support base and expand its own workers and unions networks. On their part, the beedi workers of North Kerala had been closely associated with the party left and had participated in socialist and Communist Party–led collective actions in the region since the late 1930s. They had been at the frontline of important strikes in the wake of both the Congress Socialist–led protests for independence as well as Communist Party–led mass action in the late 1940s.[46] Over time, as the number of beedi workers increased from 4,061 in 1951 to almost forty thousand in the late 1960s, they also become a major voting bloc for the CPI and then the CPI (M).[47]

While they made up an important political constituency, beedi workers were facing difficult economic challenges. The practice of decentralizing beedi manufacturing into small middlemen-managed units that many beedi company owners had adapted was badly affecting work conditions and the nature of benefits that beedi workers in the region received. In this backdrop, the CPI (M)-led Kerala government took steps to implement the 1966 Beedi and Cigar Workers' Conditions of Employment Act, which was designed to advance wage and labor reforms in the beedi industry. In order to contain adverse effects of the industry's decentralization, the act sought to provide beedi workers with a retirement fund, gratuity, maternity, and medical benefits.[48] By implementing the act, the CPI (M) government could extend and institutionalize forms of care that had played an important role in the rise of communist and socialist leaders in the decades just before and after independence. The legitimacy of subsequent CPI (M) governments, in the eyes of party supporters, and belief in the party's right to rule was anchored in precisely such extension of governmental care.

Owners of beedi manufacturing units—led especially by a Mangalore-based company Ganesh Beedi that employed twelve thousand workers—deemed the government's actions as unfriendly to business and challenged them in court.[49] As calls by workers to implement the act intensified, the company locked down its production divisions and laid off its workers, citing labor unrest and the breakdown of law and order. In order to make up for business and earnings that they were losing due to the strike and lockdown, owners of Ganesh Beedi, who had close links with the RSS, deputed one of its organizers, Chandrashekharan, to further disaggregate production, find workers ready to roll beedis in their homes, and manage this outsourced network under a different banner and system.[50] This assignment offered an important first opportunity to the Sangh to start building relationships with ordinary working-class residents of the region. In past years, beedi workers were aligned with either the Communist Party left or socialist formations; now the Hindu right was seeking to develop a relationship with them at a time when the workers' livelihood and well-being was gravely threatened.

The piece-rate system that Ganesh Beedi owners introduced through the RSS member Chandrashekharan and his colleagues provided neither good wages nor any benefits and welfare guarantee to beedi workers. Nevertheless, several workers took recourse to it in the midst of an impasse between owners of beedi manufacturing units and Communist Party–affiliated unions that were agitating for the implementation of the act.[51] Workers looking to make ends meet in challenging times were also drawn to the RSS-affiliated union Bharatiya Mazdoor Sangh (BMS). The leaders of BMS were close to the owners of beedi manufacturing units and could assure inclusion in the outsourced production network.[52] In the meantime, members of left unions picketed Ganesh Beedi offices and several beedi depots were set on fire. The attempts of BMS to draw in beedi workers of the region into its organizational network while opposing legislation for better wages and welfare provisions was precisely the kind of twist and turn in political life that the CPI (M)'s statement of policy had invoked when it spoke about mobilizing militant, self-conscious members of the fighting masses. In the days to come, three hundred members of left unions were arrested as encounters between CPI (M) and BMS members took more violent turns.[53]

The CPI (M)- and BMS-led violence consisted not only of attacks on beedi depots but also in clashes between CPI (M) supporters of other occupational backgrounds and young men drawn toward the RSS. The combative milieu not only affected beedi workers and union affiliates but started becoming more generalized into an intergroup conflict between supporters of the party left and new budding members of the Hindu right. Consequently, in November and December 1968, the region came to witness aggressive everyday encounters between young men associated with the CPI (M) and the new Hindu right recruits. According to Isaac et al., "occasional confrontations (between the two groups) soon developed into a war of attrition. Knives and bombs were freely used."[54] Ramakrishnan, the sweet-maker and RSS supporter whom I referred to in the previous section, was killed. Vijayan, the current Kerala chief minister and CPI (M) politburo member, was accused of murder but found to be not guilty. And the Hindu right, looking to expand its networks and mobilize more support, became a part of the political landscape in the midst of the "street war"[55] with left union members and others associated with the Communist Party.

On its part, the CPI (M) government sought to secure the interests of its traditional supporters by becoming more proactive in its efforts to address challenges that the beedi workers were facing.[56] In order to secure their work and welfare, the CPI (M) government took measures to launch a new company—Kerala Dinesh Beedi, a worker-owned and government-supported beedi cooperative—that could absorb thousands of beedi rollers of the region who had been rendered jobless in the last few months. Ideological claims about safeguarding the interests of the working class and a democratic imperative to obtain greater and greater popular and electoral support converged with the founding of Kerala Dinesh Beedi.

Beedi rollers associated with the new cooperative emerged as strong CPI (M) sympathizers, and the cooperative's factories came to be seen as recruiting grounds for the Communist Party. A few years later, in a series of concerted violent attacks, members of the Hindu right targeted Dinesh

Beedi factories as a means of physically and symbolically hurting the party left's political base in the region. Through a sharp battle for support among beedi workers, an intense phase of conflict between CPI (M) and Sangh members was inaugurated in the late 1960s. Violent encounters that grew out of a classical clash between industrial bourgeoisie and those seeking to represent working-class interests drew in rank and file of the two groups. More importantly, it heralded another phase of competitive contests between the party left and the Hindu right that revolved less around the question of working-class interests and much more around the problem of presence and support in local neighborhoods, towns, and villages—in other words, the typical democratic competition to gain popularity, electoral, and state power, and become major. In the next section, I locate this violence and transformation in regional and national history in order to highlight the Hindu right's more populist turn, its growth in Kerala and across the country, the declaration of national emergency, its lifting, and the repercussions on Kannur's political terrain.

A New Mimetic Conflictual Phase

The late 1960s and 1970s were years of high drama in the history of Indian democracy. The growth of the Hindu right in Kerala and the deepening of its conflict with the party left in Kannur is closely tied to the remarkable events of those years. To understand the trajectory of this conflict in North Kerala, a review of these events and the nature of political collectives and actions they affected is necessary.

As I noted earlier, the late 1960s and 1970s were a time when the Hindu right was seeking to expand its popular presence. Indeed, according to some scholars, the Sangh was adapting new populist practices.[57] Like the socialists and other groups, the BJS was increasingly trying to position itself as a party of the so-called common man, engaged in questions of the welfare and well-being of the underclasses and ready to take up agitational politics on their behalf.[58] It was a period when the Indira Gandhi–led national government, deemed autocratic and immoral, was facing growing opposition in the wake of corruption scandals and precarious economic conditions, leading to popular calls for national rebuilding. In places such as Bihar and Gujarat, Hindu right-wing students became active participants in the increasingly popular and vociferous movement led by socialist Jayprakash (JP) Narayan against corruption and the Indira government. Many in the movement hoped that its sheer force would compel the government to resign. Instead, in June 1975, the government imposed a national emergency citing threats of anarchy and a fascist takeover.[59]

It is debatable whether the JP movement's association with the Hindu right made it a potential fascist threat. However, that specter was powerfully evoked in Indira Gandhi's reasoning for imposing emergency.[60] Nearly 110,000 people were arrested under the Maintenance of Internal Security Act in the nineteen-month emergency period.[61] As Jaffrelot notes, a high proportion of those arrested were Sangh members or affiliates.[62] Two years later, motivated by a number of factors that remain indeterminate, Indira Gandhi lifted the emergency and members of all parties were released and elections subsequently announced.[63]

After this period of short suspension, electoral democracy was back. Political parties of different shades, including the CPI (M) and the Hindu right, reverted to electoral competition to obtain majority support, form governments, and cast the future of the country as a representative democracy. Nevertheless, an important political shift had taken place. The Hindu right had determinedly opposed the then unpopular Indira regime as part of a mass movement, with its youth and student wings having especially drawn national attention. Once the emergency was lifted in 1977, the Jan Sangh teamed with various socialist formations. This alliance entered into seat adjustments with (among others) the CPI (M) to put together a new government whose members had not only challenged Indira Gandhi through popular action but also defeated her party electorally. While this coalition government did not last long, all these factors won the Sangh considerable national legitimacy and support. And, although more mass agitations and electoral successes were to come, for now, for the first time in its history the Hindu right had been able to both experience the highs of agitational politics and successfully translate it into a place in the national government.

During this time, the RSS *shakha* (local branch network) expanded, as did membership in Sangh affiliates.[64] Kerala too saw a substantial rise in the ranks of RSS workers during the emergency and post-emergency years.[65] In North Kerala, young men of various families that had once supported the Praja Socialist Party leader Kurup were now drawn to the RSS and Jan Sangh.[66] Members of the RSS also began approaching CPI (M) recruits, and this triggered fresh attempts to contain the Sangh and ward off its mobilization efforts in the region. It is difficult to say exactly how many young men began attending RSS shakhas in Kannur once the emergency was lifted, but a number of accounts give us a sense of the reasons why young men were drawn to these local acculturation units as well as the tensions and violence sparked by the Sangh's recruitment drive. I became privy to some of these narratives during my interviews with RSS-BJP workers.[67]

Several interviewees who had joined the Sangh in the late 1970s and early 1980s recounted the respect with which they came to regard it for its role in the pre- and post-emergency period. They spoke of the compelling nature of shakhas, the activities, ideas, and camaraderie on offer there, while also recounting the intimidation that new members faced from their CPI (M) counterparts.[68] Some interviewees, who were particularly candid, described the ways in which new RSS–Jan Sangh recruits confronted CPI (M) workers and sought to become a presence and gain primacy in areas previously associated with the party left.[69] Two murders—of Panunda Chandran, a young RSS recruit in September 1978, and Raju Master, a leading CPI (M) figure of the area in October 1978—stand out in the accounts that Sangh and CPI (M) workers give of this period.[70] Chandran's family members were CPI (M) supporters, whereas he chose to join the Sangh. While Sangh members allege that he was killed because he had shifted his loyalties, they accuse Raju Master of orchestrating all attacks on their new affiliates.

The murder of Raju Master, in October 1978, was the first killing of a well-known local leader in the wake of the conflict between the party left and the Hindu right, which in turn set off a chain of attacks and counterattacks. And while four Hindu right workers were indicted for the schoolmaster and local CPI (M) leader's murder, police documents record comparable numbers of injured and dead from both groups in these years following the emergency.[71] In their narratives about these attacks and counterattacks in the late 1970s and early 1980s, members of each group describe the other's crimes as triggers for their own violence, each act deserving of equal, if not greater, response. This practice of one-upmanship or competing to become more equal than the other that also characterizes electoral contests was iterating itself in the lives of political workers of Kannur through violence. Underlying this process was one that resembles what the anthropologist Gregory Bateson called schismogenesis.[72] Schismogenesis refers to the mimetic power struggles, reminiscent of a cycle of machinations to be the dominant side, that has, among other things, marked a number of critical global moments ranging from the cold war to the intensification of aggression that occurred in the wake of 9/11.[73] Attempts to equalize scores at these times have been entangled with the call to obtain dominance and produce acts that seek to create a strong impact, generate considerable fear, and become memorable. In Kannur, symmetry of force was often promptly achieved while at other times it was deferred. However, violent symmetries are not always neat.

A particularly unforgettable and spectacular event took place approximately ten years after the establishment of the Dinesh Beedi cooperative—on April 6, 1979. On that day, several members of the Hindu right attacked multiple Kerala Dinesh Beedi factories and a CPI (M)-affiliated sports club in the area with crude bombs, sword knives, and sticks.[74] These coordinated attacks occurred all around the same hour in the evening. In one of the most talked about of these incidents in Taazhe Champad, two beedi workers and an alleged assailant affiliated with the RSS–Jan Sangh died while approximately ten people were injured.[75] Among the CPI (M) workers who died as a result of these attacks were two well-respected local-level workers who were rising through the ranks of the party left hierarchy; among the accused were young Sangh recruits who went on to occupy important positions in its organizational network.[76] The attacks became important reference points in the careers of many local-level workers on both sides.

The simultaneity of the strikes suggests that the violence at Kerala Dinesh Beedi cooperative factories in April 1979 was concerted and well organized.[77] A pattern of intensified attacks and counterattacks between members of the CPI (M) and the Hindu right was well underway. By this time, the violence between the two groups was not necessarily entwined with ideological and class interests of the kind that drove beedi workers' agitation and the Ganesh Beedi lockout; it was a violence of containment and one-upmanship increasingly intermixed with a bitter affective charge.

Police documents relating to the violence between members of the CPI (M) and the Hindu right during the late 1970s and early 1980s are detailed. The ex–police commissioner Alexander Jacob compiled these documents in a report on (what he calls) RSS-Marxist clashes between 1978 and 1981.[78] At several points in these descriptions of political violence, Jacob characterizes it as a "trial of strength" between the two formations.[79] The statistics of murder, attempt to murder, and rioting that he presents show that the party left and the Hindu right were head to head in the play of strength that was unfolding in Kannur during this time.[80] The incidents that he records included "the free use of country bombs, lethal weapons such as dagger, sword and spears as weapons of offence."[81]

Police investigations of these cases and Jacob's account of them have been based on official complaints that members of one or the other group filed.[82] Each group tended to present a version of events that made its members appear innocent and their opponent as the aggressors. It is therefore unlikely that the violent incidents occurred in exactly the way that members of the two parties described in their complaints. Nevertheless, the large volume of complaints, and records of deaths and injuries that they caused, give us a sense of the toll that the conflict was now exacting. Case records detailing the identity of those killed, hurt, and the accused show that the conflict between the CPI (M) and the Hindu right was drawing in young men from artisanal, peasant, and other working-class groups such as weavers, carpenters, bus drivers, and so-called coolies[83] or head-load workers. Each attack created a feedback loop. Layers of hurt folded upon themselves with time as workers of the two groups sought to equalize scores. The push for equalizing scores was now acquiring a vindictive character. The workers' search for schismogenetic symmetry was accompanied more and more by calls for reprisals escalating the violence further.

CPI (M) Workers, Preman, and Vengeful Violence

In this section, I turn to the life histories of CPI (M) supporters and workers to further elaborate on the conditions surrounding the calls for equalizing the scores of violence and obtaining revenge. Thus, I seek to offer an account of their formation as victims and agents of competitive and increasingly vengeful violence against members of the Hindu right. Here it is important to recall that the violence between members of the party left and the Sangh was playing out in a context where the CPI (M) had come to be associated with some of the most constructive possibilities of democratic life: egalitarianism, governmental care, and welfare. By focusing on the lives of a new generation of CPI (M) workers active from the 1980s to the early 2000s, I highlight how life in the party and a democratic polity produced cohesive and supportive communities but also drew its members into the world of antagonistic political violence.

In Kannur, as I discussed in chapter 1, Communist Party leaders like Gopalan had fostered practices of pastoral care as well as collective struggle since the early twentieth century. In post-independence Kerala, the CPI and subsequently the CPI (M) built on that legacy. For many families in Kannur, association with the Communist Party became an intergenerational heritage. Notable among families and young people who shared this heritage are members of peasant, artisanal, and working class Thiyya families. Over the years, many Thiyya families came to associate opportunities to emerge as equal, visible, and audible beings with access to a decent life with the growth of the Communist Party. While hardship and precarity still characterized their lives, the CPI (M)'s ascendance to the seats of Kerala government, its attempts to redistribute hutment land, and emphasis on welfare-based policies had earned it not just legitimacy in the eyes of these sections of the population but also their loyalty.

Nevertheless, some young men from such families were drawn to the RSS shakhas.[84] On the other hand, many others who sought to physically contain the turn to the Hindu right wing and, in their words, "defend" the CPI (M) hailed their deep affinity with the party. Someone who sought to safeguard the interests of the party, affirmed his closeness to it, and whose life history helps me analyze the ways in which the CPI (M)–Sangh conflict cast young men of the region is Preman. I first invoked Preman's life history and career in the party in the opening pages of this chapter.

As I noted, Preman was in his mid- to late thirties when I first met him in the early 2000s. Violent attacks and counterattacks between local-level workers of the party left and the Hindu right had become very frequent as well as spectacular at that time. In 1979, when the attack on Dinesh Beedi took place, Preman was about ten years old. In fact, he was at the Tazhe Champad beedi factory lending a hand to his father, a beedi-roller, when the attack occurred. Preman's father was extremely ill when we first met; however, in his younger days he too had been an active member of the CPI (M), propounded its egalitarian principles, and participated in jathas and demonstrations.

In the 1960s, Preman's father had been involved in violent clashes with workers of Kurup's PSP. Following the promulgation of the 1971 Land Reform Act, Preman's father traveled to Allepey and other parts of Kerala to take part in the mass movement led by the CPI (M). The movement sought to forcibly implement the provisions of the act by encroaching on government and private lands, taking possession of 10 cents (580 square feet) of land around a family's hut, erecting fences, and plucking coconuts. At that time, he was among the nearly five thousand people arrested for these acts.[85] And while land reforms devolved only hutment and not productive land on beneficiaries, Preman and his father celebrated the movement and the level of economic security it was able to obtain for them and families like theirs.[86] Their affinity for the CPI (M) stemmed from this history and was buttressed further when the Dinesh Beedi cooperative was established. Preman's father found work there, and it was the family's main source of livelihood for more than two decades.

Land reforms, governmental welfare, and employment in places like beedi cooperatives were some of the ways in which aspirations for equality and well-being were realized in Preman and his family's life. The life and living that the CPI (M)'s policies and rule afforded Preman's family often felt inadequate; Preman, who worked as a construction and daily wage laborer, was only partially employed and often unemployed. His family, including his elderly parents, wife, and three children, lived in a dilapidated and small two-room house, and they possessed no land other than that on which their house stood. Nevertheless, Preman believed that the various CPI (M)-led governments and their welfare-based development model had prevented the family from suffering utter abjection that they might have in another context.[87] There were thus, according to Preman, many reasons to regard the CPI (M) as the most deserving and virtuous of parties, whose claims to popular and electoral power he was ready to back.

Preman had joined the CPI (M)'s children's wing, or *balsangham*, in 1982 at the age of thirteen. In the years that followed, he witnessed intense episodes of violence between his colleagues in the CPI (M) and members of the Hindu right. This violence drew in Preman and his friends and contemporaries in the party in multiple ways. He spoke about those who were killed, ones who were injured, and about grueling trials and prison time. Preman also spoke at length about his encounters with that violence and his understanding of the conditions that triggered it. My interaction with Preman consisted of interviews carried out with the help of my research assistant, walkabouts around his village, and casual as well as more structured discussions with his friends and family about their backgrounds, family, work, and political life. Highlighted in these interactions was how Preman's attachment to and affinity with the party was more than skin deep. In one conversation, he described his relationship to the party as something that flowed through his blood. Preman stated, "To tell you the truth, it [the party/CPI (M)] is in my blood from early childhood.... Even in times of trouble, I would not like to be away from party organization and its different familial worlds."

If young men like Gopalan and Raghavan from higher-caste groups and families had emerged as party leaders in previous generations, Preman (and before him his father) made up the ranks. Key aspects of their biographies reveal a script that many young men of their caste–class background have lived through in twentieth-century Kerala. While Preman's father participated in the movement for land redistribution, battled members of rival formations such as Kurup's PSP, and was a part of the beedi cooperative closely associated with the CPI (M), Preman acted in plays to mobilize and organize "the masses." Niranjana's famous novel *Chirasmarana* (1977) on the young martyrs of the 1940s peasant struggle in North Kerala was, according to Preman, his favorite book.

Preman lived in an era when the search for electoral victories rather than peasant revolt had taken center stage and preoccupied the party. From a young age, he and his friends in the party would go house to house during elections canvassing for their candidate and the party. Or they would travel around the area with megaphones holding mini election rallies. Workers like Preman also facilitated the formation of associations and networks that became the site of dense sociality and close relationships among young men of their area. On his part, Preman helped start the "Red Star Volleyball Club" in his village that many young male supporters of the party were active in. Regarding himself as a "social worker," he also extended networks of care that party leaders and its governmental arm had instituted in the last few decades. According to Preman, the degree of his involvement in the lives of fellow party workers and so-called party families often became exceptionally intense. His role in the party's networks of pastoral care and self-representation as a "social worker" demanded that Preman be present in the lives of his neighbors as well as current and potential party supporters and participate in their everyday concerns, health, well-being, and various rites of passage.[88] Preman was, in his own fashion, living out forms of political masculinity that had become hegemonic in Kerala. As a local-level party worker in a contentious milieu, he had another role, namely to (in his friends' words) "defend" the party.

Preman had been active in actions to aggressively ward off persons, signs, and symbols of the opposite group. In his conversations about his "actions" to defend the party, Preman evoked the local topography of the conflict between local-level CPI (M) and Hindu right-wing workers. He noted how members of the RSS-BJP cadre often made their presence felt in the next village by painting tree trunks and walls in public spaces in their party colors, inscribing the words RSS or BJP on them, or just standing around in the village square. But if they ventured toward Preman's village and sought to make their presence felt there, they were likely to be confronted—beaten and intimidated—by him and/or his fellow CPI (M) workers. As he put it, "they come, we attack."

Attacks and counterattacks were the typical forms that the competition and conflict between members of the two groups had taken over the years. Riding on these schismogenetic attacks was the appearance of strength, the dynamics of being more equal than the other, delimiting the opponent's presence in an area and hence their capacities, and rendering them as minor figures. Hand in hand went the imperative to become a major presence and institute mobilization and organizational activities capable of generating visible and calculable support in the near and distant future. This logic had been playing in the lives of local-level political workers of Kannur for several years. Preman's statements, his readiness to attack, his desire to defend (the party), and the palpable sense of fear and anxiety he communicated in some moments were a testimony to this.

Every attack intensified the adversarial character of the political milieu and encouraged members of the two groups to herd together with their own. Political competition spurred violent contestation as well as strong bonds and relationships among members of each group positioned against the other. For young men from lower income, "backward-caste" families like Preman, party affiliations and networks provided spaces for enactments of popular sovereignty, aspirations for recognition and equality, as well as sites of obtaining and facilitating pastoral care and well-being. In a polarizing political context, party networks also inspired strong attachments comparable with blood relationships shared in a family but also projected on fraternities of male colleagues, friends, and comrades. The violence such fraternities experienced against their members laid the grounds for vengeful reprisal and the production of a hate-ridden antagonistic conflict.

Of Close Ties and Hate

The metaphor of blood ties that Preman evoked suggests a vision of affinity modeled on filiation, being not just akin but as if of the same substance or body. As I discuss in the next chapter, organicist notions and language-invoking cohesiveness and consubstantiality are much better developed among members of the RSS–BJP. At the same time, local-level CPI (M) workers also occasionally articulated similar ideas, especially as they came to find inspiration for their vision of a political community in the family. Amid communities of mutual support and in the face of competition for popular and electoral support, this "regime of sameness"[89] was reassuring. Equality was envisioned with those viewed as alike. Politics became about the assertion of this self-same subject or community made up of fraternity of fellow party members and families with a long history of association with the party.[90] When one of them was attacked, the reaction was intense and visceral.

I am reminded of a young CPI (M) worker I met whose mouth and hands trembled with pain as he recounted the murder of a fellow party worker. I am also reminded of a statement that Preman made: as he sought to explain the violence of his milieu, Preman turned around and looked at his old friend and local youth leader, Sumesh, and stated with clarity, "[If] opponents come to murder this man [referring to Sumesh] then how can I love those adversaries.... Those who deserve hatred should be hated."[91] Preman was articulating a compulsion or an imperative. In this instance, the compulsion to deliver an equal or harder blow was entwined with the relationships that Preman and his fellow party workers had formed with each other and with their local leaders. He was quite categorical: "To attack a person I am fond of is not correct." Here, reprisal was posited as an obvious reaction and those who attacked one's friends and leaders became the "hated."

The local CPI (M) leader Sumesh, like his close friend Preman, belonged to a Thiyya family, albeit one where professional success of various members had enabled the family to enjoy a comfortable middle-class life. The very genial Sumesh had risen from the ranks and was placed in an important position at the district office of the party. By the 1990s and 2000s, local leaders like Sumesh had replaced paters and patrons of yore in many parts of the district. Unlike upper-caste leaders like Gopalan or Kurup, new leaders like Sumesh were socially more equal to the young men on the ground they sought to mobilize. Therefore, they behaved less as shepherds guiding their flock and more as big brothers leading and commanding. A sense of camaraderie, friendship, brotherliness, and even love (or *sneham* as I describe in the next chapter) inflected their accounts of relationships with each other.

Communities of filial care and fraternal camaraderie formed in the backdrop of competition for popular and electoral support are not rare or exceptional in postcolonial democracies, but they have, however, taken noticeable forms in Kannur. Indeed, the fraternal and familial world of local-level CPI (M) workers contains many distinct features. Unlike members of Hindu right-wing communities or members of other so-called backward communities that have become politically significant,[92] CPI (M) workers do not often emphasize common ethnic origins and mythico-religious fathers or mothers.[93] Furthermore, to draw on MacCannell's words, the family portrait is repainted in many communities that uphold modern egalitarian ideals.[94] The emergence of a new egalitarian ethos in Kerala meant respite from traditional patriarchs and feudal overlords for many. Fraternities or masculine communities of friends and comrades have however emerged in their place. But here, too, the density of everyday social and political life has often been enmeshed with the "romance of self-repetition, similarity, resemblance, the order of the same" that, as Leela Gandhi notes, even the most "radical communities of difference" founded on solidarities of class, gender, or race are not immune to.[95] The community of friends has thus seemed like family and extensions of self; the community of male comrades has appeared as a "regime of brothers."[96]

Over the decades, a contestatory masculine culture in the aid of such a fraternal community of male comrades emerged among the local-level CPI (M) workers of Kannur.[97] Vengeful violence followed. Vengeance has its own symmetrical schismogenetic aspect that is often very harsh.[98] In the opening pages of the chapter, I narrated Preman's vivid description of strong vengeful feelings that have, in his experience, impelled cruel violence in the course of the conflict between the party left and the Hindu right. Life in the CPI (M) and a democratic polity had brought him to this fraught juncture. The CPI (M) in Kerala has played a critical part in the institution of a relatively more caring regime that provides better access to social goods than state governments in other parts of India. As compared to other prominent parties, it has underplayed the public role of ascriptive identities like religion and caste in the formation of political communities.[99] Since the late 1960s, it has also been violently contesting the growth of the Hindu right in the region.

Local-level workers of both the party left and the Hindu right involved in the violent conflict with each other share a similar class, religious, and caste background. And yet the contest between them to become a stronger presence and the major political force in the region has generated considerable violence. In various parts of India, hateful violence ridden with animus and antagonism has occurred repeatedly—against Dalits and against religious minorities, in Khairlanji, Gujarat, Muzzaffarnagar, Delhi, and several other places.[100] Events, for instance, in small towns of Uttar Pradesh in the wake of the 2019–2020 anti-CAA protests suggest that hatefulness and cruelty against minorities are aspects of attempts to truly minoritize them, render them without influence and resources, fearful, and abject.[101] That has what assertion of majoritarianism has meant in these places.

In Kannur, however, the drive to assert dominance has played itself out among two equally strong formations whose local-level workers tick the same or comparable religious, caste, and class boxes. If the CPI (M) has enjoyed considerable popular and electoral support in Kerala for many decades, the Hindu right has advanced nationally. It has won many elections and formed various provincial and national governments especially since 2000. Neither one has been reduced to a minor position, but both groups have engaged in an assemblage of competitive practices to achieve ascendance on the ground—in the towns, villages, and streets of Kannur. Competitive democratic politics has conditioned their thrust to become a major force. It has not mitigated but accentuated polarities and fixed workers of the two groups among their own close-knit kin-like networks and regimes of brothers.

The CPI (M)'s historical associations with emancipatory collective action, pastoral power, governmental welfare policies, and discourse of egalitarianism have played an important role in the formation of strong attachments with the party. In chapter 3 we will see how the Hindu right has forged similar bonds through its service activities and discourse of oneness and unity. It then becomes clearer how competition and conflict have strongly contributed to the formations of communities of affection and reprehension among members of the party left and the Hindu right. Situated in sharply opposed but internally cohesive communities, workers of the two groups have responded to attacks on them with severity. Hence, Kannur has been a site of not only agonistic contests but also antagonistic conflict as cruel violence among members of the two groups has come on the backs of a competitive democratic polity. Interparty violent conflict in North Kerala is a testimony to the ways in which the imperative to obtain majority support and become a major presence can foster divisions and violence even among people who are otherwise similar. This exceptional aspect of Kannur's long history of political conflict and its dramatic iterations draws attention to the ways in which the drive to be dominant, or majoritarianism, work to produce violent political communities in democracies. Hateful violence and cruelty have become a normal part of the Indian polity. This chapter and book are an attempt to understand how the workings of modern representative democracy have helped program the Indian polity to produce such violence.

Care, Connectedness, and Violence in Hindu Right Communities

Cultivating Internal Bonds and Conflict

This chapter revolves around the relationship between closely linked Hindu right communities and political violence. It analyzes the cohesive communities that Hindu right-wing workers have forged among themselves to create affective bonds anchored in mutual assistance, shared social vision, and identity. My examination focuses on the formation and inner life of Hindu right communities particularly from the late 1960s to early 2000s in Kannur. This period is a critical one due to the Sangh's organizational spread in North Kerala that also coincided with the germination and intensification of its violent conflict with the party left.

The Sangh has, over the years, developed a two-pronged strategy to obtain popular and state power. Cohesive communities of local-level workers and supporters, promoted through the local shakha, family contact, and social welfare programs, make up the middle term between the Hindu right's majoritarian aspirations and its violence directed against its so-called civilizational adversaries and political opponents (Muslims, Christians, and those associated with left ideologies and organizations). As various scholars have highlighted, this community-driven strategy entails the production of an adversarial majoritarian Hindu identity ranged against its purported enemies while also strengthening strong internal bonds and a sense of sameness and cohesion among its supporters.[1] The Sangh, to use Gyanendra Pandey's words, perpetuates "suspicion, fear and hostility"[2] against minority religious groups and left formations. At the same time, organizations such as Rashtriya Sewa Bharti and Vanvasi Kalyan Ashram that make up the Hindu right network seek to draw in supporters through welfare, or so-called service or *sewa* units, and coalesce them.[3]

My focus in this chapter is therefore on these Hindu right practices of dispensing care and cultivating connectedness to foster what I am calling a cohesive violent community. While acts of intimidation, attempts to murder, and murder became part of the region's political life, throughout the 1980s, 1990s, and 2000s, care and connectedness were simultaneously deployed by the Sangh to generate internal bonds among its workers and supporters. Therefore, of central importance is the dual relationship between the use of community care and the deployment of violence. I argue that it is precisely the culture of cohesion and connectedness created among Sangh members that has reinforced and contributed to violent political conflict in Kannur. I show how the violence they enacted and suffered contributed to strengthening the bonds that members of the Hindu right shared with one another. In turn, these bonds further perpetuated the conflict between the Hindu right and the party left.

In Kannur, as in other parts of the country, the Sangh has mobilized the politics of enmity together with practices of extending welfare services and offering care. Specifically, after the national emergency was withdrawn in 1977, the RSS, Jan Sangh, and other Hindu right affiliates intensified their joint efforts to further the Sangh's presence in the region. Its members adopted adversarial and increasingly antagonistic stances particularly against their counterparts in the party left, who opposed the Hindu right's attempts to enlarge its sway in the region. As we saw in chapter 2, competition for influence and popular support generated violent divisions between local-level workers of the Hindu right and CPI (M) even though they shared similar religious, caste, and class backgrounds. It is in the backdrop of this conflict that I examine how the Sangh sought and still seeks to direct the actions and dispositions of its young recruits as it molds their attachments to each other and the organization as a whole.

To explain how care and violence merge into one in Hindu right communities in Kannur, my research takes a closer look at the practices through which the Sangh has sought to create strong internal bonds among its workers and supporters, and how party members have lived out these bonds in the context of violent political conflict. I note how the violent conflict between workers of the party left and the Hindu right pushed members of each group toward their own party colleagues and supporters. As each group became a target of attack for the other, filial and fraternal care and strong kin-like ties were activated internally among CPI (M) and RSS-BJP workers and followers. Within both groups, the love that their members shared for each other was intimately linked to the animosity they shared against those who hurt their colleagues, comrades, and friends. Nevertheless, there are important differences between the communities of love and hate that workers of the party left and the Hindu right came to forge in the midst of contest and conflict. In comparison to members of the CPI (M), the Sangh developed a more charged language of oneness and repertoires of sociality to foster similitude pitched against imagined and real adversaries. In particular, valorization of shared origins, religious affiliation, and animus against purported enemies have been central to the Hindu right's philosophy, social propaganda, and political program. This divisive discourse has operated side by side with the Sangh's homogenizing vocabulary, social service units, and structures such as the local shakha where members come together daily for a program of intellectual and physical training. Implementing strong internal cohesion has therefore been the other side of the Hindu right's attempts to limit and disempower the opposition. In this way, both polarization and cohesion have been two important pivots of the Hindu right's well-honed programs to realize its majoritarian aspirations in a competitive democracy. These programs have directly contributed to making Kannur a site where the potential for conflict contained in modern democracies has been lived out in notable ways.

Care, Connectedness, and Violence: History, Concepts, and Ethnography

In order to elaborate on the particular role that practices of disbursing care and cohesive communities have played in the political conflict between the Hindu right and the party left in Kannur, I locate their emergence in the longer history of the Sangh's mobilization programs in the region. As in Kannur, these programs have had a strong polarizing agenda in other areas too. While the Hindu right in North Kerala has focused on the CPI (M) as its key political adversary in the region since the late 1960s, its activities have also been pitted against local Muslim communities. As seen in the 1971–1972 Thalassery riot,[4] Hindu right members have used staple tactics of generating strong attachments to the majority Hindu identity that RSS-BJP members purport to defend by staging conflictual situations with members of minority groups. Additionally, at various critical junctures in the late 1960s, the early 1970s, and the years following the lifting of the emergency, Sangh members organized contentious movements around majority and minority sacred geographies and symbols prevalent in Kerala.[5] Nationally, the late 1980s and early 1990s also saw Hindu right-wing organizations escalating their campaign around sacred spaces such as Babri Masjid that inaugurated a new phase of polarization between religious majority and minority groups in the country. This campaign generated several riots and incredible violence against the Muslim minority.[6] It also brought electoral gains for the BJP in different parts of the country and helped it to consolidate a bigger political majority. However, in Kerala the BJP was unable to grow electorally at this time; indeed, its vote share decreased by 0.8 percent in the 1990s.[7] Against this backdrop, the Sangh began to turn to outreach work and service activities as a way of obtaining more popular support, especially among subaltern Dalit and Adivasi groups, which it regards as weaker sections of the Hindu majority.[8] It began expanding its basic provisioning services made up of orphanages and mobile medical and food distribution units, eventually making Kerala home to fifty-two Sangh-run orphanages and one of the densest networks of Sangh service provisions in the country.[9]

In recent years detailed historical, ethnographic, and statistical accounts of the Hindu right's social welfare strategy have been offered by scholars such as Malini Bhattacharjee and Tariq Thachil.[10] Both scholars, in their respective writings, remind us that, since the early decades of independent India, the Sangh has sought to cast itself as a concerned humanitarian group that not only engaged in disaster relief during times of political calamities, such as the partition and, similarly, natural disasters such as earthquakes and cyclones, but was also involved in the lives of marginal groups by attending to their everyday welfare and well-being. In her work, Bhattacharjee highlights the evolution of the Hindu right's social welfare strategy over the decades and the discourse of *sewa* or the selfless services it mobilizes, along with the cultural appeal of this discourse. Building on these welfare activities, Hindu right leaders began displaying greater "electoral pragmatism" and started pursuing a policy of "vote maximization" through appeals to "subaltern constituencies"[11] especially from the 1980s onward.

Thachil evaluates the political rewards that the Sangh has been able to reap in various parts of the country by instituting a vast network of organizations that disburse educational, health, food, and livelihood assistance among targeted groups in various parts of the country. While it is debatable how useful this service strategy or mode of enacting pastoral power has been for the Sangh in its search for electoral rewards in Kerala,[12] my interest in this chapter is less on the vote capturing potential of the Sangh's outreach work or its organizational dimensions. Instead, I am interested in the cohesive forms of community that the welfare approach has instituted among those who took part in it, namely local-level Hindu right recruits who joined the neighborhood RSS branches or shakhas. These recruits were over time absorbed further into the Sangh ranks and eventually became the victims and agents of its violent conflict with the party left. In this move beyond the question of vote gain through welfare assistance, I examine the role of communities of young male Sangh supporters in asserting and often promoting violence.

In discussing the role that services and outreach works have played in the lives of Hindu right workers, I turn to the Foucauldian terms "power of care" and pastoral power that I have invoked in previous chapters.[13] The term *care* helps me capture the quotidian and corporeal character of relations activated in the work of meeting others' needs.[14] Most especially, I focus on the forms of connectedness and attachments that acts of care have initiated and perpetuated among Hindu right workers and supporters in the midst of political violence. While feminist political theorists like Joan Tronto envision care as the cornerstone of a better democracy, various arms of the state as well as nonstate actors like members of the Hindu right deploy care alongside violence. Care then becomes the relational force of the Sangh's cohesively produced communities. These acts of care have afforded the Sangh power to not only mold individual bodies, minds, and energies but also shape its members' sense of being part of the communal whole—their experience of not just themselves but each other as interlinked beings.

Foucault noted how pastoral power iterated in acts of shepherding is meant to ensure the welfare of a group through acts of kindness.[15] He mapped how such pastoral power has become a pivot of the modern state when translated into acts of governmentality. As I noted in the introduction to the book, pastoral power has also been tapped into and mobilized by prominent leaders of twentieth-century Kerala who have drawn on it to build a loyal network of supporters and assert hegemonic forms of political masculinity. Multiple concrete and discursive acts of mutual assistance, instruction, and care at various sites have been instrumental in fostering attachment to the Sangh community. In the hands of local Hindu right leaders and workers, attending to individual persons and the well-being of particular families became a form of attaching them to each other, to local prominent Sangh figures, and to the group as whole.

If the local shakha is one place where Sangh workers tended to get together, specialized training camps, each other's homes, verandahs, and gatherings on festive occasions such as *rakshabandhan* or the RSS founding day have been the others. Much like the pastorate, the Sangh has tutored its members on how to relate to each other, their friends and families, and the world around them, as well as how to conduct, regard, and assess themselves. What lies in these acts of tutelage and inculcation of self-management is both the individualizing and totalizing capacities of pastoral power.[16] These twin seemingly contradictory modalities through which individual Sangh workers experience and apprehend their particularity as well as become part of the same discursive or interpretive community are crucial for understanding the relationship between Hindu right workers in Kannur and political violence in the country more broadly.

To highlight this phenomenon, Arafaat Valiani, in his ethnography of the RSS in Ahmedabad, describes how martial rituals and ideas of virtuous masculine civil conduct disseminated in the shakhas don't generate blind conformity but a self-conscious individual striving to enact and perfect them.[17] In a similar vein, RSS-BJP workers I engaged with in the course of my research had an acute sense of how they measured as Sangh workers, nationalists, and agents of pastoral care in their own right. Their adeptness at physical exercises taught at the shakha reminded them of their individual possibilities and limits; at the same time, Sangh workers described how attachments they forged with each other coalesced as a collective "spirit." I became privy to these thoughts and formulations in the course of long interviews and conversations with Sangh members at local RSS *karyalaya* (office) and *sewa kendra* (service center) or in the verandahs of their homes. My research assistant, with whose help I conducted these conversations and interviews, was a key enabling agent in these settings.[18]

A number of workers whose lives and careers I studied with the help of my assistant joined the Sangh in the conflict-ridden years of the 1980s and 1990s and came into their own in the early 2000s. In 2003, Kannur hosted the province's annual officer training camp (OTC). The camp brought together male recruits from the region for three weeks of training in Hindutva ideology, in virtuous behavior or *samskars*, physical exercises, drills, and marches.[19] My research assistant and I gained access to the camp for two to three days, affording us the opportunity to converse with and observe their conduct at the camp. Several RSS workers I had become acquainted with in the course of my research on victims and agents of the violent conflict with members of the party left became instructors and managers of the camp involved in training the next generation of recruits. The camp's space of intensified interaction and extraordinary levels of sociality among RSS members honed my insights into the practices that link individual "I"s with the collective "we." The two apparently disparate processes of individuation and absorption in the larger community, I surmised, were especially relevant for Hindu right workers inhabiting Kannur's violent political context.[20]

In the course of conversations with RSS-BJP workers, I gathered how the pain of the violence they have suffered and the memory of the violence they have enacted sharpened each worker's experience of his particularity. At the same time, networks of pastoral care and sociality with other Sangh workers restored these workers to the larger Hindu right community or totality. The legal status of Sangh workers as guilty or not guilty of inflicting violence along with their physical and emotional well-being became closely tied to their integration within the Sangh community. Furthermore, instances in which RSS-BJP workers spoke about their injuries, scars, and pain highlighted how Hindu right communities experience and mobilize their victimhood while also disclaiming their violence. Both moments, I suggest, have played an important part in forging tightly knit loyal units among Sangh members. These cohesive communities of RSS-BJP workers and supporters, reared on acts of pastoral care and the Sangh's organicist notions of connectedness and unity, are crucial for realizing its majoritarian aspirations. Such acts of care and connection are a product of the Hindu right's attempts to produce a vast machine of committed members whose everyday well-being, as well as their sense of self and identity, are linked to its organizational network and ideology. Members of these communities have done the work of canvassing greater popular and electoral support for the Hindu right. They have also aggressively restrained and repressed the opposition in a competitive democratic environment while attending to those who have suffered violence. Therefore, acts of care, I suggest, do not simply accompany the Hindu right's violence but are integral to the communities who perpetuate and enact this violence.

Producing "Sneha-Bandhams": Affective Bonds and Hindu Right Communities

I commence my analysis of the constitution and character of the Hindu right's cohesive communities in Kannur with excerpts from my conversations with Sadanandan Master, a well-known and regarded figure in local Hindu right-wing circles.[21] A onetime schoolteacher and CPI (M) sympathizer,

Sadanandan Master went on to join the RSS in his early twenties. At the receiving end of a brutal attack by CPI (M) supporters in 1994, he has since recovered and risen through the Sangh ranks,[22] and in 2016 he stood for election to the legislative assembly as a BJP candidate. In Sadanandan Master's life, pastoral care, encounters with political violence, and the search for popular support and electoral success have converged in vivid ways. Erudite and well versed in Hindutva theory and practice, he spoke to my research assistant and me at length about his turn to the Sangh, his encounters with severe violence, and his welfare work for the RSS-BJP. Significant parts of our conversation with Sadanandan Master took place at the OTC training camp, where he was a key instructor surrounded by young recruits. Drawing on his words and biography, I seek to plot the correlation between care, violence, and the search for political ascendancy that members of the Hindu right have lived out in Kannur.

I begin with the power of care that workers like Sadanandan Master have sought to mobilize to generate greater support for the Hindu right. As I noted earlier, it is debatable how useful the welfare or social strategy has been for the Sangh in its search for electoral rewards in Kerala. But even as pastoral power has been slow to produce electoral success, the Sangh's service activities enabled it to concertedly lay grounds for recruiting cadres, building networks, and drawing individual members and their families into its umbrella of organizations. The discourse of giving, receiving, and reciprocating, and thereby becoming one with the other, has played an important role here. This language has helped Sangh workers perpetuate its vision of a united community and pull their colleagues and supporters together with tighter communal bonds. As Sadanandan Master explained, the nature of ties that the Sangh sought to create among its workers and supporters were akin to familial affection. Cultivation of familial feelings, he elaborated, was central to the Sangh's work of ideological and political mobilization. However, the Sangh recognized that before such sentiments could be fostered, it had to engage with people's everyday challenges—by facilitating access to schools, employment, and various welfare entitlements. In other words, it had to mobilize pastoral power, disbursing as it were the masculine big brother's largesse.[23]

Sadanandan Master called this mode of generating support and receptivity to Sangh ideas its "psychological approach." As he said, "we don't seek to make them (future supporters) understand the Sangh ideology directly. Instead, (we) seek to gain their trust. That is what it is!" Explaining the strategy further, he noted, "Three-four of us go over to a house, engage with their (family members') day-to-day concerns such as the education of their kids. If there is anyone unwell in the house and there is a problem getting medicines, we do whatever we can. They are ordinary people; our 'line' is to gain their trust and not just propagate ideology. How should their trust be gained? How should they be approached? That is what we do in the 'house contact program.'"

Sadanandan Master went on to describe the final stage and the principle underlying this approach and said, "When we win over their confidence, it becomes possible for us to draw them in. That is the Sangh's 'strategy.' In shakhas, the *swayamsewaks* (volunteers or local-level workers) sing of the principle of rising (gaining popular support) by offering personal *sneha bandham* (bonds of love). To convert personal relations into ideological relations . . . the Sangh adapts this mode of working in every village."

Sadanandan Master thus invoked a concept and emotional quality that many in Kerala summon in their everyday lives: *sneham* coupled with *bandham*. According to Monier Williams's definition, sneham may be understood as "attachment, fondness, friendship, tenderness or love" and bandham as the ties that are produced by these feelings.[24] These ties serve as the furrows through which affects associated with sneham can flow. In Kerala, intimacies born of close kinship relations, neighborliness, and friendship are all associated with sneham.[25] But sneham, or these feelings of affection and love, have to be enacted and embodied in order to exist,[26] and actions such as sharing food and giving gifts, which are metonyms of oneself, are central to this enactment. In this light, self and substance are portioned through gifts between friends and neighbors, brothers and sisters, parents and children, husbands and wives, as well as landlords and tenants creating a "field of *sneham*"[27] or care and love between them. By engaging in small acts of giving and sharing, Sangh members mobilized the power of care and its capacity for forging networks of friendship and affection. While each moment of extending care and facilitating well-being addressed particular individuals, it also tied them together as part of a larger whole.

These acts of care built on the discourse of sneha bandham, which deems the unrestricted flow of sneham within and between persons (even persons divided by strong hierarchies) as a condition of their health and well-being. This discourse suggests that without sneham and without acts of sharing and giving that signify the unity of one with another, a sense of being ill at ease, depleted, and even flawed may emerge. But as one finds within themselves what is also present in or given by another, wholeness and fullness are said to be engendered. Here it is important to remember that feelings and affects float and pass among and within us as palpable, fleeting, and inarticulable sensations that sometimes move so quickly that they cannot even be fully comprehended.[28] However, with the weight of time, use, and history behind them, terms such as *sneham* congeal and stabilize affects of oneness, placing these bonds in an established circuit of meanings. Like many of his colleagues, Sadanandan Master drew on these intensities and "habits of relating"[29] to vivify, through the vernacular, the Sangh's vision of collective life of the Hindu majority as a united body. That is the work that sneham did especially for workers such as Sadanandan Master. It helped him and others build on the Sangh's service activities and masculine pastoral power, and order affects ranging from vague apprehensions of friendliness to its more intense kin-like potentials.

Buttressed by concepts such as sneham, filial, fraternal, and friendly relationships, circuits of care became an important instrument through which the Hindu right sought to cultivate a cohesive and loyal group of local-level supporters in Kannur. Feelings of connection and communion among them gained a special valence in a competitive democratic environment where the Hindu right was competing for ascendance. Those affects and emotions held together local-level workers and supporters who sought to aggressively contain and minoritize the opposition as well as those who suffered attacks and counterattacks in a schismogenetic vengeful context. Conflict and violence were in the air.

In the midst of that conflict, acts of care and the languages of connectedness, affection, and love that sneham offered were especially significant. As I describe in the following pages, these bonding acts mitigated the pain of those Hindu right workers who suffered the opposition's attacks and impelled vengeful counterattacks. Additionally, dense interrelatedness among Sangh members also helped to obscure individual responsibility for violence. In all these ways, the closely connected communities of RSS-BJP workers and supporters, which workers like Sadanandan Master helped forge, became agents of the Hindu right's majoritarian aspirations and contributed to the perpetuation of the antagonistic contest between the Hindu right and the party left.

Harrowing Violence and Sangh Sociality

The OTC where my research assistant and I spoke to Sadanandan Master at length became an important site for understanding the relationship between cohesive Hindu right communities and political violence. The camp was one of two OTCs that were conducted in Kerala in 2003, and four hundred men were instructed there. This particular camp was held in a large high school, which was vacant at the time due to summer vacations. Atop a small hill, the school was housed in a building that faced a big playing field where the camp's closing-day functions were held in a gathering of nearly one thousand people. In the field stood a metal pole that was ordinarily used to hoist the national flag on India's Independence Day. However, for the duration of the camp, it carried the saffron RSS flag. Symbols hailing the Sangh community had taken over the space otherwise kept for signifiers of the nation-state. The RSS recruits followed the routine of morning exercises, lectures, group discussions, and evening drills that the RSS's *Shiksha Varg* (education wing) has laid down for all such gatherings. They shared meals, sleeping arrangements, and leisure time living out, as it were, the Hindu right's vision of a close and cohesive community. It is against this backdrop that Sadanandan Master discussed the Sangh's approach and strategies for generating close ties and a shared collective life.

As I noted previously, early in his political career Sadanandan Master became the target of a terrible attack in which he lost both his legs. This assault was part of a chain of attacks and counterattacks between CPI (M) and RSS-BJP members in which various workers of the two groups lost not only use of their limbs but also their lives.[30] Sadanandan Master's account foregrounded these harrowing features of political violence in North Kerala but also focused on the atmosphere of the OTC where we were conversing. He recounted the violence he suffered while simultaneously drawing on the camp's ethos and the community of supporters forging around him. The love and attention he received from them, and what that tells us about the nature of unity and the consciousness of that unity among Sangh supporters, stand out in my analysis of his narrative. Like most other Malayalam speakers, Sadanandan Master dropped the subject pronouns when he spoke, and I have subsequently added them in parentheses to make his statement easier to read in English.[31] As Sadanandan Master noted, that day in January 1994 after finishing up at the school where he taught, he went to his uncle's house to discuss the arrangements for his sister's upcoming wedding. In his own words:

> I headed out from there around 7:30 p.m. You need to catch a bus to my place. I alighted from the bus around 8:00–8:15 p.m. at a place called Uruvachal. [You] have to walk two kilometers. There were very few other vehicles in that area. [I] got off from the bus and began to walk.

The electricity had gone off. Someone grabbed [me] from behind. It was extremely planned. They held so tightly, [I] could not even move. The bus had left by then. It is a bazaar visited by many people. [I] remember that when I was grabbed there was a bomb explosion. There was a loud sound.

Then there was one batch [of assailants] to hold me and another batch was there to disperse people. That seems to have been the plan. People got scared and hurried away. Shopkeepers downed their shutters. Many people stayed inside the shops. Within seconds [I] was left alone with them.

Then they held me from behind and laid me on the road. Then they were doing all this. [I] don't know how much time they took. It was very dark. [I] could not even understand what they were doing. My head was pressed hard on the road. *Vettaano atiyaano vyakthamaakunnilla sariykku* [Being hacked or being beaten, it was not really clear]. [I] was tugging away to escape. [I] was trying to shake them off but none of that happened. They had held so tightly. Then I felt that everyone had left.

In a low voice Sadanandan Master continued:

[I] tried to get up and saw this: at that very "spot" my legs were in a state that both the feet had been cut off. An extremely terrible . . . me. . . . Then [I] gave out a very loud cry, cried a lot—that is how [I] remember it. Blood was flowing just like that.

There was no one around, not even one person. Someone might have been there but did not come forward; it is a strong CPI (M) "pocket." [I] was shouting for water, shouting "water, water." Nobody came forward. [I] lay like that on that road for almost fifteen minutes. Then after fifteen minutes, the police came and took me to the hospital. I was acquainted with the policeman who arrived. . . . [I] clearly remember that he stopped to get me water from a shop. [I] was nearly unconscious by the time we reached Thalassery.

At the hospital, [I] would recover consciousness every now and then. . . . Important workers reached Thalassery. The magistrate had come to note the "dying declaration." [I] was going to die—was in such a condition. . . . Blood was just flowing away. [I] can't remember the rest of it very well. [I] was given blood at Thalassery and then taken to Medical College.

The next day [I] recovered consciousness around 11:00 a.m. After taking off [amputating] the foot, took out the rest of the leg as well to put on the [artificial] limb.

These were the details of the attack on him that Sadanandan Master recounted in the conversation we had at the OTC. In subsequent statements, he went on to describe the contribution of the Sangh and its workers to his recovery. His recovery from the attack became a site for close affective bonds to be forged between all of them. The schoolmaster spoke about his deep awareness of how these bonds or bandham were essential to him. As noted earlier, for Sadanandan Master and others, Sangh work is indeed about creating these bonds. In our first three- to four-hour-long conversation, he had described working for the Sangh as an *anubhuti* (an edifying aesthetic experience). "It's not false or artificial," he said. In the same vein, he continued:

> There are many experiences that you get from the Sangh.... When this accident . . . no . . . attack occurred, about twenty *swayamsewaks* gave blood for me. I believe that the blood of those twenty swayamsewaks is running through me.
>
> Swayamsewaks were the ones to look into all the hospital matters, to look after my very basic needs. These artificial limbs of mine were made in an organization in Bangalore run by the Sangh. The person running the outfit is also a swayamsewak—from Orissa. I feel that a whole order has been created—everything was done for me by swayamsewaks, the one to make this limb was also a swayamsewak.

Sadanandan Master noted that there have been times when he felt that he had paid a heavy price for his work in the Sangh. His work entailed walking and traveling from one town and village to another, conducting the so-called family contact program, and building those close personal relations that are central to the spread of the Sangh. That work had been impeded, and, as Sadanandan Master said, sometimes he felt deep anger against his assailants. At the same time, as the schoolmaster articulated it, his coworkers and junior colleagues protected him from an overwhelming sense of dejection by stepping in to compensate for the disabilities he suffered. His colleagues and friends in the Sangh gave him blood, looked after him in the hospital, made and fitted artificial limbs, and enabled him to recover. Such exceptional relationships continued to reproduce themselves in all other walks of life too and were especially evident at the OTC. At the camp there were, as Sadanandan Master described, "many workers with a large, open heart willing to do anything for me: to wash my clothes, if I have to go anywhere they provide vehicle, take me there, just to fetch something there is someone here." The ready and unflinching manner in which the Sangh workers assisted Sadanandan Master was, according to him, one of the most remarkable aspects of their actions. Such was the lifeworld of RSS workers, according to the master, that no one directed the Sangh workers to behave in a particular way and there was no threat of punishment. Just being a Sangh worker was enough for, what many workers call, a "spirit" to be generated or, one might say, an order of the same to be created and a community of spirit to be forged.

Sadanandan Master dwelled on and described in romantic terms the ways in which a collective spirit permeated among Sangh workers. It can also be said that through romantic statements about the Sangh community—made in the wake of encounters with terrible violence and in the presence of bodies and selves marked by them—members of the Sangh experienced and reproduced an order of the same. For while Sadanandan Master was one of the most evocative victims of political violence in Kannur, there were others at the camp who bore various marks of injuries suffered due to it. Sadanandan Master drew upon his erudition to talk about the Sangh and the bonds between its members eloquently; others in the camp echoed these sentiments and lived the relationship between encounters with violence and the bonds that the Sangh works hard to forge among its supporters.

Sangh workers' narratives and scenes from the OTC that I present next illuminate the relationship between the discourse of oneness and unity and violence that the Hindu right has fostered while pursuing its majoritarian ambitions and aggressively containing and minoritizing the opposition. Conversations about violence that various Sangh workers had endured or enacted are central to scenes from the OTC that I describe here. Discussions about and around attacks, injuries, victims, and assailants highlight ways of communing and forging bonds with each other that Sangh members came to share in the midst of conflict and violence. Those members like Sadanandan Master who had suffered violent attacks were sympathetically absorbed into and capacitated by the Sangh community, and those who ordained and carried out attacks were absolved of their individual responsibility.

The thread of the conversations I pick are from a day at the OTC in 2003 when my research assistant and I had been introduced to many people residing and working at camp. We were sitting under the trees of the playing field, drinking tea, and exchanging banter with some young but well-known RSS workers from the nearby towns and villages. From a distance we saw the older, silver-haired worker Kesavan walk out of the school building where the camp was being organized. Like Sadanandan Master, Kesavan had also suffered nearly fatal injuries in the course of an attack allegedly by CPI (M) members. He had recovered and now managed an RSS-run home for underprivileged children close by. His wife, son, and daughter were also with him. Kesavan waved at us, and his wife and children smiled self-consciously but warmly. Unlike Sadanandan Master, Kesavan had not been severely disabled by the attack. He did, however, walk with a limp, and his left arm, bearing the hand with amputated fingers, was always folded close to his chest. Some of the men we were talking to asked if I knew about Kesavan's work at the school or *shishu mandir* where economically disadvantaged Hindu families sent their children to be nurtured and educated. Earlier in the day, children from shishu mandir had come for an excursion to the camp. Others in the group expressed surprise at the attack on Kesavan; after all, he was not well known when the attack occurred. Furthermore, there had not been many attacks and counterattacks at the time when he was assaulted. This inspired a discussion on assaults like the ones on Kesavan and Sadanandan Master, and citations of various bits of information about the attacks against them mingled with condemnation of the CPI (M)'s violent postures in general. The Sangh members' statements about the reprehensible nature of CPI (M) workers' actions set the latter up as deserving candidates for vengeance and counterattacks. At the same time, it became clear that the scars on Kesavan and Sadanandan Master's bodies and their disabilities were triggers for the formation of this collective of Hindu right workers. The workers seemed to experience their own sense of self and oneness through the pain of their friends and associates who had suffered violent attacks and by extending sympathy and assistance to them.

Sadanandan Master, on his part, had described the moment when he apprehended the violence that the Hindu right's opponents had inflicted on him in these words: "An extremely terrible...me.... Then [I] gave out a very loud cry, cried a lot—that is how [I] remember it. Blood was flowing just like that.... [I] was shouting for water." RSS workers at the camp interpreted and talked of the quality of Sadanandan Master's pain in their own fashion. They had heard about, and now they recounted, how he lay there on the road, asking for water for what they believed to be nearly fifteen minutes, crying out "water, water." Their words highlighted the process of semeiosis[32] that was underway as the statements about and signs of violence that Sadanandan Master and Kesavan had experienced took on a sensory aspect for their colleagues and friends. Their meanings were not always clearly classified or sharply articulated, but many people felt them as palpable affects—for instance, as the *bhayankar* (tremendous and dreadful) feeling that overcame them when they heard about what had happened to Sadanandan Master. Gradually, however, talk of dreadful feelings passed and was replaced with a sense of the relative well-being that Sadanandan Master had also achieved since the incident. The road to his recovery, Sadanandan Master continually maintained, was paved with generosity and efforts of the RSS-BJP workers he had recruited and worked with. He said that over time he came to feel more and more integrated with, and inalienably related to, other workers and the organization as a whole. On their part, RSS-BJP workers also talked about the deep respect they had for Sadanandan Master and the ways in which they sought to assist him. In this way, along with the signs of violence on Sadanandan Master's body, members of the Hindu right continued to commune with each other. Sadanandan Master's injured body itself became the locus around which new selves and a collective spirit appeared.

Individual experiences of violence thus became the medium for connecting the Sangh workers with each other and the larger whole. Violence was an important glue holding its members together, intensifying not only their attachment to particular victims but also attachment to the RSS-BJP in general. Such visceral attachments, I suggest, have cemented loyalties for the Hindu right in a competitive democratic setting, furthering its violence and becoming integral to its twin strategy of cohesion and polarization to obtain popular support and state power. As I noted earlier, cohesion and polarization are two sides of the Sangh's goal of competing to become (and now maintain its position as) the major ruling force in a democratic country. Consequently, violence in this scheme is not a pernicious side effect of the Hindu right's political program and policies but a vital part of its work of producing divisions between various groups and close internal bonds among its own members and supporters. And instead of countering this divisive collective spirit and violence, the democratic system in India has rewarded the Hindu right with state power.

Of Collective Spirit, Dharma, and Blameless Perpetrators

Sadanandan Master was not the only Sangh worker who invoked its strong collective spirit while describing encounters with political violence. It was a trope that emerged frequently in my conversations with workers of the Hindu right. Accounts of the relationship between the fellowship that Hindu right workers shared in the shakha, a collective spirit, and interparty violence especially surfaced in a discussion I had with two RSS workers at the Sangh Thalassery office in the early 2000s. One of them, Sasi, had been recently acquitted of the murder of a CPI (M) worker; the other more senior Sangh worker had been accused in several murder and attempt to murder cases but had not been convicted. During our conversation about prominent attacks against CPI (M) workers that members of the Hindu right were implicated in, and the complex of motives that impelled them, Sasi watchfully claimed that he did not entirely comprehend the character of those who enacted violence. In the next sentence, however, he went on to speak suggestively about the affects that have animated Sangh workers' violence and the social worlds that have produced them. In his words, "It's hard to say what kind of people they are—the ones who commit murders. At the same time, their willpower inspires to do so. At that moment, such courage and power comes. It happens unknowingly. It's a 'spirit.' Through the evening shakha and the *balshakha* [children's shakha], when twenty to twenty-five people get together, stand around, and discuss different things, a 'team spirit' enters all of them. To sit around the shelter, just talk about anything, that's all there is to it."

Sasi described this collective or team spirit as a function of everyday interaction that RSS members have with each other since their days in the balshakha. He also considered this spirit as the force driving the violence that Hindu right workers had enacted. At the same time, the language of collective spirit offered RSS-BJP workers like Sasi a vocabulary to disclaim responsibility for their grievous acts. To some extent, these disclaimers are similar to popular, journalistic, and legal descriptions of collective violence as acts of combusting rage that flare up to destroy everything in their wake. At several critical conflictual junctures in the last few decades, partisan public figures and police officers sympathetic to the Hindu right have mobilized this language of combustion and rage to describe the violence of its members, suggesting that their violence is spontaneous and that the lines of responsibility for the violence cannot be traced.[33] However, it is important to note here that Sasi's references to a collective spirit that drives Hindu right workers' violence contained allusions to not just anger or rage but also a slowly cultivated group sentiment born of sociality, care, and camaraderie at the shakha. Furthermore, Sangh's modes of sociality and practices of extending care come on the backs of a well-developed discourse of cohesion and harmony among its supporters who it seeks to coalesce in tightly knit communities. My interactions with Sangh members at the OTC revealed how the accompanying language of connectedness and communion with one another made it possible to avoid, or what I call sublate, individual responsibility for grievous violence. In other words, while the Sangh workers' sense of responsibility for violence was not entirely effaced, their individualities were dissolved enough in the dense sociality of Hindu right communities for that responsibility to be denied and negated.

In a competitive democratic landscape, this language of connectedness helped to produce a loyal community of supporters and assist the Hindu right in its majoritarian project. In conflictual settings like Kannur, it also helped to create a nameless and blameless group of perpetrators. Individual culpability of agents of political violence were dissolved in a carefully produced "we" or community of fellow Sangh workers and supporters. This was a community of Sangh supporters made one with each other through everyday interaction, acts of pastoral care, and the discourse of sneha bandham, cohesion, and sameness. Various Sangh workers I met in the course of my research in the early and late 2000s in Kannur emphasized that an internalized sense of rights and duties toward one another and the group as a whole guided these forms of sociability, drawing on the concept of *dharma* to encapsulate that sensibility. Dharma, as one RSS worker Ajayan noted in a conversation with my research assistant and me, ignited an awareness about a shared life force that united them with one another and all living beings.[34]

The concept of dharma has an important place in the Hindu right's organicist conceptions of society, and its workers like Ajayan have imbibed and interpreted them in their own ways. One of the founding fathers of the RSS, M. S. Golwalkar conceived dharma as the "universal code of right conduct that awakens the common inner bond" between people and keeps them in a "harmonious state" even in the absence of an external authority. For, it adjusts conduct so that individuals start to realize the "real image of man imbued with sublime principles of innate oneness and harmony."[35] The individual thus becomes an instrument of attaining "permanent social good" even as the individual realizes that he himself is "impermanent."[36] This notion of dharma has been passed down in the Sangh's shakhas and training camps.[37] Hindu right supporters are hence encouraged to identify social good with their prescribed way of life and interests of the Hindu majority and pitch this against Muslim and Christian minorities as well as all other formations that question and oppose their vision. These adversarial postures against opposing groups and communities deemed to be foes have served the Hindu right well in its attempts to become a major political force. Workers like Ajayan have participated in the resulting violence as well as invoked the concept of dharma to explain the sense of oneness and unity they share with other members of the Hindu right community.

In one of our first long conversations with him, Ajayan, who joined the Sangh in the early 1980s, described how during the clashes of the 1980s and

1990s Sangh members had taken on CPI (M) workers in different neighborhoods. Upon containing CPI (M) influence, Sangh workers were able to institute their own mobilization activities to become the main political force in those areas. In other more reflective discussions, Ajayan spoke about his turn to the dharmic mode of living and consciousness of his oneness with others. He elaborated on the ways in which, after joining the Sangh, he had started recognizing and acknowledging how he was akin to others striving for the same social good. In this process of playing an active role in the Hindu right's pursuit of support and ascendancy, Ajayan had risen through the Sangh ranks.

Ajayan was an important office-bearer of the Sangh when I first met him in the early 2000s. He had been given crucial responsibilities for running the 2003 OTC, where my research assistant and I visited him. Some years prior to the OTC, Ajayan had also been accused of the murder of a young CPI (M) worker and had been out on bail for more than two years, but now the trial for this murder was about to start soon. Both my research assistant and I addressed him as "Ajayan *ettan*," or older brother Ajayan. We addressed many other people in this fashion but had developed an easy rapport with him. When we visited the Sangh's officer's training camp, Ajayan met us at the gate and took us around with pride and pleasure. On this occasion, he spent an entire day with us. He familiarized us with the camp's many activities and introduced us to many people—the cooks, the cleaners, the physical and intellectual instructors, the officials, and many local-level RSS workers who had come from different parts of Kerala. The story of Ajayan's participation in the terrible murder of a CPI (M) worker sharply interrupted this genial atmosphere.

The dead CPI (M) worker was a metal welder who was killed in his workshop three years earlier. Ajayan's account of this event came after a long and tiring day of meetings as we sat sipping tea under the trees. He told his story so simply and quietly that the horrific details of the events seemed muted by his relaying of them. Ajayan had been instrumental in recruiting a young orphan boy, about twelve years old, into the local shakha. One morning, when the boy was distributing some Sangh flyers, the metal welder and other CPI (M) workers accosted him and beat him up. The murder of the metal welder was retaliatory. In his retelling of the story—an account in which he never used the first person to discuss the actual act—Ajayan said, "[I] had just got ready to step out in the morning when [I] heard about it [the boy's beating]. There are many RSS pockets nearby. It happened." He then recalled going to the workshop, the metal welder being held down and being "cut up."[38]

My research assistant and I thus became privy to the description of yet another violent attack and counterattack that has made up the conflict between the Hindu right and the party left in Kannur. Through the years, competitive agonism had turned into antagonistic violence driven by the call to equalize scores as well as seek vengeance. Ajayan, who had been integrated into the Sangh's close-knit community of supporters from an early age, had been part of clashes with members of the party left, and had gone up the Hindu right ranks, was recounting details of one such moment of vengeful violence. In the same instance, he was also eliding responsibility for it.

Ajayan spoke in Malayalam, the language most commonly used in Kerala, and, as in many statements rendered in other Indian languages, the first-person-singular pronoun "I" was missing from Ajayan's description of otherwise clearly defined actions.[39] Furthermore, use of the first-person-plural "we" or the third-person "they" instead of the "I" would not have altered the Malayalam verb forms.[40] The fact that the first-person pronoun "I" was missing might have been a function of the Malayalam linguistic form, or it could have been Ajayan's way of protecting himself from the legal consequences of an admission. It could also indicate the dissolution of the individual "I" into the collective "we" that has marked the life of Hindu right-wing workers and the cohesive communities they form with one another. I suggest that all three aspects underpinned his statement. When Ajayan dropped the "I" as he spoke about the metal welder's murder, he was conforming to widely pervasive linguistic protocols. He was also, I believe, guarding against a substantive admission of individual responsibility. Most importantly, while the memory of the violent attack was vivid in his mind, he was at liberty to obfuscate his role in it within the Sangh community, where the individual self was seen to be akin to the other, merged with the whole and dissolved in the collective.

Ajayan spoke extremely quietly as he recounted the incident, and my research assistant and I had to strain a bit and concentrate to hear him. All around us was the community that the denizens of the camp constituted, and Ajayan was, dare I say, in the midst of the community that the three of us formed. There seemed to be a slight note of regret in Ajayan's voice while he was also seemingly aware of the discordance his story had generated. He had evoked details whose horrific nature would have particularly come to the fore if they had been described in minutiae. In his rendition, however, the regret, the discordance, and the horror could not be effectively located in specific words or phrases. These had been spread thin or evened out by the manner in which Ajayan narrated the incident as if it could have been experienced by anyone in the community and done by anyone in the community. "It happened," "it" being impelled by the attack on the young boy, done for his sake and the good of everyone.

If I had spoken about the incident with some other accused in the case, or Ajayan's coworkers in the Sangh, the distress and dissonance associated with it might have been altogether drowned out. It might have been subsumed by the so-called team spirit in which violence came to be enacted apparently unknowingly and with little thought except about those who had to be avenged. Or, it might have been overlain by narratives about how the Sangh should rightfully come out on top of its opponents. Many RSS workers might have cited the RSS camp, its offices, and shakhas, and the ambience in those spaces, as evidence of sneham or love among them.

Soon, Ajayan's close colleagues and friends joined us, and they shared a team spirit of their own as exchange of friendly banter, local, and national news commenced. Ajayan also animatedly discussed everything. As each person's words resonated and poised well with the others', a web of agreement, accordance, and mutually affirmative ties slowly began to be knitted. Ajayan's story had created a "mood"[41] that was filled with the possibility of shock, suspicion, and impending disruption of all routine. That mood was slowly passed over. Instead, space was made for that realm of familial feelings and community in which, as described earlier, solidarities are experienced, individual peculiarities and differences are minimized, and an enabling sense of self-constitutiveness as part of the totality is regained. As for Ajayan and his story of the CPI (M) worker's murder, he seemed all the more blameless and unburdened of it. The absent first-person "I" of his narrative outside the OTC camp never came alive.

Ajayan, my research assistant, and I talked about the events of the murder on two more occasions. These conversations revealed the ways in which the cohesive caring community of fellow Sangh workers that surrounded Ajayan both impelled his violence and enabled him to disclaim responsibility for it. Unexpectedly one day, Ajayan drove us past the scene of the said murder, a workshop, and slowed the vehicle down offering us the opportunity to view the site of the attack, albeit from afar. However, from that point forth Ajayan's narrative, in great detail and apparently very spontaneously, conformed to his line of defense in the upcoming trial. The place of the missing first-person "I" was now taken by someone who was enmeshed in a complicated tale of alibis and absences from the site of the murder. Caring friends and supporters served as defense witnesses ready to back Ajayan's alibi. A singular knowing and acting subject could no longer be abstracted from this cohesive community. "It" happened, but Ajayan no longer knew about it. The person who might have witnessed and participated in the murder of a CPI (M) worker had become one with many others in his community and was thereby lost and renounced. The trial court too acquitted Ajayan.

Affection, Reprehension, and Democracy

In the competitive game that is representative democracy, violence has been committed in order to equalize scores and gain the upper hand, as well as to avenge one's own. Hindu right-wing communities brought together through the workings of pastoral power have mitigated individual suffering, pain, and the weight of culpability that have come in the wake of this violence. So far, while the Sangh's service activities and pastoral power have not generated enough backing for the RSS-BJP to emerge as winners in elections in Kannur, they have drawn in recruits, animated and molded their inner lives, and produced grounds for connection, communion, and forms of sociality in which the singular "I" can be dissipated in the collective "we." An attack on one thus became an attack on all, and the pain and burden of one became the pain and burden of all within this community. This included the individuating pain and burden of both suffering and enacting violence.

The force of these connections has, I believe, allowed the Sangh to emerge as a particularly effective majoritarian face of democracy. Its search for ascendance has been supported by a long-standing campaign to transform the social subjectivity of the majority Hindu population in a way that would assure it "permanent political majority."[42] That search for ascendance is not extraneous to democracies but is part of their basic definition and structure. This is evident in Kannur where competition to become a ruling force divided members of the party left and the Hindu right who shared similar class and caste backgrounds into sharply polarized communities of affection and reprehension, each one seeking to become preeminent in the region and contain and minoritize the other. The forms of agency and attachments fostered among youth in the region by these two parties made their practices of containment and minoritization increasingly cruel and vengeful. However, surrounding that cruelty and vengefulness has been care, pastoral power associated with influential forms of political masculinity, camaraderie, friendship, and community. Among members of the

RSS-BJP combine, well-developed discursive and organizational practices to disburse care and achieve cohesion have played an important role in producing those connections and hateful communities.

Following that final interaction with Ajayan, I returned to Kannur three more times for research purposes between 2009 and 2017. However, wary of the weight of individual responsibility as well as the web of complicity and evasion that surrounded many local-level political workers of the Hindu right and the party left in the region, I minimized my direct research interaction with them. In place of oral accounts of injuries, attacks, and blows—suffered and delivered—I turned to written tracts of local leaders and third-party narratives of local political history. Most importantly perhaps for my argument concerning the link between cohesive communities and violence in the region, I observed party gatherings and meetings from a distance. The 2017 Hindu right campaign against the party left is notable in that regard.

As I described in the introduction, Kannur became a topic of media headlines in October 2017 when the BJP organized a long march across Kerala's towns and villages raising the issue of security and protection from what it called "red and Jihadi terror,"[43] referring to the violence of the CPI (M) cadres and that of so-called Islamic radicals. By doing so, the Sangh was hoping to mount a significant challenge to the communist party government at the helm in Kerala. A number of key leaders of the party participated in the march, including the recently elected chief minister of Uttar Pradesh, Yogi Adityanath, well known for his hateful rhetoric against religious minorities and his implementation of repressive discriminatory state practices targeting them. As a culmination of its campaign, the party organized a public rally in Thiruvananthapuram, Kerala's state capital, which I attended. Sharp vitriol against the Hindu right's regional political foe, the CPI (M) and its imagined civilizational adversary, the Muslims, laced a number of speeches given by the selected speakers.

The BJP had hoped for participation of at least fifty thousand people in its campaign. The numbers of people who attended the rally were far less than expected, but they still reached a few thousand.[44] Noticeably, people did not attend the meeting as individual supporters of the Sangh but as families complete with grandparents, children, aunts, uncles, and cousins. And while there was bitterness against the Sangh's opponents in the speeches delivered at the rally, there was an air of festivity, warmth, and cohesiveness among the audience who was listening to them.

The sight of this affable crowd of middle- to lower-income families listening to antagonistic and aggressive speeches—all underwritten by possibilities of violence against communists and Muslims—reminded me of the first such gathering of Sangh supporters that I had attended in 2003. That meeting took place at the end of the OTC that I described earlier. On the last day of the camp, as is customary, the recruits' wives, children, aged parents, and extended families arrived to hail the Sangh, watch them drill, march, display their skill in use of bamboo staffs (*lathis*), and listen to speeches on nation and nationalism as the Hindu right interprets it. On both occasions—at the public rally in Thiruvananthapuram in 2017 and at the end of the training camp in Kuthuparamba in 2003—the closely connected community of supporters, which the Sangh has forged in Kannur, Kerala, and many other parts of the country, was on display. This community whose members have been tied together by acts of care and assistance, posited as akin and alike to one another has, as I have shown in this chapter, played a key role in obscuring responsibility for violence done in its name.

In the last few years in a pandemic-ridden world, questions of care, welfare, and well-being have gripped the globe. In the meantime, India—the world's largest democracy—has emerged as a particularly prejudiced and dangerous place. It is a treacherous place for those who oppose the Hindu right and those whom the Sangh regards as its civilizational adversaries. Reports of everyday acts of bigotry and violence against Muslim minorities suggest that the Sangh's supremacist ideology has been imbibed by members of the Hindu majority in many different parts of the country. Accounts of poor Muslim vegetable vendors being refused to ply their trade and sick Muslim men and women being denied medical care in the midst of the pandemic[45] are piled atop descriptions of state persecution and torture and plans to implement inequitable citizenship laws, which I discussed in the introduction. In other words, the Hindu right has been effective at not only obtaining electoral and state power but also inculcating exclusionary, divisive, and violent dispositions and practices toward minority groups. Members of the majoritarian Hindu community who practice this violence extend care and social welfare to their own while actively eliminating or letting die those they oppose. Despite such violence, in a context where democracy means multiparty competition and majority rule, the BJP-led regime remains stable and constitutionally legitimate. Representative democracy, therefore, stands out as a political system that fosters and rewards divisive and violent politics of reducing the opposition to a minor position.

Part I of this book has plotted the career of such divisive democratic politics in Kannur. In chapter 1 I described how the competition to gain ascendance drew in members of various parties including the socialists, communists, and Congress. I described how aggressive righteous masculinity and acts of pastoral power marked the contentious political field that was created during the 1940s, 1950s, and 1960s in North Kerala. In chapter 2 I explained how the drive to compete and become a major influence in the different neighborhoods, towns, and villages of Kannur expressed itself not only through fierce efforts to contain the opposition but also the fervor to equalize the scores of injuries and deaths and obtain vengeance. The majoritarian communities that Sangh workers have formed stand out in chapter 3 for the organized distribution of care they are grounded in, for the discourse of oneness and unity that underpins them, as well as the politics of enmity and minoritization they mobilize.

Against this backdrop, local-level workers of different parties led by influential men sought to coercively contain their competitors while party leaders tousled and navigated their way through electoral alliances and divisions to obtain a numerical majority in the legislature and gain state office. These tussles and agonistic contests translated into antagonistic conflicts between CPI (M) and RSS-BJP workers especially from the late 1970s onward. This was the period after the brief imposition of emergency rule when multiparty democracy returned and the Hindu right began pursuing greater popularity and electoral presence in Kerala and other parts of the country. While democracy as the competition between different parties to become rulers was restored, its links with violence became more complete. Since then the Hindu right's modes of homogenization and polarization have produced exceptional violence in various parts of the country. Exceptional conflict between CPI (M) and RSS-BJP workers in Kannur offers us clues to apprehend possibilities of majoritarianism and minoritization, marshaling of care, and violence already present in democratic polities.

II

Judicial Responsibility and Subterfuge

Law's Subterfuge

AFFORDING ALIBIS AND BOLSTERING CONFLICT

Commencing part II of the book, this chapter examines the legal processes that have perpetuated political conflict in North Kerala. I map the ways in which the criminal justice system has worked as a form of subterfuge in the competitive and violent struggle between the party left and the Hindu right. In the wake of trials meant to redress wrong and hurt that this conflict has inflicted, the justice system has clouded over conditions and complicities that have produced political violence. This is borne by a number of cases related to murder and attempts to murder in which workers of the two groups have been the victims and alleged assailants. The Raju Master (1978) and Divakaran murder (1981) trials that I discuss in this and the following chapter exemplify the ways in which judicial proceedings obfuscate the structure and context underlying political violence. As I illustrate through an analysis of these trials, the criminal justice system has also extended the conflict between CPI (M) and RSS-BJP workers in Kannur. Courtrooms have become a site for reenactment of the aggressive contest between the two groups in which one side comes out on top while the other is defeated and made minor through use of injurious and hurtful means.

Here lies the ruse of criminal law: the justice system has depoliticized political violence and projected responsibility for it onto individual members of the two groups it deems misguided (at best) or pathological (at worst). Legal principles and practices associated with the work of securing justice in modern democracies have thus afforded an alibi to political structures, processes, and party formations that have conditioned intergroup violence in Kannur and other parts of the country. This depoliticization and criminalization of individual members has also helped the party left and the Hindu right advance their own search for dominance. In trial and appeal proceedings, workers of the two groups have made concerted efforts to produce legally valid narratives that would not only exonerate their own members but also implicate workers of the opposition. Members of the two groups have purposefully targeted their counterparts in the opposition by charging them with acts of grievous violence, putting individuals through long, arduous criminal trials and seeking convictions as well as (in some instances) capital punishment.[1] The conflict between the CPI (M) and the RSS-BJP in Kannur has therefore been reenacted in the courts. Instead of dispelling the violence between the party left and the Hindu right, the criminal justice system has become a part of the contest to be a major force in the region and minoritize the opposition.

Deployment of law in Kannur's political conflict is not a unique invidious instance where legal objectivity and fairness have been undermined. Instead, as I describe in this chapter and the following one, criminal courts are structurally and historically programmed to become an instrument for the perpetuation of violent strife, while masking the larger institutions and processes that generate political conflict in the first place. In particular, this chapter maps the recent history of this twofold subterfuge: a large assemblage of institutions and practices enabling both parties in Kannur to escape responsibility for generating violence, while letting individual workers, often occupying the lower echelons of socioeconomic and party hierarchies, bear the brunt of political strife. I situate this judicial duplicity, which Kannur has witnessed, in the broader workings of an Indian legal system that has created a disjuncture between acts of political violence and their context, thereby depoliticizing the violence and obscuring the conditions that have produced it. At the same time, the hierarchies, divisions, and interests that make up the social and political milieu have colored jurisprudence and the course of trials.

Police, trial, and appeal courts have frequently shielded culpable members of dominant groups and the Hindu-majority community for their violence against members of minority and marginal groups. At the same time, as I discuss below, they have directed the punishing force of the law against the latter. The Indian legal system has thus taken a majoritarian turn: it has often afforded impunity to members of the dominant community while persecuting minorities and those who challenge its hegemony. Against this backdrop, this chapter discusses two criminal cases involving members of the party left and the Hindu right in Kannur who, for years, have been engaged in their own contest for dominance. Each case relates to critical turning points in the history of political violence in the region. Initiating shadowy practices, members of the two groups in both cases manipulated and mobilized the criminal justice system in ways that advanced their respective projects of becoming the major political force in the area.

While I discuss backstage practices of fabricating evidence and tutoring witnesses that members of the two groups have engaged in, I do this not to uncover guilt or innocence in a way that a criminal court judge might, but to describe how legal teams associated with the party left and the Hindu right sought to produce "effects of truth" in trial courts.[2] These truth-effects in turn affected the fate of individual CPI (M) and RSS-BJP local-level workers, exculpating them in several instances and subjecting them to painful punishment in others. As the details of individual actions came to be scrutinized, questioned, or defended and the fate of accused political workers hung in the balance, each case became a site for a replay of the contest between the two groups. Judicial attention remained focused on the culpability of individual workers of the party left and the Hindu right. In the meantime, larger political structures, principles, ideologies, and practices underlying the violence between the two groups remained shielded.

This analysis lays the groundwork for chapter 5, where I analyze the paradigms of apprehending responsibility and evidentiary requirements central to modern criminal justice. It is these paradigms, I propose, that have enabled Indian democracy to refuse accountability for the violence in its midst as well as to perpetuate it. Guiding doctrines for affixing responsibility in Indian criminal law that lend themselves to this subterfuge were instituted in the late nineteenth century. They have persisted in current times. As I plot the genealogy of critical criminal codes and regulations and examine their effects on trials in Kannur, the methodological individualism underlying criminal law and its understandings of action, intention, motive, and *mens rea* stand out. This methodological individualism has reduced complex phenomena like political violence to a forensically decipherable intention to hurt harbored by the few accused. This focus on individual crimes, follies, and pathologies has consequently helped modern democracies and their party formations displace and disavow responsibility for the violence they have fostered. Together, the two chapters that make up part II of the book are about that criminalization and the resultant displacement of responsibility for political violence. To conclude, I look at the relationship between democracy and violence from the eyes of the local-level workers of the party left and the Hindu right who have been made criminally liable for it.

Criminal Liability, Depoliticization, and the National Context

As I describe in part I of the book, local-level Communist Party and Hindu right-wing cadres' violence has been anchored in their attempts to safeguard the interests of their respective formations, in the competition between their parties to become ascendant at the local and regional levels, and in the lives of the communities and constituencies their supporters forge. I have argued that this association with collective efforts to protect different group interests and/or gain state power makes the violence political and not simply a criminal act.[3] In the courts, however, the violence inflicted by cadres has been depoliticized and understood as little more than a crime akin to many others listed in the Indian penal code. But this very casting of political violence as a criminal act opened the door for producing truth-effects in court that one party or the other found more desirable. Hence, members of both parties teamed up with lawyers to mobilize procedure and rules of evidence, and craft testimonies and arguments to obtain acquittals for their own workers and convictions for members of the opposing group—who they had rightly or wrongly accused in incidents of political violence.

Consequently, trials of local-level party workers made it possible for larger democratic structures, principles, and practices to evade their share of responsibility for political violence. They also became a stage for a reenactment of the conflict between members of the party left and the Hindu right to become major and make minor. The law, therefore, did not serve as a means of containing and mitigating political violence but perpetuating it. Inside the courts—where each side sought to produce its own truth-effects about the violence—the fate of individual accused workers hung in the balance for years through various phases of these trials and subsequent appeals. Outside in towns, villages, and neighborhoods of Kannur, the cycle of violence between the two groups was maintained and turned even more vengeful. However, Kannur is not the only instance where criminal law has played this duplicitous and damaging role. In order to grasp both the particularities of the relationship between democracy, political violence, and criminal law as it has unfolded in North Kerala and apprehend its broader implications, I outline some key features and moments in the history of the postcolonial Indian state's response to political violence.

A critical duality has marked the adjudication of political violence in postcolonial India where both majoritarian formations as well as marginal communities have mobilized violence to assert themselves. In response, the justice system has both depoliticized political violence by reducing it to the criminality of a few and become a means of affirming the dominance of the majority community over those it has sought to minoritize. Majoritarianism has become the feature of not only the executive but also the judiciary in different parts of the country. A particular relationship between the identity of the perpetrators, the political community they belong to, and the responses of the criminal justice system has developed. This is especially evident in Gujarat, where Hindu right perpetrators of the 2002 pogrom against Muslim minorities have come to enjoy immunity and impunity.

New research on lower-court trials in the wake of the anti-Muslim violence in Gujarat has shown how everyday legal procedures and practices have been mobilized to shield culpable individuals from criminal prosecution and conviction. Police investigations of violent events, their modes of documentation designed to purposively produce evidentiary uncertainty, partiality of prosecutors, and manipulation of legal reasoning and procedure in the trial courts have played a critical role in securing this impunity.[4] While legal accountability for majoritarian violence has been elusive[5] and culpable members of the Hindu majority community have often escaped judicial punishment, a punitive legal regime has especially besieged members of minority groups, such as Sikhs from Punjab and Kashmiri Muslims, who have challenged hegemonic ideologies and state policies.[6] This regime has also targeted with violence individuals belonging to other collectives that have sought economic and political self-determination in places as far ranging as Telengana, Bastar, and the North-Eastern regions. Members of these groups have been persecuted through a series of special laws and authoritarian legal provisions that have eased due process and evidentiary requirements for arrests, detention without trial, criminal prosecutions, and convictions.

Ujjwal Kumar Singh and Jinee Lokaneeta have argued that these special laws are in fact not exceptional. Indeed, these apparently extraordinary laws have been "interlocked"[7] and "integrally connected"[8] with routine legality reflecting, refracting, and reproducing commonly seen unjust judicial practices and police violence directed at minorities and other marginal dissenting communities. Members of these groups have thus been imprisoned, charged, and convicted under both extraordinary and ordinary criminal laws in disproportionately large numbers in postcolonial India compared to members of the upper-caste Hindu majority community.[9] Even in instances where they have been acquitted, the acquittals have come after long, grueling legal battles inflicted on under-trials and their families.[10] In addition, perpetuation of such judicial violence has gone hand in hand with extrajudicial killings of dissidents deemed as insurgents or "terrorists." Analyzing the Indian state's responses to political violence, the scholar, activist, and lawyer K. G. Kannabiran noted how underlying the state's deployment of legal and extrajudicial violence is the equating of violent politics with crime—that is to say, scaling down and individuating political violence. In Kannabiran's words, "Politics is treated as a crime. The subversion of law begins with the reduction of politics to a crime. After such subversion, the law becomes a pretext for violence."[11]

In multiple writings, Mamdani has also offered an insightful critique of the tendency to reduce political violence to a criminal act.[12] The ways in which criminalization often obfuscates context and issues underlying acts of political violence by ignoring them while establishing individual guilt or innocence, and consequently depoliticizing the violence, is crucial here. Rather than comprehend and confront the causes of political violence, equating it with criminality confounds our ability to understand it. That failure to apprehend political violence is at the heart of the law's subterfuge.[13] Criminalization and depoliticization, according to Mamdani, encourage us to avert our eyes from the larger factors that have produced the violence and encourage us "to think of violence as its own explanation."[14] All eyes are focused on the perpetrators rather than the concerns that drove their violence. An impression is consequently created that punishing the perpetrator will resolve the problem of political violence. But the violence of punishment does not lead to a meaningful solution. It heralds, as Mamdani notes, "a quagmire" that "feeds the cycle of violence."[15]

The genocide in Rwanda and the conflicts in Darfur, Congo, and northern Uganda are the backdrop against which Mamdani makes his argument about the ways in which depoliticization and criminalization have fed the cycle of violence.[16] Here various groups switched roles as victims and perpetrators in a prolonged interethnic contest that morphed into civil wars and mass atrocity. In India, the nation-state has emerged as the hegemonic political community, and the struggle for dominance and state power has largely been resolved in favor of those who promote nationalism's upper-caste Hindu inflections—from the Congress party at one time to its more extreme right-wing proponents associated with the Sangh in recent years. As noted previously, groups anchored in other identities and economically informed political movements—in the North-East region, in parts of Central India, and among the Sikhs of Punjab and Muslims of Kashmir—have deployed violence to challenge this hegemony. But rather than apprehend the causes and context of that violence, courts have scaled it down to the criminality of a few, depoliticized political violence, and cited punishment or the law's violence as key solutions to counter it. In many influential quarters, the temptation has been to think that eliminating the perpetrator will resolve the problem.

This focus on perpetrators of political violence and punishment as the solution to political violence has been particularly apparent in the promulgation of exceptional laws such as the infamous Terrorism and Disruptive Activities (Prevention) Act (TADA).[17] Writing in 2000 in the wake of debates about another such law, prominent civil rights lawyer and activist K. Balagopal made a crucial point: namely that political militancy in India has attracted repressive laws not just because it is militant or terrifying but precisely because it is politics. Indeed, it has attracted extraordinary laws and judicial violence because it is a form of politics that has especially threatened hegemonic and dominant social forces. Singh makes a similar observation when he describes the ways in which a range of laws—from the Preventive Detention Act (1950) to TADA and POTA (Prevention of Terrorism Act 2002) have been mobilized to aggressively defend a particular definition of "the people" and the "us" who are seen to constitute "the" national political community. Such definitions in conjunction with the public and judicial discourse that has accompanied the promulgation of these laws have consigned collectives who don't conform to hegemonic nationalism's yardsticks as the "others" historically external to it.[18] We might then say that the very move to criminalize political violence and promulgate harsh laws has played a role in the political contest between the hegemonic and the marginal, or the major and the minor. Political violence has therefore been depoliticized through the law; at the same time, the law and its violence have been mobilized to reinforce nationalist dominance and hegemony of majoritarian ideologies, and visions of the country over others.

Criminal Justice and Political Justice

In Kannur, a similar but different situation has prevailed for several decades: local-level workers of the CPI (M) and the Hindu right have been the agents and victims of the contest that has been playing out between the two groups especially since the late 1960s and 1970s. As I noted in part I of the book, most members of the two groups belong to the same lower-caste historically disadvantaged Thiyya community. In other words, most CPI (M) and RSS-BJP local-level workers in Kannur are not divided against each other along caste, class, ethnic, religious, or racial lines. Thus, while their identities as members of the Sangh and the Communist Party guide their worldviews, affinities, and actions, the conflict between the two groups cannot be read as a conflict between an ethnic or religious majority against a minority community. At the same time, the strife between them exhibits multiple features of the drive to become the more dominant, major, or hegemonic force and make the other minor. The search for ascendancy that typically permeates political life in electoral democracies—the imperative to conjoin the different scales of dominance (local, regional, and national) and gain state power while containing and weakening the opposition in multiple ways, has driven the workers to the point of grievous vengeful violence usually associated with long-standing religious, ethnic, or racial enmity.

This violent struggle to become major and make minor between the party left and the Hindu right in Kannur is ongoing. Unlike the national stage and other parts of the country where Hindu right-wing formations have gained considerable influence over people's lives and become electorally and institutionally dominant, the struggle between major and minor in Kannur remains to be settled. Members of the two groups have been living out this conflict through physical confrontations, attacks, and counterattacks as well as in the courts. With this spread to the courts, the judicialized conflict between the party left and the Hindu right in Kannur has enfolded many others into it—from schoolteachers to electricians to cycle mechanics and street vendors—who have appeared in court on behalf of the prosecution or the defense. They have been drawn into painstakingly long criminal trials through which political violence has been depoliticized, and the law has been deployed by political parties against each other. Over the years, these trials have become a routine aspect of political life of Kannur. While Gujarat, Delhi, Bastar, Kashmir, and the North-East may be cited as extraordinary examples of the role that the law has come to play in majoritarian assertions, Kannur represents the everyday judicial life of political strife in India, one where force of law is regularly mobilized against opponents, acquittals for violence are also routinely obtained, and democracy reconciles itself with the violence it gives rise to. What has, however, been undone in all these cases is the possibility of getting justice—criminal and political.

Criminal justice proceeds from the principle of individual responsibility. It concerns itself with hurt and affront caused to the victims and seeks to recompense them by punishing specific perpetrators. The pursuit of criminal justice in cases of political violence frequently overshadows the question of political justice, or forms of justice that especially attend to the future of the polity, even as they take note of hurts and affronts caused in the past. Inherently, political justice implies reform of the system that produces the violence and engagement with issues that drive it.[19] In India, even as peace has been obtained in some conflict-ridden regions, meaningful reform has remained elusive at the national level, regionally, and locally.[20] In a national context where victims of majoritarian violence, for instance in Gujarat and Delhi, have been exerting themselves to secure criminal justice and members of minority communities have been reeling under authoritarian laws and unjust police practices, progressive activists have also struggled to apply themselves to the task of securing political justice. The goal of remaking the contours and character of political practices and institutions that have given rise to political violence remains outside the purview of legalized definitions for justice. Instead, as elaborated previously, the judicial system and its adversarial structure have become the site of reinstituting divisions and hierarchies between various communities, groups, and political formations.

In Kannur, this occurred as the local context itself became suffused with efforts by political workers to frame charges against those they deemed guilty and secure acquittals for their own. The politics behind the violence between members of the party left and the Hindu right was acknowledged in these cases, but it was also rendered simplistic as lawyers and judges posited politics as an already established relationship of animosity mapped along the dividing lines of an adversarial system between the accused and their supporters, and the victims and their sympathizers. While judges waded through investigation reports and apparently "truthful" and "untruthful" witness testimonies to determine individual guilt and innocence, the possibility of understanding conditions that produce the politics of enmity, grasping its formation and tracking its emergence in Kannur, or how antagonisms enfolded the persons charged was repressed. No one held up a mirror to the prevalent political system that had conditioned the conflict between the two groups. The phenomena of political antagonisms and enmity—now lived out in the courts—was taken at face value and never probed. The criminalization of political violence thus flourished with the naturalization of the idea of politics as an adversarial contest to become major. Eventually, the deployment of law to gain the upper hand in the contest to become major and make minor further confounded the possibility of both criminal and political justice.

The two cases from the late 1970s and early 1980s, which I analyze in this chapter, set Kannur on this judicial path that belied the possibility of both criminal as well as political justice. These cases are among the 250 Kannur district court judgments delivered between 1978 and 2003 (a critical period in the history of interparty strife in North Kerala) that I examined in the course of my research. In the first instance, this research entailed going through old files and folders of the district court records office, and paperwork archived in the offices of lawyers who had prosecuted or defended the accused. Copies of judgments relating to cases of interparty violence that I so obtained gave me insights into how attacks and counterattacks were framed and reconstructed in the courts. Judicial understandings, articulation, and "disarticulation" of the politics behind the violence stood out.[21] On the "frontstage" of the trials, lawyers and judges offered a depoliticized understanding of political violence. Interviews about several critical cases with mid-level workers of the party left and the Hindu right who had liaised between the accused, witnesses, and the prosecuting and defense legal teams helped me apprehend aspects of the "backstage" where testimonies were formulated and rehearsed, and party workers and accused prepared to appear before the court.[22]

Wherever possible I followed up on these cases with the relevant witnesses and accused to grasp the ways in which they experienced and sought to influence the course of the trial. Interviews with street vendors, passersby, and residents who purportedly witnessed a violent attack, murder, or attempt to murder, and who I could access several years after the trials, were often halting and awkward. I was not always able to forge the same rapport with these witnesses as I was with workers of the party left and the Hindu right who had been accused of violence or been its victims. The latter had become familiar with me and my research assistant in the course of my research trips to Kannur. The long hours we spent at various party offices in the district, in the offices of lawyers they knew and trusted, and in the front yards of some CPI (M) and RSS-BJP workers' homes, created conditions for relatively more candid conversations. That candor was however scarce among witnesses who, in many instances, had affinities with one group or the other. They had appeared as prosecution or defense witnesses in well-known incidents of political violence and were understandably wary of revisiting details of the cases and their testimonies with a researcher and a stranger. Nevertheless, some were forthcoming.

My familiarity with local-level party leaders whom the witnesses trusted and lawyers aligned with their respective groups encouraged some of them to speak to me about cases in which they had testified. Their accounts have facilitated my descriptions of the backstage of criminal trials involving members of the party left and the Hindu right. Both cases that I discuss in this chapter ended in acquittals and heralded many such outcomes in the years to come. The first case involves the murder of an important local-level CPI (M) leader and schoolteacher, Raju Master, on October 26, 1978. Four RSS workers were accused of murdering him, and their district court trial was concluded on August 25, 1981, with all four workers being acquitted.[23] The second case relates to the murder of two CPI (M) workers in an attack involving the use of crude bombs as well as weapons such as a *kathival* or knife-sword. Several persons accused in this case went on to become important local figures in the various Hindu right-wing formations, including the BJP. Each of these cases revolves around a critical incident in the late 1970s when the Hindu right began making a concerted effort to become influential in the region and the contest between the two groups began to take increasingly violent turns.

Cases, Investigations, and Motives

My decision to focus on the 1978 Raju Master case and the 1981 case involving the murder of two CPI (M) workers is, of course, guided by the materials—judgments, interviews with accused, and interviews with witnesses and those who were injured but survived the attack—that I could gather about them. Both attacks also have an important place in the local narratives about the history of violence between the party left and the Hindu right. With respect to the Raju Master murder case, it is important to note that, according to members of the Hindu right and other residents of the area, Raju Master had facilitated several attacks on RSS–Jan Sangh members. They particularly held him responsible for the murder of Panunda Chandran, who had recently left the CPI (M) to join the student wing of the Hindu right. Raju Master's murder was thus both a form of reprisal, a way for the Hindu right to proceed with its own mobilization work, and a function of the violent contest to become ascendant that had begun unfolding in North Kerala. But as we see in this and other cases, the courts failed to grasp the context in which the murder took place. Indeed, the grievous side

TABLE 4.1. SUMMARY OF 1978 AND 1981 CASES

Case name	Period	Number of accused	Weapons used	Lower court trial duration
Raju Master murder case	Late 1970s– early 1980s	4	"Kathival" (Knife-sword)	4 years
Case number 2	Late 1970s– early 1980s	6–8	Crude bombs, swords, and sticks	4–7 years

of democratic competition behind this act of political violence remained veiled throughout the trial. Instead, the trial became the occasion for each party to pursue its own goals and strive to come out on top by obtaining acquittals for its own members, and the harshest punishment for members of the opposing group.

Table 4.1 outlines information relevant for my analysis of the two cases. This account especially revolves around the prosecution's witnesses and arguments against the accused.[24] In the interests of maintaining anonymity, however, I do not provide exact and complete details about the witnesses and accused and have changed some names of people associated especially with the second case.

In the Indian criminal justice system, it is the state's responsibility and prerogative to initiate proceedings through a state-appointed prosecutor, who in turn draws on police investigations to support his arguments. In other words, the police investigation along with the state's and prosecutor's approach to a case have a formative effect on the course of the trial. In their work on criminal trials relating to the 1984 anti-Sikh violence in Delhi and the 2002 anti-Muslim violence in Gujarat, Vrinda Grover and Moyukh

Relevant accused	Relevant witnesses	Judgment
1. Aji (A1) 2. Sasi (A2) 3. Pannianur Chandran (A3) 4. Mohanan (A4)	Schoolteachers (PW 1 and 2); Gopalan Nambiar (PW 3); an electrician (PW 4)	Acquittal
6 RSS–Jan Sangh workers	Cycle repair shop owner, Sunandan; explosive experts	Acquittal

Chatterjee respectively focus on some troubling aspects of police investigations and their practices of documentation.[25] They describe "omnibus FIR(s)" or First Information Reports that the police filed in these instances of political violence as they bunched various attacks on minority communities together and attributed them to amorphous mobs made up of hundreds of unnamed assailants. Assailants belonging to the majority community with links to the ruling political parties were not identified individually and could not be held accountable for their violence. Here responsibility for the violence was scaled to the level of an amorphous crowd. In several other instances where police actually named the attackers, "shoddy and casual investigations"[26] failed to generate credible evidence to corroborate the prosecution's case against culpable individuals. Criminal justice has hence been elusive while police investigations have laid the grounds for the impunity that many involved in acts of majoritarian violence have come to enjoy.[27]

In Kannur, police have not filed such illegal omnibus FIRs. Indeed, each violent incident has been recorded as a discrete event and has not been available for clubbing together with several others. While in some instances, attacks by one group or the other have involved fifteen to twenty individuals, it has been hard to afford blanket anonymity to them. Therefore, in a large number of cases that I examined relating to CPI (M) and RSS-BJP workers' violence in Kannur, individual accused have been named and their age, occupations, and villages listed. To this extent, police have followed criminal procedure and apparently attempted to affix individual criminal responsibility. But as in cases in Gujarat in 2002 and in the anti-Sikh violence cases in Delhi in 1984, police in Kannur have often failed to produce material evidence to corroborate their allegations and assist the prosecution's case.

A pertinent question relating to evidence that comes up repeatedly surrounds the weapons used in the crimes. While weapons allegedly used by local-level CPI (M) and Hindu right-wing workers have been recovered and presented before the court in many cases, in all of the cases I studied, the police failed to obtain forensic evidence to link the weapons to the accused. In some cases, the recovery of weapons seemed more like a performance to stage efficiency in crime detection rather than a practice that has any evidentiary value.[28] This resulted in one trial court judge in the well-known Jaykrishnan Master case criticizing the police severely for simply standing over a cache of weapons and beaming at the media's cameras while failing to use the weapons to determine the identity of the guilty.[29] He was especially scathing in his judgment wherein he concluded that police investigations were "twisted" to assist the defense, "shatter and damage" the prosecution's case, and make "the entire trial a mockery."[30]

Police and judicial authorities have sought to assign responsibility on specific individuals; at the same time, they have frequently failed to generate adequate supporting evidence to facilitate convictions and punishments. Thus, in the absence of substantial material evidence, the criminal trials of workers from both the party left and the Hindu right have revolved around the testimony of victims and apparent witnesses of the violence. However, in a large majority of cases, the testimonies of prosecution witnesses have also failed to secure convictions. In a context where the possibility of political justice is remote, the absence of convictions and failure to hold individual agents of violence in Kannur accountable signal the ways in which the limited ends of criminal justice have also been defeated in Kannur. Instead, the courts became a stage in which each party sought to marshal the law against its opponents. This relationship between the criminalization of political violence, the modes in which various parties sought to mobilize law, witness testimonies, and acquittals especially comes to the fore when we look at the first of the two cases I focus on in this chapter—namely, the Raju Master case.

Raju Master, a schoolteacher and an influential CPI (M) local leader, had developed a formidable reputation by 1978 when he was killed. He played a crucial role in the early years of the competitive struggle for supporters between the CPI (M) and a revitalized RSS–Jan Sangh. According to Sangh workers I met in the course of my research, Raju Master not only sought to dissuade young men of the area from going over to the Hindu right but also reportedly intimidated and assaulted those who did. Such incidents, RSS-BJP workers maintain, provoked Raju Master's murder. Sangh workers credited themselves with the murder of the CPI (M) local leader but, at the same time, claimed that their accused colleagues had not committed it and accused prosecution witnesses of giving false testimony against them. As they did so, Hindu right-wing workers invoked a category common among many political workers in Kannur—that of the "made accused."

The phrase *made accused* is murky. It indicates that someone was charged for committing a crime but raises doubts about the veracity of those charges. In other words, while noting that someone was indicted, it obscures the fact and nature of their actual culpability and creates the impression that they might have been wrongfully accused. I repeatedly encountered the phrase in the self-narratives of local-level political workers of both parties, and started to grasp its implications as one worker after the other—of the CPI (M) and the Hindu right—observed, *Njan prathiyakkappettu*, or "I was made accused." Others simply said *Njan prathiyayi*, or "I was accused." Neither phrase indicated the speaker's actual culpability but simply that charges were (rightly or wrongly) filed against them, most probably at the behest of the opposing group. In a context where police personnel lacked the "wherewithal" to investigate complex cases and, according to many accounts, accepted "lists"[31] of culpable people provided by the accusing group, the category of "made accused" had a special place. Various workers claimed that they were "made accused" while also invoking their participation in violent events. But most simply said that they had been "made accused" and a cloud hung over the question of their individual responsibility for a murder, attempt to murder, or act of criminal intimidation. Acquittals in trials marked by sloppy police investigations and allegations of false testimonies did little to lift those clouds over such (made) accused.

The accused in the murder of Raju Master were RSS–Jan Sangh workers Sasi, Aji, Mohanan, and Pannianur Chandran (see table 4.1). The oldest among them, Mohanan, was twenty-six years old. In keeping with the code of criminal procedure (CrPc), their trial commenced with the presentation of the prosecution's case, and, in his presentation, the prosecutor divided the entire event into smaller sequences. I describe these sequences and the many empirical details that the prosecutor presented, the defense lawyer contended, and witnesses confirmed, contravened, or remained silent about. These frequently dramatic details were central to determining guilt or guilt-lessness of the accused. At the same time, micro-sequences and details about who did what, how, and where, and who saw or did not see a violent crime played a depoliticizing role—zeroing in on the culpability of individuals and obfuscating the ways in which larger political structures, formations, and practices contributed to the violence. They also performed a crucial role in each party's attempts to pursue the judicial outcomes they desired—getting their own members exculpated and their opponents convicted.

With respect to the Raju Master case, the prosecutor began his narrative with the following ground-level specifics: late afternoon on October 26, 1978, Raju Master and a colleague were walking home from the school where they taught when four men stopped them in their tracks. One of them, accused number one (A 1) Aji, asked Raju Master what the time was. Raju Master replied that it was 4:10 p.m., and the master and his colleague proceeded on. They had walked a few steps when A 1 Aji stepped behind Raju Master, swung a *kathival* (knife-sword), and inflicted a cut on the master's neck.[32] Raju Master cried out "*amme*" (mother) and ran. Raju Master's colleague, fearing for his own life, fled in the opposite direction and into a roadside flour mill. Diagonally across from the flour mill was a house whose resident became a prosecution witness and whose testimony played a critical role in the case.

According to this witness and the prosecutor, Raju Master tried to climb the steps of the house, but A 1 Aji and two others restrained him. He fell on the steps and once again Aji cut him with the kathival. The other assailants had kathivals in their hands, and after inflicting injuries on Raju Master, they all fled as many people in the area, who eventually became prosecution witnesses (PW) 2, 3, and 4, gathered. Soon after, by chance, Raju Master's brother arrived on the scene and quickly hailed a passing taxi, taking Raju Master to the Thalassery Government Hospital where he succumbed to his injuries at 7:00 p.m. The prosecutor claimed that five people witnessed the murder, and these five eyewitnesses were called to confirm the prosecutor's account in the court.

The judge had his task cut out for him: on the basis of witness testimonies, he had to determine whether A 1 Aji attacked the master as alleged by the prosecutor, whether the other accused were present during this attack, and whether they restrained Raju Master and inflicted injuries on him. In order to make his determination about the case, the judge had to attend to the micro-sequences of the event and the actions of the accused; he did not, however, have to consider the accused workers' motives and impulses. Kannur district court judges repeatedly subsumed motives that impelled an act of political violence under the phrase *political enmity*. But the use of this phrase in court, without consideration of the conditions and contexts that had produced this enmity, had a depoliticizing effect. The phrase was, as I discuss below, invoked but also rendered vacuous.

In keeping with the code of criminal procedure, the focus was on criminal liability and testimonies that could link various micro-sequences of the act in question with persons who allegedly performed them. According to the CrPC and formative judicial precedents, in that moment when the judge is convinced of the facts of the case as told by the witnesses, and "when there is convincing direct evidence to prove the guilt of the accused," the motive behind the accused person's act becomes inconsequential.[33] In cases of political violence in North Kerala, judges followed this approach to determination of guilt or innocence. Evoking another Supreme Court judgment delivered in 1998, the Kannur District Court judge in a later case wrote: "Every act of the accused is clothed in a motive. It is not always easy to prove motive for an offense. Often the motive is locked up in the mind of the offender. The imputation of a motive for a crime is therefore not imperative in each case."[34]

An instructive early Supreme Court judgment that I cited above also states, "The prosecution is not obliged to establish motive for the commission of a crime, and in some cases, motive may be known only to the perpetrator and no one else. But absence of proof of motive would keep the Court on its guard to examine the prosecution evidence with great care."[35] Prosecutors in North Kerala heeded this advice, detailing the sequences of the criminal act and associating the performance of each sequence with an individual or group of individuals. Other accused could be made "vicariously liable"[36] for that performance, but attention was seldom on the workings of the larger networks and groups that they were a part of. The terms in which workers understood and legitimated their violence also remained obscure. While the accused were identified as members of political groups, the field of forces and relations of power within which they worked were not elaborated. Nor were the accused described as bearers of particular histories and ideological inclinations. An extremely economical reading of the workers' actions and motives meant that there was no critical reflection on conditions in which "political enmity" and their violence was generated. All that remained of their politics in the courtroom was this hollowed-out interpretation of an already given condition of animosity or enmity with no background or context. Nevertheless, this depoliticized understanding of politics continued to haunt the trial, its adversarial structure, as well as witness testimonies central to the innocence and guilt of the accused.

Testimonies and the Problem of Credibility

Raju Master was killed in the middle of the day near his school; however, no one was held criminally responsible for the murder. The larger factors that created a violent political milieu in Kannur at the time also remained unexamined. The criminal justice system's methodological preoccupation with individual action and empirical details offered an alibi to political structures, principles, and practices that led up to the murder. They also became a tool for specific parties that could manipulate the outcome. Instituted to deliver criminal justice, the trial court served as a deceptive instrument for extending the conflict between the party left and the Hindu right. Each group sought to call up micro-details of witness testimonies and evidence to their own end. They sought to buttress or undermine these testimonies to support the prosecution or defense case. The charge that witnesses' testimonies were scripted and false emerged repeatedly—in judicial pronouncements and in the conversations that I had with workers of both groups.

I begin my analysis of the testimonies with the statements of a key prosecution witness: a young electrician who had identified three of the four accused as Raju Master's assailants during an identification parade. The defense lawyer deemed the young electrician's testimony as untruthful, and the trial court judge accepted this argument. Suspicions were also raised about other prosecution witness testimonies, leading the judge to acquit all the accused in the Raju Master case. I cannot say with certainty if, how, and the extent to which the testimonies I discuss were scripted at the behest of the two groups. It is however notable that criminal law's reliance on the empirical minutiae of events made it possible for legal teams representing the victim and accused parties to produce and question the latter's guilt and culpability. In criminal trials where truth, responsibility, and justice are anchored on assembling legally valid positivist details in coherent testimonies, prosecution and defense teams sought to produce as well as undermine them. This was the judicial field of forces in which the contest between members of the CPI (M) and the Hindu right played.

In Raju Master's case, the prosecutor relied heavily on the young electrician's testimony to affirm his case against the accused.[37] In fact, this witness had claimed that he was acquainted with the accused and had even informed the police of their names. He was, however, what in the court's parlance is called a "chance witness." Unlike other witnesses who resided in the area or worked close by, the electrician had no obvious reason to be at the scene of the crime; he was not a "natural witness" of the crime. His credibility as a truthful witness could only be established if other eyewitnesses testified to his presence at the scene of the crime and if the judge was convinced about his reasons for being there. Otherwise, he would be deemed untruthful. This tussle over the chance witness's credibility became a key part of the contest in court among members of the two groups in the Raju Master case: it was the tussle between the prosecutor and members of the CPI (M) who were seeking conviction and punishment for the accused, and Hindu right workers who were striving for their acquittal. In a context in which attacks and counterattacks between the two groups were becoming more frequent and a greater number of cases were going to the courts, cases like the trial of the four RSS–Jan Sangh workers accused of Raju Master's murder added their own nodes of strife between the two groups.

As in other political violence cases, the Sangh deputed some key local-level workers to work with a legal team in the Raju Master case. When I met the senior local RSS-BJP worker who assisted the defense team in the Raju Master case, he too recalled how the precarious position of the young electrician who appeared as a chance witness assisted the defense team and the accused Sangh workers. The electrician had given a statement to the investigation officer that was part of the evidence presented to the judge, and in court the electrician was asked to explain why he was at the scene of the crime. The witness detailed why he was near the school where Raju Master taught, the vehicle he was traveling in, why and how he alighted from it, that he heard the cry "amme," and upon turning around witnessed the accused attacking the now dead CPI (M) local leader. However, as the judge observed, the police officer investigating the case had recorded no such reasons during their initial interview. The witness' protestations that this was an omission by the officer, and that he had in fact explained his presence to him, did not help. Lack of police corroboration hurt the prosecution's case.[38]

Additionally, when asked to repeat his reasons for being at the scene of the murder during the cross-examination, an inconsistency emerged in the electrician's statement that generated greater skepticism about his testimony. The electrician explained that he found himself near the scene of the murder because he was taking a "short-cut" to reach his destination. His destination, however, was in the northeasterly direction. Consequently, the question arose: why was he traveling eastwards away from a road leading straight toward his destination in the northeast?[39] This simple logical fallacy cost the electrician dearly. The judge immediately became suspicious of the electrician's testimony and wondered aloud if the electrician's reasons for being at the scene of the murder were not a "cock and bull story invented from the witness box."[40]

Another crucial mistake further discredited the electrician's testimony. He had claimed that he could not only pinpoint Raju Master's assailants but could also name them. In court he successfully identified and named three of the four accused, but he faltered when it came to the fourth one. The defense lawyer highlighted the errors in his testimony and accused the electrician of lying at the behest of the CPI (M). The electrician's denials failed to impress the judge; he was ready to believe the defense lawyer's word about this witness. As the judge noted, "The witness had admitted that he was formerly a Marxist Party [CPI (M)] sympathizer. That he was not one now could not be believed. It is more than evident that he (the electrician) has given evidence . . . just to oblige . . . the Marxist Party."[41]

With these words, the indignant judge further stated how the law's call to truth was being undermined inside the court. Precedents related to the Evidence Act warn judges that if one part of the testimony is false, they should not assume that the entire testimony is untrue. In other words, they warn judges not to adapt the principle *falsus in uno, falsus in omnibus* (false in one, false in all) while determining the truthfulness of testimonies.[42] However, the trial court judge in this case chose not to heed this advice. He had his reasons: he had come to believe that the clash between the two groups had moved from the streets to the courts, and that the political animosity between vengeful workers of the two groups also drew in witnesses who testified in court in favor of one side or the other.

While it is likely that the electrician was testifying on behalf of the CPI (M), it is also possible that this was an instance where a defense lawyer was able to successfully mobilize the law's positivist evidentiary standards to undercut a judge's faith in a witness's testimony. Testimonies often become fallible and imprecise over time and (to the best of my knowledge) no substantial evidence was offered to support the suspicion that the electrician had testified at the behest of the CPI (M). Nevertheless, the missteps in his statements were real and substantive. Supplemented by the defense lawyer's assertions, they led the judge to conclude that false witnesses were being positioned in the courts by political groups. The case was thus made for disregarding the testimony against the accused RSS–Jan Sangh workers by the chance witness.

With the defense team and the Sangh gaining the upper hand, the Hindu right workers accused of CPI (M) local leader Raju Master's murder were on their way to being acquitted. As the tussle over the details of individual testimonies and actions in this instance of competitive violence consumed the courts, the complicity of the larger political structures and practices that created the grounds for the violence were rendered more and more obscure. Judicial reenactment of the struggle between the party left and the Hindu right to come on top proceeded alongside the depoliticization of their violence.

Web of Suspicions and "Untruthful Witnesses"

Continuing to contribute toward the Sangh workers' acquittal for the murder of Raju Master were other witnesses and their evidence (or lack of it). A judicial subterfuge was hence instituted in this salient early case. I detail their testimonies to describe the judicial frontstage on which the contest between the CPI (M) and the Hindu right played out in the Raju Master case. What unfolded on the frontstage signals the efforts that the two groups were putting in the backstage to fight each other—judicially via presentation of evidence and witness testimonies. One key prosecution witness who also apparently witnessed Raju Master's murder was Gopalan Nambiar (PW 3). Like the electrician, Nambiar claimed that he saw the attack on Raju Master and singled out (in the identification parade and in the court) the accused RSS–Jan Sangh workers as the schoolteacher's assailants. Nambiar lived close to the house toward which Raju Master ran when he was attacked. In court Nambiar reported that he was sitting in the verandah of his house reading a magazine when he heard someone cry out "amme" and saw Raju Master being chased down the street by the assailants bearing *kathivals* in their hands. During his testimony in court, he identified three of the four accused as Raju Master's assailants. According to his statement, A 2 and A 4 (accused number 2 and accused number 4) pulled Raju Master down from the steps he was trying to climb, while A 1 Aji "cut" him with a knife-sword five to ten times.[43] He thus confirmed the prosecution's case against three of the four accused.

When I talked about the case with one of the accused, he confidently spoke about those who had and those who had not seen the incident. While discussing Nambiar's testimony he noted: "Gopalan Nambiar had not seen [what occurred]. Other people—the master's colleagues [PW 1] and "lady teacher" [PW 2]—saw what happened. Gopalan Nambiar was a Communist Party man, he gave false evidence; he had not seen anything, but he tried to speak as if he did."

In another conversation about the case, the RSS-BJP worker deputed to assist the defense lawyer also discussed Nambiar's testimony. He added that Gopalan Nambiar could not be "approached" (by the Sangh about the case) because he was a member of the Communist Party. This statement led me to wonder if RSS-BJP representatives had in fact "approached" other prosecution witnesses about the case. Two prosecution witnesses (PW 1 and PW 2) acknowledged that they had witnessed the murder, but in court they declared that they were unable to identify the assailants. Did the two witnesses say so because Sangh workers had "approached" them while Nambiar, as a "Communist Party man," remained unapproachable? Was this an instance when the defense team actively sabotaged the prosecution case? Or was this an instance where the Communist Party man was giving false testimony to implicate the accused from the opposing group?

I cannot answer these questions unequivocally. Nevertheless, I raise them to highlight the web of suspicions about party affiliations and witnesses that came to envelop cases of political violence in Kannur. Suspicions about veracity and truthfulness were important tools through which prosecution and defense teams and members of the party left and the Hindu right fought their battles in court with another. Consequently, my own arguments in this chapter about the ways in which members of the two groups were reliving their conflict with each other on the judicial stage are anchored in allusions, cryptic statements of complicity in acts of violence, and manufacturing of testimonies. It is through this cloud of obfuscations that I have sought to piece together details of crucial cases and understand the role of criminal law in instances of interparty violence.

In the Raju Master case, suspicions dogged both the electrician and Nambiar's testimony. Like the electrician, Nambiar also faltered while identifying one of the accused in court; during the identification parade he had seemed uncertain about another two. Therefore, like the electrician, he too was discredited as a CPI (M) sympathizer and an untruthful witness. All the accused benefited from the dismissal of key prosecution witness testimonies, and the trial court judge acquitted them. The trend of acquittals in cases of political violence in Kannur thus developed. In case after case as persons charged with murder, attempt to murder, or intimidation have been acquitted, criminal justice has not been delivered and the question remains:

who committed the crimes? Simultaneously, long trials continue to be held, and police personnel, lawyers, and judges remain preoccupied. The rule of law has been followed even as its procedures, means, and methods have afforded opportunities to defense lawyers to create suspicions about witness testimonies and their credibility. It has also provided a performative stage for others who have offered false testimony on behalf of one group or another. Trial courts thus became sites for a complicated subterfuge that masked both the context and causes of political conflict as well as advanced and extended the violent contest between the party left and the Hindu right in Kannur.

Trials by Suspicion

Some members of the two groups clearly linked the political conflict playing out in the streets to the machinations and maneuvers occurring in the courtroom. Political work in the time of conflict meant, among other things, scaling down responsibility, affixing it on marked out individuals, producing and performing testimonies in court to obtain acquittals for one's own party-men and convictions for members of the opposition. In the words of one prominent RSS-BJP worker from the area, "*ethokke rashtriyamanu; sakhshikalay nammall shrishtikunnatha aairikyum*" (This is all political; [therefore] we will be creating [tend to create] witnesses). This Sangh worker was among the four accused of Raju Master's murder, who were acquitted due to questionable reliability of prosecution witness testimonies.

In Kannur, a large number of workers from both groups have been accused as well as acquitted while doubts about their innocence or guilt have continued to circulate. Suspicions have produced acquittals and led to accusations and prosecutions in long and grueling trials. Indeed, suspicion has played a particular role in the Indian legal system, and it is important to understand its place to appreciate the relationship between criminalization, politics, law, and forms of justice on offer here. Suspicion occupies a dangerously prime place in Indian extraordinary laws like the "Armed Forces Special Protection Act" (AFSPA) that has been imposed in places such as Kashmir and the North-East for many decades. As Lokaneeta notes, "One of the main provisions of the AFSPA is that it allows the armed forces to shoot on mere suspicion. Under this law, the armed forces can arbitrarily arrest, detain, seize property, and use force, including lethal force based on 'mere suspicion.' And in turn the law protects the soldiers from prosecution through an explicit provision to enable immunity resulting in enduring impunity."[44]

Like Lokaneeta, Singh also highlights the place of suspicion while discussing other extraordinary laws and the Preventive Detention Act that various Indian governments have used to deny fundamental rights to their opponents and dissidents.[45] Drawing on the noted critical legal theorist Upendra Baxi's description of the Preventive Detention System, Singh alerts us to the "jurisprudence of suspicion"[46] and the parallel legal processes that it has spurned in the country. This system, notes Singh, is "geared towards repressing (primarily political and ideological) opposition. It thrives on minimal due process and gives preeminence to executive decision-making and 'satisfaction' in the initiation and affirmation of extraordinary proceedings."[47]

In Kannur, the criminal proceedings that workers of the two groups have sought to facilitate against each other have not been based on extraordinary laws. In some cases, TADA has been invoked, but in most cases workers of the two groups have deployed routine legal procedure and evidentiary tests of the criminal justice system to hurt members of opposing groups. Extraordinary laws contain provisions that permit the use of excessive force on simple suspicion and lower the evidentiary bar to determine guilt. Members of the party left and the Hindu right in Kannur have however drawn on ordinary provisions of criminal law to cast doubts about and accuse their counterparts of grievous violence subjecting them to arduous and long trials for acts punishable with capital punishment. Mere suspicion of different degrees of involvement in the violence as well as deductive and conjectural knowledge has guided testimonies that witnesses have worked hard to "create" under the tutelage of representatives of the two groups. To quote a senior local CPI (M) worker whose words echoed those of his counterparts in the RSS-BJP combine: "In our area when there is a murder, there are always attempts to influence the witnesses. Sometimes they might even be coerced. Same thing happens on both sides. It happens on this and on that side too."

In the Raju Master case, prosecution witness testimonies aroused judicial skepticism and led the judge to acquit the four accused. A large proportion of cases involving CPI (M) and RSS-BJP workers in Kannur have ended in acquittals for similar reasons. Members of both groups have worked hard to undermine prosecution witness testimonies; they have also produced testimonies to gain the upper hand and repress the opposition by subjecting its members to criminal trials and their attendant pressures and punishments. In the following discussion of a 1981 double-murder case, I especially foreground moments in which one such testimony was produced, and highlight the complex nature of the motives, suspicions, and affects that accompanied its performance. The conflict between the party left and the Hindu right manifested in the workers' enactment and experience of violence; it also manifested through suspicions, reasonings, and the web of feelings that accompanied court testimonies and presentations. The 1981 double-murder case helps us grasp this life of persistent political violence in Kannur.

The case in question involved an attack in the late 1970s by six Hindu right workers on CPI (M) supporters, killing two of them. To maintain the anonymity of the accused and witnesses who spoke to me about the case, I omit several concrete specifics related to it—including the exact date when the attack took place and the names of persons involved. I have also changed identifying details about the witnesses who spoke to me. This case was a complex one, involving several prosecution witnesses and many experts in different fields. According to the prosecution, the assailants had employed country-made bombs as well as swords and sticks to carry out their attack. Consequently, the trial was marked, not only by the presence of medical doctors who could describe the nature of injuries and causes of death but other professionals including experts on explosives. To pass the tests of facticity, each testimony had to complement and corroborate the other, and testimonies in court had to be consistent with witnesses' previous statements. Furthermore, they were judged in light of the expert evidence presented. Among other things this implied that the witnesses' description of their own and others' injuries, and the weapons used to inflict them, had to correspond with the medical experts' opinions about the injuries and weapons used. Once the witnesses passed these tests, their evidence against the accused could be regarded as credible.

Just as in the Raju Master case, several witnesses in this case claimed that they could not only identify the assailants by sight but that they also knew their names and the neighborhoods in which they resided. However, not all the witnesses seemed credible when they sought to back up these claims with their testimonies in court. Some witnesses consistently associated one set of violent actions with one set of people, and even put the right name to the face. But others faltered; their testimonies in court were not always consistent with evidence they had given on other occasions, including identification parades. All these inconsistencies proved beneficial for the defense team looking to obtain acquittals for the accused.

However, one prosecution witness who seemed to be on the mark was the cycle repair shop owner Sunandan. A slightly built, sharp, and astute man, Sunandan was proud of his testimony in court. As he recounted, "they (the accused) frequently changed seats in the court. They sat in different orders to confuse us. Then the lawyer asked their names. Nevertheless, we identified them correctly." But Sunandan's ability to "correctly" identify some of the accused along with his youth and mental agility did not win him credibility in court.[48] It too was eventually disqualified. Here I draw on Sunandan's testimony as presented in the court judgments and an interview that my research assistant and I conducted with him. The former enables me to analyze the frontstage of the trial where lawyers presented and questioned evidence and testimonies, and judges made assessments about truthfulness, falsehoods, responsibility, and guilt. The latter helps me describe the backstage of the case where suspicions about culpability were rife and acted on to assemble legally valid accounts that would hurt members of the opposing group.

Debates about minute evidentiary details, individual actions and culpability, witness testimonies, and their authenticity clouded over the underlying context and causes of political violence between the party left and the Hindu right. In the meantime, the battle to become ascendant between the two groups was advanced through backstage machinations. Sunandan's testimony, the suspicions it raised in the course of the trial, and his statements about it enable me to highlight the nature of such fabulations. It is, however, important to remember that the term *fabulation* is mine. For Sunandan, even his lies contained a truth and a possibility of justice.

Sunandan's Testimony: Of Justice, Truth, and Lies

Sunandan was one among many witnesses in the 1981 double-murder case. He was also injured in the attack. I believe he agreed to speak to us forthrightly and candidly due to my friendship with a local CPI (M) leader he looked up to. Our conversation about the case took place at his cycle repair shop outside Kuthaparamba town. He had run the shop for more than twenty-five years and had been a CPI (M) supporter for even more. Sunandan had, in other words, lived through difficult and eventful years in the conflict between members of the party left and the Hindu right. He had seen the competitive agonistic violence between the two groups translate into vengeful antagonist conflict, and as a partisan he played his part by testifying on the prosecution's behalf in this crucial double-murder case.

The lawyer defending the Sangh members accused of murdering two CPI (M) workers closely scrutinized Sunandan's testimony, and the judge weighed the matter. The salient point of contention was the moment at which Sunandan too was attacked, the amount of smoke in the air that the country-made bomb explosions had generated, and the resulting levels of visibility or invisibility. The explosives expert was skeptical about witnesses' ability to see and recognize the assailants. He maintained that the smoke from the bomb explosion had enveloped the entire scene, and everyone there must have been caught in its haze and therefore could not have seen who carried out the attack. The presiding judge accepted the expert's argument. The experts' opinion implied that Sunandan's testimony implicating the accused RSS–Jan Sangh workers was false.

When I met him, more than two decades after the trial, Sunandan strongly protested this conclusion. According to him "definitely, there was smoke, and it also made our eyes water. But the smoke was thin and quickly moved upwards. It did not obstruct our view.... We could see the culprits." This statement might make us think that perhaps Sunandan was indeed telling the truth and the judge was wrong to disbelieve him. In the course of a conversation with my research assistant and me, however, he offered details that further obscured the distinction between truth and lies. Explaining why several other prosecution witnesses could not identify the accused correctly, Sunandan noted: "Some witnesses faltered while giving evidence. Everyone's stories did not completely match up. We could not provide clear proof. All of us spoke in different ways. There were also many witnesses who had been brought from outside, who had no real experience [of the event], and were not from the area."

Through these words, Sunandan identified himself with the group of witnesses whose testimonies failed the test of consistency and facticity, who "spoke in different ways" and therefore "could not provide clear proof" of the event. This discrepancy may be explained if we remember that testimonies are indeed narratives, which (by their very character) may differ from one another even as they speak about the same event. Sunandan's statements, however, point in a different direction: he stated that witnesses were in fact "brought from outside," they "were not from the area," and they "had no experience [of the event]." That was the reason why, according to Sunandan, they could not identify the accused correctly and why several witness testimonies differed from the others. Moreover, noted Sunandan: "Only some of them [the accused] were real culprits. It's just that the case was made against the leaders. They did not carry out the attack. Making various people accused was a practice amongst both the groups."

With these words, Sunandan admitted to committing at least partial perjury. He claimed that some of the accused did not actually participate in the attack; at the same time, we know that he testified against them. There were several contradictions afflicting his and other witnesses' testimonies, and Sunandan acknowledged them by admitting that some of the accused that he and others testified against were not "real culprits" (*yatarth kuttukaran*). Nevertheless, Sunandan was extremely indignant that his testimony was deemed a lie. Speaking with righteous anger and resentment, he said, "I don't believe in courts. We had spoken in the court so that the guilty would be punished. But what we said in court was considered a lie."

Sunandan thus articulated his and many other party workers' understanding of guilt, justice, truth, and lies. Culpability, according to Sunandan, did not imply direct, empirically proven participation in a violent act. Party workers and sympathizers such as Sunandan believed that guilt by association or based on suspicion of various degrees of involvement could and should be assigned. His testimony did not qualify as truthful in the trial court, but his beliefs about responsibility and punishment align with various provisions of Indian criminal law. For, just as in the Preventive Detention System and actions sanctioned by laws like the AFSPA, Sunandan too believed that suspicions against particular individuals were enough to regard them as responsible for a crime. And just as extraordinary laws and the Preventive Detention System have been used to suppress political opposition in different parts of the country, so also witnesses such as Sunandan and other members of the party left and the Hindu right (who tutored witnesses to demonstrate evidentiary certainty in court) have sought to mobilize rules of law against members of groups they regard as their adversaries and sought to contain and minoritize.

Simultaneously, Sunandan was hinting at something else: some of the people he had given evidence against were not ordinary supporters of the Hindu right. They were not just suspected of being vaguely involved in the attacks against the CPI (M) but were in fact believed to be the leaders who were conspiring and actively facilitating the violence there. However, conspiracy charges were extremely difficult to prove. Hence, in several cases, important local figures thought to be planning and facilitating the attacks in various ways were accused of actually physically enacting the violence. Members of both groups listed names of people they suspected to be involved in the violence to the police. At their behest, police officers included the names in the official catalog of accused. As one CPI (M) worker observed while discussing such charges: "That they [the leaders] get acquitted is another matter. The case might be rejected, but can we spare a man who conspired, and not even write his name among the accused?"

The prosecution's case against accused Sangh workers in the 1981 double-murder case was indeed rejected and they were set free. But the acquittal came after a long, demanding trial during which the (made) accused were subject to a painful legal process. To (make) accused was a way of affixing responsibility on the basis of subjective suspicion. It was also a way of addressing the culpability of the leaders who were believed to be the conspirators behind the violence in Kannur and of repressing the opposition. Mostly, the cases against these "made accused" did not hold up in courts. This has resulted in acquittals in an inordinately large number of cases along with uncertainty about whether the alleged assailants were "real culprits," merely (made) accused, and/or "leaders" who plotted and aided the violence in different ways. Murders, attempts to murder, and criminal intimidation have taken place, but there has been little judicial verification of the individuals responsible. Consequently, criminal justice as a determination of responsibility for the violence and meting out of punishment to culpable individuals according to due process has been scarce. It has not resolved or mitigated the violence. Instead, the criminalization of political violence has provided opportunities to reenact the conflict between the two groups and the competition to become major and make minor on the judicial stage.

Law's Artifice and the Question of Justice

The rule of law is a critical cornerstone of modern democracies. However, the process involved in the determination of criminal responsibility often obfuscates the context and causes of political violence. At the heart of the judicial subterfuges described in this chapter has been the long-instituted pattern of positing courtroom solutions for political violence and determining individual responsibility through the micro-sequences of a violent act. In Kannur, trial court judges have acknowledged the politics that accompanied the conflict between members of the party left and the Hindu right albeit to flatten such politics as enmity enacted and embodied in violent encounters and events. They have attenuated the meaning of politics and ignored the question of political justice, thereby offering an alibi to democratic structures, principles, parties, and practices that have conditioned the violence. At the same time, as the Raju Master case and the trial in the 1981 double-murder case show, the courts have themselves become a site for everyday legal bolstering of conflict and antagonisms. Testimonies have been maneuvered and manipulated, and in case after case the courts have acquitted accused local-level workers and leaders of both groups. Violence between the two groups has therefore been accommodated and the vengeful competition to *become* major perpetuated. Impunity in cases of the anti-Sikh violence in Delhi in 1984, Gujarat violence in 2002, and the long history of extraordinary laws in the North-East region and Kashmir are other more dramatic instances of the ways in which majoritarian aspirations have been realized through the workings of law.

Underlying judicial accommodation and perpetuation of political conflict and violence is the principle and practice of criminalization and individuation. In the next chapter of the book, I plot the genealogy of individuation in criminal law crucial to the workings of modern democracies. This history further highlights how individuation of responsibility obscures the field of social, political, and affective forces that condition conflict. Against this background, I unpack ideas of political agency and responsibility that local-level workers of the party left and the Hindu right who have enacted or suffered violence articulate. Their understanding of responsibility and justice does not shy away from the question of individual responsibility, but it also does not use individual responsibility as a tool to mask broader causes of political conflict and extend it through judicial means. Instead, the statements on violence and responsibility given by the workers assist in peeling away the law's artifice and outline what justice, which accounts for the conditions that produce violence in democracies, might look like.

Individuating Responsibility

THE PROBLEM OF INTENTION, INJUSTICE, AND JUSTICE

This chapter examines the history and effects of individuating legal responsibility for political violence. The pursuit of justice for interparty violence in Kannur has largely meant prosecution of local-level political workers lower down the caste-class hierarchy.[1] They have been accused of criminal intimidation, attempt to murder, and murder of members of opposing parties, and each person has been charged and adjudged in his particular capacity. Individuation of criminal responsibility is central to democracy's promise of objective justice. Democratic rule of law undertakes to treat all citizens equally. It assures them that they will only be judged on the basis of their actions in keeping with systematically designed legal procedures. These procedures, criminal law textbooks tell us, help to rationally determine culpability on the basis of an individual's intent to afflict harm. Someone's social background or reputation will not make them offenders in the eyes of the law. In the annals of Indian legal history, the Indian Penal Code (IPC) (first enacted in 1860) is hailed as a crucial step that presaged such a democratic criminal justice system for the country.[2] It formally instituted individuals as subjects of modern criminal law—to be judged on the bases of intended conduct. But this form of criminal justice, I argue, has fallen short on several fronts. It has especially failed to address the problem of political violence in postcolonial India.

Criminalization of political violence has meant that causes underlying long-running cycles of political violence have been ignored. Rather than transform conditions that produce violence, the justice system has been designed to affix responsibility on select individuals. As they set out to try individuals, judges are meant to determine culpability on the basis of their intention to violently hurt the victim. However, in many instances, individuals have been criminalized not so much for their conduct as for their imputed character. Individuals have been deemed suspicious on the bases of their social class and political affiliations.[3] Legalized state repression of political opponents has intensified since 2014 when the BJP took over the reins of the national government. Subsequently, a new phase in that repression has been unfolding. Between 2016 and 2018 alone, 3,974 people were arrested under the "draconian" Unlawful Activities and Prevention Act (UAPA) that suspends due process while expanding executive powers.[4] On the basis of available charge sheets and information about these cases, it is safe to say that a large majority of those arrested have been unjustly charged under the law because the ruling party deems their social backgrounds and politics as threatening.[5]

A critical contradiction has thus inhabited rule of law in India: it has promised to follow what legal theorists call the capacity-based model of fixing punishment. In other words, it has undertaken to judge individuals on the basis of their intentionally committed cognizable actions; at the same time, the justice system has repressed individuals deemed suspect on the basis of their ascribed character and political sympathies. Furthermore, in cases involving political violence, criminalization has precluded the possibility of transformative political justice. It has made individuals responsible for long-standing cycles of group violence rather than address the conditions that have produced it. But neither the refusal of political justice through a singular focus on individual actions nor the perpetuation of injustice through character-based assignment of responsibility are new developments. I describe them as an imperial bequest embodied in the provisions of the IPC and in colonial-era laws that projected entire communities as criminal. The penal code formalized the focus on individual intent to affix criminal guilt; laws revolving around so-called criminal communities collectivized responsibility. Together they set the grounds for the emergence of a rule of law that does not mitigate political violence but reproduces it.

In the course of my analysis of these laws, I describe how the colonial history of individuated capacity-based understandings of responsibility and character-based punitive preventive detention laws is tied closely. In postcolonial democratic India, they have been conjoined in novel ways that I parse out through a brief overview of the UAPA and the repressive "jurisprudence of suspicion"[6] that this act has reinvigorated. As I described in the previous chapter, subjective suspicions have also played an important role in the long-running conflict between the party left and the Hindu right in Kannur. Workers of both groups have actively participated in attacks and counterattacks and have been tried for the same. Simultaneously, they have manufactured testimonies and mobilized the justice system to punish each other through long, grueling trials. Media and public discourse have played their own part in circulating derogatory character-based assessments of workers lower down the social and political hierarchies who have been accused of different acts of political violence. All along, the singular focus on individual party workers and their particular responsibility for the violence has obscured the larger causes underlying it.

Party left and Hindu right-wing workers' affectively charged renditions of responsibility for political violence figure prominently in the concluding sections of the chapter. Most political workers who appear in this chapter have been prosecuted for murder; some of them have been charged multiple times. Each one has been through trials that have proceeded from the question of individual intent to violently hurt another. Hence, in their own accounts, workers of the two groups grapple with the question of intention to afflict harm. Their reflections vivify the limits of individuating responsibility in cases of political violence. They also help us imagine a thicker concept of intention and justice capable of transforming the conditions that produced the violence. This thicker concept of justice calls for engaging with the causes underlying long-running cycles of political violence in Kannur. In trial after trial, lawyers and judges described the workers' violence as political but were unable to reflect on its context and causes. The problem, as I discuss in the following pages, has been an epistemic one. In the first instance, it has to do with the ways in which the penal code defines individual action.

The Courts, the Code, and the Problem of Intention

In cases of culpable homicide amounting to murder, the IPC stresses only two variables as the bases for determining fault: the issue of intent and levels of awareness that an action might lead to death. Intention is central to the very definition of action offered in the penal code. It states that "an act means an event which is subject to the control of the human will." Such will or intention of the actors then "has to be gathered from the circumstances of the case and the nature of the acts."[7] Drawing on the code, criminal jurisprudence in India has regarded situations such as grave and sudden provocation and good faith private defense as exceptions. In these instances, according to the IPC, a violent act leading to death may not be classified as murder. In other words, the nature of death needs to be interrogated before judges can call it murder.[8]

Consequently, trial after murder trial in Kannur opened with the question of intent. Judges had to determine if the victim's death was the result of an intentional act. In other words, was it indeed murder? To answer the question, they turned to reports about the victim's injuries and the testimony of the medical experts, who explained how these injuries had led to death and if an intent to kill could be discerned from the injuries and the blows that caused them. The medical specialists' response to this question was crucial for the judges. On the basis of their answers about intent, the judges deduced a common objective to kill. Once intent had been ascertained and the accused were deemed to be of reasonable mind capable of cognition and volition, the judges proceeded with the trial. They drew on other circumstantial evidence and witness testimonies to ascertain if the accused persons were indeed the ones who had killed the victim and punish them accordingly. But law and criminal procedure did not call on them to do more.

The penal code does not acknowledge worldly elements in the structure of individual will.[9] After requisite levels of volition and cognition have been established and a crime has been classified as murder, it does not pose questions about the sentiments that accompanied it. Judges do not have to examine its context; neither do they have to ask what caused it. In trials related to cases of political violence too, Kannur district court judges had to only establish if the accused were the ones who had in fact committed the crime. The judges understood that individuals are formed by their milieu. They repeatedly noted that "political enmity" drove the actions of the men they were being called on to try. But in their renditions, political enmity became a stock phrase whose history, meaning, and lived reality were never explored in court. The courts' domain remained forensically parsed-out individuated actions of afflicting injury and causing death. Local-level individual CPI (M) and RSS-BJP workers were made answerable for other workers' deaths. But what this process failed to answer was the question of why their victims had been killed.

In a few cases, presiding judges expressed their anxiety about the process of delivering criminal justice that they had been trained to faithfully follow.[10] They acknowledged that they did not understand much about what had transpired in the instances of political violence that they were being called on to judge. Judicial procedure limited the scope of their understanding. Several written judgments hence became a testimony to these inadequacies. Among the court records on violence between CPI (M) and RSS-BJP workers that I collected in the course of my research, one such judgment stood out. Anxieties about the limits of judicial understanding vividly emerged in this well-known case surrounding the murder of a Sangh sympathizer in 1981—a time when the conflict between the party left and the Hindu right was intensifying.

Four CPI (M) workers were charged with murder. The judge in the case had worked through the evidence presented to him to discern the accused Communist Party workers' intent. In keeping with the penal code, the presence of a vicious will or "guilty mind" that had apparently led to the victim's "dastardly murder" was the starting point of the trial.[11] Subsequently the judge found the accused guilty on the basis of the evidence presented and sentenced them to life imprisonment. As he passed the judgment however, he paused a little. By the judge's own account, he was dissatisfied with his judgment. He noted that he had in fact not learned much about the murder in the course of the trial. He had reviewed the medical expert's opinion about the victims' injuries, stacked them against the accused workers' alleged actions, and identified the intent to kill. The judge noted that he was aware of the political animus prevailing between members of the party left and the Hindu right. Nevertheless, all these details failed to explain the "high-handed and dastardly" character of the murder.[12] The thin nature of the account he had received solved the problem of determining legal intent. It helped him establish guilt, and due punishment was imposed. At the same time, the judge was keenly aware of his failure to grasp the complex of motives surrounding the crime. Its gruesome character brought home the limits of his understanding. He could not apprehend the affects that impelled it and the context that caused it.

Faced with comparable cases of "dastardly" murder, prosecutors in some instances sought the gravest punishment (death penalty) for political workers of the party left or Hindu right accused of terrible murders. They described the accused workers as "most brutal,"[13] "hardened," and "blood thirsty"[14] individuals. Such pronouncements were in keeping with past precedents that reserve capital punishment for the most so-called diabolical persons.[15]

While judges called on to determine individual guilt or innocence focused on the presence of cognitive capacities and will to kill, prosecutors seeking maximum punishment interpreted violent acts as reflections of the accused persons' essential character. All of them were acting in accordance with a judicial episteme that upholds the idea of individual intention as a sufficient category to explain criminal actions.

Popular guidebooks on the penal code, which have shaped the education of lawyers and judges in the country, similarly hail formulations of responsibility that focus on an abstracted concept of individual will. Taking their cues from philosophies of action underlying English common law, these books expound on the importance of disjoining intention from the socioeconomic and political backgrounds of the accused. They regard the 1860 IPC's limited rendering of individual agency as a gift to the country embodying the possibilities of an objective justice system. This system, they assert, has progressed from character-based practices of fixing responsibility to capacity-based paradigms.[16] The former judged people on the basis of their background and reputation. They were thus ridden with social prejudice, whereas capacity-based practices of determining culpability emphasize volition, cognition, and scientifically oriented jurisprudence.

Capacity-based paradigms proceed from theories of *mens rea* or the "guilty mind" as hermetically sealed to develop a forensic interpretation of intention and deduce culpability. These apparently progressive theories appear in guidebooks about the penal code as an unproblematized legal heritage of the colonial encounter. In the next section, I turn to one such popular guidebook on the Indian Penal Code to further scrutinize that epistemic heritage. Throughout, I discuss forms of criminal justice that Indian lawyers and judges have been taught to hail. Their pursuit, I argue, has not only inhibited other more comprehensive forms of transformative justice but also facilitated persecution and injustice.

Penal Heritage: From Character to Capacity

The text that I discuss to illustrate my point is S. N. Misra's *Indian Penal Code*, which has gone into more than ten editions since its first publication in 1981. Representative of many other commonly consulted works on the penal code, Misra's guidebook helps me outline the discursive field that Indian criminal law, lawyers, and judges inhabit. Like these other works,[17] Misra tells an oft-repeated history of criminal responsibility as it creates a predictable teleological narrative charting the evolution of individuated paradigms through the centuries, from the fourteenth to the twentieth. Throughout, Misra cites works of European and English philosophers, utilitarians, and positivists ranging from St. Augustine, William Blackstone, Jeremy Bentham, Fitzjames Stephen, John Austin, and H. L. A. Hart, moving almost seamlessly between clauses of the penal code, their writings, and Indian, English, and American criminal case law. The common law doctrine of *mens rea* helps him to reflect on "mental elements in crime."[18] Misra acknowledges that the doctrine of *mens rea* is not invoked in the penal code. Nevertheless, he turns to it to elaborate the understanding of intention distinct from motive that the code proceeds from.

Citing the seventeenth century British barrister and judge Edward Coke's writings, Misra provides frequently cited history of the doctrine's intellectual evolution. He reminds his readers that the notion of *mens rea* finds its earliest articulation in St. Augustine's sermon: *ream linguam non facit nisi mens rea* (the tongue is not guilty unless the mind is guilty). And, after Coke's elaboration on the idea of *mens rea* and the "guilty mind" (or the "vicious will" as Blackstone interprets it), Misra notes, the maxim that "no man is guilty unless his mind is guilty"[19] found place in many English court decisions. He then goes on to describe its importance for these decisions and for legal philosophy in general.

In the penal code, as we know, intention prompted by the operation of the will—distinct and abstracted from underlying motive—is regarded as sufficient to determine responsibility and assign punishment. Drawing on Austin, Stephen, Bentham, and the doctrine of *mens rea*, Misra posits motive, will, and intention as three distinctive beads in the chain of causality. In a crucial section titled "Volition, Motive and Intention," Misra suggests that Stephen's words drawn from his canonical text on English criminal law are representative. Here Stephen describes intention as "an operation of the will directing an overt act." Motive, he says, "is the feeling which prompts the operation of the will, the ulterior object of the person willing, e.g., if a person kills another, the intention directs the act which causes death, the motive is the object which the person had in view, e.g., the satisfaction of some desire, such as revenge etc."[20] Determination of a guilty mind read through the prism of intention and the operations of will is, writes Misra, "one of the main characteristics of our legal system." The Indian legal system, he notes, abides by theories that consider intention as an independent "objective standard" to determine culpability.[21] It thus follows the principle that all intended violations of penal law must be proscribed and punished regardless of the sentiments and moral debates surrounding the action.

The principle of proportional punishment, to paraphrase Didier Fassin, posits an indisputable "moral and legal link" between crime and penalty. It upholds the call for punishment as "self-evident" and necessary to obtain the ends of criminal justice.[22] Underlying such an imperative is the understanding that a forensically discernable conscious intention—which can be ascribed to an individual—exists. And central to that prescription is the presumption that one chain of causality can be pulled out "from within an indefinite network of causality." Such an actor is then "made answerable to power," judges, and law.[23] Like many other instructors in criminal law, Misra asserts these epistemic suppositions when he posits a clearly delineable actor behind every action. Individuals appear in his rendition as self-determining subjects without shades of any complex emotions—anxieties or elations—that mark their ordinary lives. In so rendering them, instructors and commentators like Misra gloss over doubts about the autonomous character of individual free will that have in fact haunted the writings of the very legal theorists he cites.[24] I argue that accounts such as his also produce other blind spots. They fail to reckon with the actual working of law in the past and the present—in India as well as in other parts of the world whose judicial experience they regard as edifying.

Where English criminal law is concerned, the feminist legal theorist Nicola Lacey is instructive. Her research on the justice system in England and Wales from the eighteenth to the twentieth century highlights the blind spots in accounts of its linear advance from "moral grading"[25] to "factualized" technical understanding of responsibility anchored in psychology and forensics.[26] Lacey's revised history of British criminal law compels us to revisit Indian criminal law's own claims of progression toward individual capacity-based paradigms of framing responsibility. Lacey reminds us that evaluations based on social reputation not only dominated mid-eighteenth-century English criminal law but have continued to be entangled with determinations based on cognition and volition in the twentieth and twenty-first centuries. Contrary to its claims, the justice system is not objective. As we know, it continues to ascribe responsibility on the basis of assumed character at many stages of the criminalization process.[27]

Subjective suspicions based on race, class, gender, and ethnicity dog the course of investigations and the instance of prosecution as well as sentencing and actual implementation of punishment in many parts of the world.[28] In postcolonial India, members of lower-caste groups and Muslim men have been especially vulnerable. A jurisprudence of suspicion guided by partisanship and bias has also haunted various stages of the criminalization process in cases of political violence. Since 2014, when the current BJP government came to power, the criminal justice system has especially become a tool for persecution of minority communities and those who oppose the present regime. Nevertheless, rules of law that uphold individualized rational paradigms of responsibility continue to offer Indian democracy an alibi for its own role in perpetuating violence.

Lacey links the turn to individualized volition and cognition-based understandings of responsibility to the emergence of the nation-state in the nineteenth and early twentieth centuries.[29] This was a period when state power was increasingly centralized and government institutions designed to mold individual behavior proliferated. The latter went hand in hand with the influence of utilitarian beliefs on public discourse, which saw rationalized criminal law and the prison system as tools for shaping dispositions. Figures such as Bentham, James Mill and Macaulay played a key role in the extension of these ideas to India. They facilitated the establishment of legal and administrative institutions, which focus on individuals as the site of their reasoning and practice.[30] As I noted earlier, the IPC bearing the promise of scientific jurisprudence was seen as an especially impressive progressive achievement in this regard.[31]

The penal code was the culmination of a range of developments that go farther back to the eighteenth century, through which colonial authority was consolidated in India. In the first instance, this legacy revolves around positing individuals as self-determining subjects of criminal law. The idea of self-determination also implied that individuals could be divorced from their communities of upbringing and belonging. These twin moves enabled colonial authorities to institute their own sovereign right over their subjects' destinies. In this imperial context, native life was subject to much skepticism as well as outright derogation. Hence, even as the penal code was being formulated to establish individuals as subjects of criminal law, the colonial state was imposing legal injunctions against entire collectives and their ways of being.

In the next few pages, I draw on the work of various scholars to further clarify aspects of that history that, I argue, continue to haunt the country. I especially examine the ways in which colonial jurisprudence in the eighteenth and nineteenth centuries regarded individual agency, and how individual actions were apprehended in order to obtain objective justice. I also describe how the justice system became an instrument of persecution targeting various sections of society. This history and duality give reason to pause. They call on us to reevaluate democracy's investment in modern judicial paradigms of criminal responsibility. A reconsideration of the judicial order also compels us to reimagine it in a way that it might cease to be a tool for advancing political violence and become more adequate to the task of truly mitigating it—by ameliorating the conditions that produce the violence.

State, Subjection, and Suspicion

The IPC formally inaugurated a judicial order anchored in capacity-based understandings of responsibility. After independence, it became the official criminal code of the republic of India. The paradigm of responsibility, which underpins it, sees individuals apart from relationships they inhabit. The career of Anglo-Muhammadan courts, through which the East India Company-State began exercising its juridical powers in the late eighteenth and early nineteenth centuries, help us grasp the paradigms and practices that the IPC was built on but also sought to discard in favor of more cohesive authoritative laws.[32] Anglo-Muhammadan courts were set up to mediate between the emergent colonial state and a population whose forms of life company officials did not understand but whose destinies they now sought to direct. They drew on and commissioned translations of compendiums such as *Al-Hedaya*, deeming them to be the bases of a "monolithic" authoritative code.[33] In that move to both textualize Islamic law and reify it, British colonial authorities undermined existing Islamic legal practices and their underlying philosophy.

The technical vocabulary that the courts used was Islamic, but assumptions about personhood and the place of law in society were English.[34] Very importantly, contrary to the prevailing judicial ethos, judges in Anglo-Muhammadan courts failed to see individuals as part of a network of relationships but regarded them as singular abstracted units—accountable not to their communities but solely to the company state and its laws.[35] Islamic modes of engaging with crime prevalent in the pre-British Mughal era involved consultations with family members of the offending and the hurt parties. Depending on the social status of victims, the hurt caused could be repaired through reparation as well as pardon. The Anglo-Muhammadan courts that began emerging in the mid-eighteenth century noted those practices but also ignored them. They increasingly neglected to ascertain or meaningfully abide by the wishes of the victims' families; neither did they query the nature of weapons used as stipulated in Islamic law nor examine the relationship between the assailant and the victim at the time of affixing punishment as was the prevailing practice.[36] The judicial method that the

Anglo-Muhammadan courts adapted failed to incorporate procedures that might allow victims and their families to forgive the accused or seek restitution, effectively equating justice with punishment alone. The focus was now on the individual willfulness behind an act or lack thereof albeit disconnected from its "social habitation."[37] In other words, the social lost its concreteness and became a vague and general category in the administration of criminal justice. As the emergent eighteenth-century colonial state neutralized familial and group claims over its subjects' judicial destinies, it sought to articulate its own sovereignty much more categorically. State and law commanded native life, and all persons were to be judged solely as individuals on the bases of their intentionally committed actions.

The individualizing moves of the Anglo-Muhammadan courts thus became precursors to the IPC's emphasis on volition and cognition as singular variables for determining responsibility. But the command over native life also took other diametrically opposite judicial forms with profound implications. Rather than separate individuals from their social location, an array of laws emerged that determined people's fates according to their backgrounds. These legislations gave legal life to social stereotypes about criminality and made them the basis of state subjection. I am referring to the Thugee and Dacoit Suppression Acts promulgated in the mid-nineteenth century, their eighteenth-century precursors, and the Criminal Tribes Act (CTA) promulgated ten years after the IPC.[38] It is instructive to understand the history of these character-based acts and juxtapose them with the capacity-based IPC. This exercise helps contextualize the twin-faced character of the legal system that offers apparently progressive modes of dispensing justice while perpetuating injustice against multiple collectives.

Colonial India turned social stereotypes about various collectives— hereditary robbers and guilds of bandits and thieves—into judicial categories. Precolonial conceptions described these guilds as bearers of their own ethics, professionalism, and guiding gods and goddesses. Many colonial administrators, on the other hand, regarded these groups as treacherous fraternities that could not be dealt with through normal provisions of the IPC and the CrPC.[39] They were guided by imperatives of pacification and a deep suspicion of native life.[40] In their search for state "paramountcy," administrators ranging from magistrates to the police inspector generals demanded special provisions to contain this "habitual criminal class."[41] The resulting laws preserved a semblance of due process while granting special powers and executive control to punish, contain, and discipline members of groups designated inherently criminal.

The designation came to condemn a vast array of people—ranging from peripatetic craftspeople to dispossessed peasants—especially after 1857 when concerns about containing insurgency and expanding imperial control gained renewed urgency. For local-level colonial officials in many districts across the country, powers obtained through laws such as the Criminal Tribes Act became a means of securing "colonial tranquility."[42] As Piliavsky reminds us, "between 1871 and 1949, an ever-growing number of communities were systematically registered as 'criminal tribes,' and settled in labor colonies where they were subjected to special surveillance and penal measures that included roll call, raiding, absentee passes, warrantless arrests, and thrashings."[43] Surveillance through registration and preventive arrests became part of the repertoire of police action through which the state made claims of obtaining public security. Consequently, at the time of independence in 1947, 3.5 million people belonging to 128 communities were designated as congenitally criminal.[44]

Subsequent national and provincially enacted laws have retained many of the old special policing and penal provisions directed against members of listed groups even as they have replaced the term *criminal tribe* with *habitual offenders*.[45] Formal legislation and informal policing practices continue to treat members of these erstwhile criminal tribes (who are now close to twenty million) as potential felons and subject them to surveillance and abuse. Lawyers working at the coalface of the criminal justice system have shown how through design and default police personnel seek to realize a number of goals—from maintaining public order to implementing forest protection measures and (most recently in the course of the pandemic) securing public health—by scapegoating members of these groups. Dalits, socially and economically vulnerable migrants, Muslims, and sexual minorities have also been similarly targeted.[46] Character-based assessments of responsibility are thus alive and well in the midst of attempts to obtain criminal justice through individualized capacity-based paradigms of responsibility as laid out in the IPC and judicial principles such as *mens rea*.

The IPC stresses individual cognition and volition as key variables for adjudicating crime—rationally and scientifically. Laws such as the CTA and bad-livelihood provisions of the CrPC projected criminality onto entire collectives. The IPC excised contexts of violent actions from view as it stressed individualized assessments of the guilty mind on the basis of will and knowledge. It thus obviated the possibility of political and transformational justice in instances of individual and group violence. In the meantime, laws revolving around *thuggee* and so-called criminal tribes made social antecedents the rationale for repressive but legalized subjection of vast communities of people for decades to come. These laws helped lay the grounds for legalized injustices of postcolonial democratic governments, which have targeted minorities and other dissenting marginalized groups. Their history offers a critical insight: that the jurisprudence of suspicion underlying character-based assessments has gone hand in hand with individualized responsibility capacity-based provisions of the IPC. Character-based assessments have led to the containment and criminalization of groups that dominant sections of the polity find threatening; in the meantime, capacity-based paradigms promise objective criminal justice. They are cogs of the same wheel that granted legitimacy to the colonial state while securing its sovereignty. They perform a comparable role in postcolonial democratic times.

The relationship between capacity and character-based understandings of responsibility is hence close. Capacity lies at the heart of ideals such as equality before law and rationalized unbiased judgment; in the meantime, character-based evaluations come alive in everyday policing as well as through emergency provisions and exceptional laws to produce webs of surveillance and subjugation directed at communities of persons deemed particularly suspicious. Capacity-based codes help cover the tracks of character-based repression. Both are part of the same authoritative institutions. Character-based modes of assigning responsibility that so subjugate particular groups get their cloak of democratic legitimacy from a criminal justice system that upholds the unbiased application of *mens rea* and cognition and volition as key considerations while fixing accountability and punishment.

This interlinked system of individualized justice and collectivized injustice has profoundly impacted the polity in Kannur and the country more broadly. The logic and practices of character-based judgments have been working in tandem with executive and police discretion to produce repressive albeit democratically sanctioned force of law. In the last chapter, I described how the postcolonial Indian state has mobilized police and law against members of communities and political formations that have challenged hegemonic nationalist narratives and state power. Since 2018, a new wave of arrests of Dalit, minority, and Adivasi tribal rights activists, human rights lawyers, academics, and university students who oppose the majoritarian and exploitative character of the Indian state has taken place under the aegis of the UAPA.

Like the colonial-era CTA and the Habitual Offenders Act, the UAPA proceeds from the presumption of guilt. It suspends due process and habeas corpus, granting considerable powers to the police to arrest and initiate extraordinary proceedings against those whom it deems suspicious. Individuals can become suspects even in the absence of a violation or crime; the mere suspicion that individuals intend to carry out unlawful activities can make them prosecutable under the UAPA. In other words, an act of violence does not have to actually take place for the police and judiciary to charge a person for it; intention to commit an unlawful act can make a person culpable for it.[47] In the meantime, the act leaves the term *unlawful* ill-defined. The UAPA thus makes two critical moves as it affixes intention to commit unlawful acts on specific individuals on the bases of particulars bits of evidence while defining unlawful in vague terms. Mobilizing vague definitions of unlawful, the National Intelligence Authority has, for instance, cited plans to organize photo exhibitions that inform students about violence against minorities, as well as the singing of songs parodying the Hindu right and Prime Minister Modi as suspicious signs of collusion and conspiracy to carry out punishable activities.[48]

Charges of intending to commit unlawful activities bring together capacity and character-based paradigms of fixing responsibility to produce a novel view of the guilty mind. The UAPA leaves the definition of unlawful wide open; at the same time, it deems imputed intent to engage in these nebulously defined unlawful activities as a sufficient basis for prosecution. So prosecuted, individuals can be held in prison for an indefinite period while they await trial. Various instances in which police in different parts of the country have drawn upon the UAPA and its detention without trial provisions to keep a number of political and human rights advocates in prison have gained attention. Varavara Rao, eighty years old and bedridden with COVID, was granted bail in March 2021 on medical grounds after over thirty months in prison and repeated appeals; eighty-three-year-old Father Stan Swamy, suffering from Parkinson's disease, was less fortunate and died in July 2021 while still in police custody awaiting trial after nearly nine months' imprisonment; at the time of writing, others such as student activists Umar Khalid, and Meeran Haider remain behind bars more than two years after their arrests.[49] Months and years of preventive detention have become their punishment. Against this backdrop, state-sponsored media have been demonizing these activists as members of an incendiary extreme left Jihadi network guilty of everything from bringing disrepute to the nation to assassinating the prime minister. This propaganda helps to deem the activists suspect even in the absence of credible evidence that links them with any plans to carry out unlawful activities.

The Hindu right–led majoritarian Indian state is thus currently criminalizing and minoritizing not just its designated civilizational adversaries such as Muslims but also a range of critical activists belonging to other sociopolitical formations who challenge its policies. It has been employing a two-pronged strategy that reproduces the spirit and substance of repressive colonial-era provisions. Like the imperial legal order of the eighteenth and nineteenth centuries, this strategy combines character- and capacity-based paradigms of assigning criminality. While media houses do the work of manufacturing social disapprobation against those who oppose the current regime and cast them in menacing stereotypes, the police have invoked laws such as the UAPA against them. The UAPA suspends due process and freedoms granted in the constitution; at the same time, it prosecutes each person separately on the basis of individually imputed intent and (reportedly manufactured) weak evidence to do harm.[50] The individuated capacity-oriented paradigm of responsibility—a key pivot of a criminal justice system that promises equality in the eyes of the law—hence permits the violence of character-based judgments to be perpetuated. Building on a legal system that coalesced in the colonial period, rules of criminal law allow cruel minoritization of opposition to unfold in a democracy.

Minoritizing Dissent and Opposition

Kannur has been witnessing a version of this minoritization of opposition via rules of law at least since the late 1970s. Since that time, members of both the Hindu right and the party left have mobilized capacity-based provisions of the penal code to accuse individual workers of the opposing party of grievous violence.[51] Witnesses that they have "created" in court to so indict members of the opposition have not always held up to close judicial scrutiny. Consequently, district and higher courts have over time acquitted many accused workers of the two groups. But these acquittals have come after long, taxing trials. Fabricated testimonies have helped to subject workers of the two groups to the rigors of the criminal justice system for acts such as murder—punishable with capital punishment.

In the meantime, outside the courts, public and media discourse has been replete with speculations. Rumors have circulated against members of the party left as well as the Hindu right, which have demonized workers of the two groups. Various media outlets that claim to be nonpartisan have described workers of both groups as "bloodhounds" gone "wild" on the "killing fields" of "literate Kannur."[52] These caricatures have created the impression that all judicial and extrajudicial punishments (including vengeful killings) might be appropriate for these apparently vile beings.[53] When attacks and counterattacks have occurred, some police officials have sought to zealously classify local-level party workers as "known goondas" and "rowdies" apparently habituated to crime. They have enforced preventive detention measures against them and made the case for denying bail to workers so arrested.[54] Inside the courts, prosecutors have pronounced party workers found guilty of violence as such deeply "depraved" and "diabolical" persons that they deserve to be penalized through death.[55]

Character-based judgments have hence played their part in the adjudication of the conflict between members of the party left and the Hindu right. They have operated alongside the penal code's capacity-oriented paradigms of determining responsibility that emphasize empirically sound evidence of individual intention to commit specific crimes. Like the BJP government's current campaign to criminalize and repress its critics, the conflict between the Hindu right and the CPI (M) has seen the play of both capacity- and character-based paradigms of assigning responsibility. It is however important to note significant differences between the workers of the party left and the Hindu right whose lives and violence I write about in this book and the student activists and human rights defenders whom the police are currently targeting. My focus on local-level party workers' encounters with the law in Kannur helps illuminate its operations against renowned critics of the Indian state and vice versa. That said, the life trajectories of CPI (M) and RSS-BJP workers such as Preman, Sumesh, Sadanandan Master, and Sasi, who appear in various chapters of the book, have been very different from human rights activists imprisoned under the UAPA.

Activists arrested in the last few years under UAPA include influential young and old critics of the prevalent sociopolitical order. People such as the civil liberties lawyer Sudha Bhardawaj[56] and Anand Teltumbe and Gautam Navlakha are renowned for their peaceful and nonviolent advocacy against economic and caste-based exploitation, state violence, and majoritarian and supremacist ideologies. On the other hand, the RSS-BJP and CPI (M) workers whom readers meet in this book have been part and parcel of their respective parties' struggle to become predominant and gain state power. Many of these local-level party workers have lived and worked in the interstices of the competitive and corrosive democratic polity that scholar-activists such as Teltumbe have critiqued. They have been instruments and victims of the violence that this political system has produced; at the same time, that violence has been reduced to their individual criminality. These workers who frequently belong to lower-caste groups have been held responsible in their individual capacities for decades-long interparty violence. Like the dissidents that the Indian state is currently targeting, several local-level party workers have also been prosecuted on the basis of weak evidence and testimonies that lack credibility. In the meantime, the larger context behind the violence between the two groups has been effaced.

The criminal justice system has thus helped larger democratic structures disavow their role in producing political violence by criminalizing it. Pursuit of criminal justice has precluded the possibility of political justice—of remaking the democratic model that has conditioned the long-running cycle of interparty violence in Kannur. This violence, as I have argued, is an exceptional-normal phenomenon that highlights the hurtful character of democratic competition to become ascendant and obtain majorities and state power. In Kannur, interparty conflict has especially affected the lives of the young unemployed or partially employed men from disadvantaged caste groups who make up the lower echelons of both the CPI (M) and the RSS-BJP. They have been its executors as well as its victims, and they have also been held liable for it. In the final section of the chapter I turn to these workers' own affectively charged accounts of cognition, volition, and agency activated in the instance of violence. Some CPI (M) and RSS-BJP workers, such as Preman and Ajayan, whose narratives I draw on, have also appeared in previous chapters. As I describe in the next section, Preman, Ajayan, and other party left and Hindu right workers acknowledged their role in the violence but also disclaimed intention to commit it. But disclaiming intention to enact violence does not imply disclaiming accountability. The workers' vivid renditions of their agency can, I argue, help us formulate a nuanced understanding of intention and responsibility in the instance of political violence. They compel us to confront the broader political system and democratic structure and practices, which have conditioned interparty violence in Kerala and other parts of the country. We are thus called on to rethink the forms of justice on offer to truly mitigate it.

Workers' Agency and Other Forms of Justice

The call for truly mitigating political violence implies not simply reducing it to individual criminality but addressing the structures that underlie it. The idea of individual accountability is present in the CPI (M) and RSS-BJP workers' narratives that I present here. At the same time, their layered interpretations of violent political agency go beyond simple capacity- and character-based modes of criminalization. It cannot be captured in forensic accounts of individual intention to enact violence; neither can it be reduced to their alleged pathological dispositions. Instead, the workers' narratives allow us to locate their actions amid a range of intersubjective relations. These local-level party workers associate politics with those viscerally experienced relations that imbue thoughts with multiple affects ranging from fervor to sadness.[57] Such affects tend to remain ineffable, but the workers signal them while talking about themselves and their violence. Folded therein is the workers' complex understanding of intention to enact political violence.

In the first instance, their statements remind us that intention is neither singular nor continual. Read through the workers' embodied sensibilities, party workers' intention to enact violence appears broken by loss of self and ridden with apprehension. They describe themselves as heaving in the instance of violence as well as being simultaneously frustrated and even fearful, wary of being acted on even in the instance of their action. These complex renderings call for grasping the ways in which their agonistic and antagonistic contexts have produced the workers' violence. They shed light on the fraught contradictory nature of democracy itself, which on the one hand repudiates violence and, on the other hand, fosters it. Rules of law help to conceal that fraught nature; the workers whose statements I present next reveal it.

I begin with Preman, the local-level CPI (M) worker whose biography and encounters with violence throughout the 1980s and 1990s I recounted in chapter 2. The son of a beedi worker with close affinities to the Communist Party, Preman's career revolved around local CPI (M) campaigns for popular and electoral mobilization. His everyday life was embedded in close-knit ties with fellow workers and local leaders of the party. Preman was clear and categorical about the reasons underlying the murders his colleagues had been accused of as well as his own violence. "Those who deserve hatred should be hated," he said. He further identified the candidates for hate as those who attacked a leader whom he loved and respected.

Preman's sentiments carried a certain imperative—as it were—to enact violence. He went on to detail an actual instance of violence when he (and/or his coworkers) wreaked multiple blows on an opponent gravely injuring him.[58] It is hard to account for the number of injuries inflicted during an action like the one that Preman described. In Preman's mind, its cruelty was mitigated by the fact that this violence was not just an action but also a reaction—a reaction to other perceived brutal attacks. The context that Preman and his coworkers inhabited was made up of such cruelties. Workers of the party left and the Hindu right targeted each other as they fervently competed with one another for popularity and electoral ascendance. They sought to become vivid presences in the small neighborhoods, towns, and villages of Kannur, and so gather supporters who could be counted on during elections. Competition for political support was entangled with performance of adversarial masculinity. It also involved forging close bonds with fellow party men who had long intergenerational affiliation with the organization. Each attack on these men spurred a new chain of counterattacks giving rise to hate-ridden antagonistic conflict between the two groups.

A Hindu right-wing RSS worker, Rajeevan, described how difficult it was for political workers like him reared in this milieu to distance themselves from the conflict. Rajeevan had been accused and acquitted in two murder cases. The acquittals were a source of relief, but the cases had taken a heavy toll on his family, who urged him to stay away from the Sangh and ongoing conflict with the CPI (M). While talking about his family's attempts to dissuade him from engaging in political work and the accompanying violence, Rajeevan noted: "At some points when they would talk like this [seek to dissuade him from political work], I would get angry with them. Because the way it [a violent incident] happens is that when you are doing Sangha work, the mind is so completely immersed in it. Or why would this happen... for an ordinary worker... what can he do to stay away?! What can a person do... right there on the spot... how to stay away?!"

At the same time, even as Rajeevan acknowledged the ways in which he could not "stay away," like many workers of the left and the right, he too disavowed and repudiated the intention to actually enact violence or kill. In his own words, "That a murder has to be committed.... I have never done anything with that intention. I have been working with the Sangha for 10–20 years. From my perspective, nothing like this has happened [no murder has been committed with the intention to kill]."

Rajeevan had lived through the conditions that necessitated violence; he had experienced the fervor to become visible on the public stage and compete for electoral victories. In the process, he had shared close camaraderie with his colleagues that had translated into strong affective bonds. Violence had become a way of living competitive fervor and bonds, which Rajeevan associated with the world of the political. He recognized his family's demand to "stay away" from the conflict but also asserted that he could not stay away from the violence that his political work brought in its wake. Nevertheless, almost seamlessly, in the very next instance he disavowed any intention to enact violence.

Like Rajeevan, various CPI (M) workers also disavowed the intention to murder while acknowledging their participation in acts of violence including murder. I encountered an especially complicated but vivid rendition of this disavowal during my conversation with Saleem, an important local CPI (M) worker who was especially active in the 1980s and was charged in several attempt to murder and murder cases. While talking at length about the political conflict in Kannur, Saleem described the Communist Party's inclination to "take a [violent] stance against the Sangh," its inclination to respond "a bit hard" against the Hindu right, and the subsequent emergence of "political enmity" between them. Furthermore, he spoke about his own involvement in several "retaliations" and violent actions. At the same time, in the course of the conversation Saleem declared, "I will never support murder at any cost. I had this apprehension even while I was a full-time worker . . . when I knew well that the next day someone would be finished."

It is the issue of apprehension versus support for murder that workers like Saleem and Rajeevan deemed central for the intention to kill or murder. Saleem, Rajeevan, Preman, Ajayan, and many others contrasted such an intention or support for murder with contexts that impelled them toward it. But they did not employ this contrast between intention and impulsion because one apparently suggested the presence of free will and the other extenuating compulsions. Instead, I suggest that they were articulating a different understanding of action and agency—one that is always entwined with its contexts and generated in an intersubjective space. For workers of both the party left and the Hindu right, the space and moment of violence were marked by moments of lurching forward with ineluctable passions but also grave apprehensions. A realm of action unmediated by these affects and the workers' context did exist in their imagination; however, they regarded such actions as products of a hermetic intention that the courts emphasized.

The local-level workers of the left and right that I spoke to did not identify with this judicially coherent and notionally sealed intention. Their actions, as the workers described them, could not be delinked from the travails of political life that they were immersed in; the intentions behind the actions were not singular and continual but frequently broken by loss of self and ridden with misgivings and trepidations. These workers were aware of the democratic virtues of respect, friendship, and tolerance as modes of dissipating conflict; they spoke about these virtues all the time, and they even earnestly subscribed to them and hence did *not* intend to enact violence or murder. At the same time, workers like Saleem and many others were also aware of the role that adversarial zeal played in political life. They did not seek to bracket off or pathologize the visceral affects it produced. Instead, they lived it—constantly associating democratic politics with agonism and its translation into antagonism.

Democracy had gained a foothold in the lives of these young men from lower-caste peasant and working-class families through its promise of equality and popular sovereignty. It fell short on all these counts but still offered visibility in various public stages and the opportunity to be part of larger political communities. The workers strived hard to ensure enumerable support for their parties. Containing the opposition became part and parcel of this work. Many affects circulated among them—competitive ambition and ardor, but also hurt and anxiety, as well as a vengeful spirit—generated while carrying out everyday work of popular and electoral mobilization in an electoral, representative democracy. Both these registers in which democracy operates—abjuring violence normatively and yet creating the conditions for it—found place in the words of political workers like Preman, Rajeevan, and Saleem. Hence, they both acknowledged their participation in the violence and repudiated any intention or inner feeling to enact it.

Law, on the other hand, has sought to simplify things. In a context where justice is equated with proportional punishment of individuals, capacity- and character-based modes of fixing responsibility have stepped in to depoliticize political violence. Capacity-based tenets of the penal code have obscured the affects accompanying the workers' actions. Instead, courts have focused on the forensically circumscribed intent of the accused to inflict harm. This intent has become the basis for prosecuting individual members of the party left and the Hindu right and trying them for decades-long conflict between the two groups. In the course of the trials, lawyers seeking the maximum penalty against convicted workers have cast grave aspersions on their characters. In the meantime, media and public discourse has reduced the conflict to depravities of select persons born of cultural legacies and membership in misguided political communities. Few have asked about how the agents of violence and their communities came to be. How did workers of the party left and the Hindu right come to embody their respective parties' drive to become major political forces? Importantly, how did the parties become involved in the project of becoming ascendant? That is to say, how did cultivating a homogeneous consenting community of supporters and aggressively undermining and reducing opposition to a minor position become a crucial preoccupation of the two groups. The vagaries of criminal trials and preoccupation with individual culpability have left little room for posing and answering such questions.

Individuation of culpability has obscured the role that modern democratic systems play in producing political violence. Particularizing it has made it a personal and cultural pathology. Furthermore, the criminal justice system has itself become a tool for repressing dissenting individuals and groups. But justice can also take other forms—one whose end goal is not to merely affix individual culpability on the bases of capacity or character but one that proceeds from the contexts that accused persons inhabit. This book has especially focused on the democratic context of the workers' violence—on the ways in which contemporary democracies as an assemblage of competitive practices anchored in the majority principle produce interparty violence. Democracy here stands for multiparty politics and rule of representatives. In Kannur, the search for electoral and popular power has drawn in generations of young men willing to attack and counterattack so that their parties might stay on top. Nationally, public life and institutions are becoming brutally majoritarian.

I believe that, against this backdrop, the call for a form of justice that can meaningfully mitigate democracy's violence implies transforming democracy itself. Such a transformed democracy cannot be grounded in the binary between majority and minority, nor rely on abrasive competition to determine the collective good. The search for justice here must not begin and end with fixing individual guilt and punishment but address itself to structures that produce divisive binaries and aggressive competition and, hence, seek to ameliorate the very causes of political violence.

Conclusion

India and Other Democracies: Past and Present

A few days before India marked its seventy-second "Republic Day" on January 26, 2021, the noted public commentator and historian Rajmohan Gandhi wrote an insightful piece on the prevailing political climate in the country.[1] The article was published in the widely read South African news magazine *Daily Maverick*. In his article, Rajmohan Gandhi associated India's present violent juncture with the rise of an "imperialist" ethnonationalist "spirit" in the country. Ethnonationalists, he noted, tend to believe "that a nation belongs more to its dominant section than to everyone." Such an ideology implies that "the US belongs to its whites, India to its Hindus, China to its Hans, and so forth." Gandhi identified Donald Trump in the United States, Narendra Modi in India, Recep Tayyip Erdoğan in Turkey, and Jair Bolsonaro in Brazil as "well-known symbols of ethnonationalism's growth." In India, he lamented, ethnonationalism had undone the democratic energy of institutions ranging from the legislature to the judiciary as well as the media. All of them, he accurately observed, have become complicit in perpetuation of "ill will" against minorities especially Muslims, Christians, and Sikhs whose liberties have been steadfastly eroded.[2] A few days after

Rajmohan Gandhi's article, another well-known public intellectual, Pratap Bhanu Mehta, wrote in a similar vein about the fate of Indian democracy in the pages of a national daily. Penned in the wake of a police crackdown on farmers (many of them belonging to the minority Sikh community) protesting the government's agricultural policies and the media campaign demonizing them, Mehta's words were stark. He wrote about the BJP-led state's divisive and repressive strategies to deal with those who opposed it. He also condemned public discourse, which acquiesced to these strategies. Together they seemed to have, noted Mehta, set Indian democracy "on the road to perdition."[3]

The word *perdition* evokes a painful abyss. It reminds us of horrors of the past—the intense violence that accompanied the partition of the country, the period of national emergency in the 1970s, the anti-Sikh violence of 1984, the pogrom of Muslims in 2002, and the decades-long police- and military-led suppression that Kashmir and parts of the North-East region have faced. It also makes us wonder what the new installment of perdition might look like. The imperialist ethnonationalist spirit might claim many more victims (as it is already doing). Many more institutions might also become complicit in perpetuating the Hindu right's violent majoritarian agenda. I agree with Mehta and a number of other commentators that this agenda is driving Indian democracy to a very grim place.[4] But as Rajmohan Gandhi reminds us, India is not alone. Many other polities—from the United States to Turkey to Brazil—are currently suffering the vagaries of polarizing politics that seeks to secure the domination of one group over others. Many regions have suffered from such politics before.[5] But what Gandhi does not mention is that like Prime Minister Modi, Erdoğan and Bolsonaro were elected democratically with large margins.[6] And while Trump lost the popular vote by 2.1% in 2016, he too had won the presidency through a well-established electoral system. His defeat in 2020—in large measure due to the large Black minority vote against him—reminds us of other possibilities that electoral democracies create. For, they are not only the route through which supremacist leaders have obtained power but might also be the way to secure their exit. In the near or distant future, India and other places that are veering under the weight of exclusionary ideologies might also be able to cast away their domineering leaders. This does not however detract from the fact that democracies are a constitutively vulnerable place for numerical and social minorities.

As I argue in this book, the binary between majority and minority is central to modern democracies. Their competitive milieu creates the grounds for the emergence of aggressive majoritarianism on the one hand and disempowering minoritizing practices on the other. I do not see the grim path that Indian democracy is on as a pathological aberration that RSS-BJP's ethnonationalism is solely responsible for. Instead, this book turns the mirror back on modern representative democracy—and the potential for homogenization, polarization, and violence that it contains. The Hindu right particularly embodies that potential, but it has also inflected the workings of the Communist Party as well as several other political formations. My study of political conflict in Kannur shows how democratic competition set communities of young subaltern men affiliated with various political parties on a violent course. The fact that young men at the forefront of the conflict between the party left and the Hindu right in Kannur share similar religious, caste, and class backgrounds makes it exceptional. Their righteous rage, aggressive action, and the communities of support that they have forged also stand out. At the same time, the first three opening chapters of the book read local-level party workers' aggressive rage not as a perversion peculiar to them, their parties, or the region, but as an expression of something more general—the adversarial search to become a major force in a political system. Democracy, in this context, becomes the name of the political system where pastoral power and abrasive forms of hegemonic masculinity are mobilized to foster majoritarianism.

Modern democratic practices and institutions began gaining ground in the 1920s in Kerala. In chapter 1, I turned the clock back to that period and detailed North Kerala's particular political context through the decades when interparty contests there became increasingly conflictual. In chapters 2 and 3, I described how the CPI (M) and the RSS-BJP impacted the political field in Kannur and the lives of those who inhabit it. Both parties offered different kinds of public presence to members of "backward castes." They also held them together in communities of pastoral care, love, and hate. As the competitive pursuit of popular and electoral majorities between the two groups intensified, young blue-collar men from disadvantaged backgrounds came to occupy the frontlines of the conflict between the party left and the Hindu right. Democratic contests became the grounds for the emergence of an agonistic masculine culture and its translation into antagonistic, schismogenetic violence among them.

Police, courts, and several sections of the media pinned the blame for the violence on these young local-level political workers. By affixing responsibility on selected workers, the courts did not mitigate the violence but in fact advanced the conflict between the groups. Chapters 4 and 5 showed how criminalization depoliticizes political violence and also furthers it. Such depoliticization prevents us from understanding its character and hence meaningfully transforming the structures that produce it. If not individual agents of violence, we indict figures like Trump, Modi, and Bolsonaro, and the organizations and ideologies they represent. Responsibility for the rise of violent majoritarianism and vengeful group conflicts lies with all of them. But it also lies somewhere else—namely with a mode of organizing political life that rewards similitude and division, producing cohesive but adversarial communities pitched against one another. Rules of law that obfuscate the complicity of this democratic political system afford it an alibi or a free pass. It is however important to remember that the modern democratic system did not always have such a free pass. In India, its principles and practices came under intense scrutiny several decades before they were completely instituted. As I discussed in the introduction, critics of the ways in which electoral democracy was being transplanted in the Indian context included influential figures like Sir Syed Ahmad Khan, B. R. Ambedkar, and Mahatma Gandhi.

In 1888, just two years after founding of the Indian National Congress, Sir Syed wrote about the "potentially oppressive" character of democracy, fearing that it might translate into "crude enforcement of majority rule."[7] Majority rule, Sir Syed worried, would give rise to "more conflict and disagreement" as contentious matters might be decided by "the weight of numbers rather than negotiation and goodwill."[8] Some years later Ambedkar and Gandhi aired their anxieties and offered their disparate proposals for obtaining a more equal polity. Both of them forewarned us about the ways in which the modern democratic system might enable the rise of a dominating communal spirit. They understood that the democratic dispensation anchored on and run through the will of the majority is, by definition, a precarious place for social and numerical minorities. Today when the democracy they feared has come to pass, I believe we need to attend to questions that figures like Sir Syed, Ambedkar, and Gandhi raised.

Ambedkar argued that in India's caste-ridden social landscape, unfiltered majority Hindu rule would lead to marginalization of Dalit and other minority communities. Undoing the imperialism of caste Hindus and obtaining self-rule for Dalits meant undoing the former's capacity for lordly majoritarianism.[9] Like his counterparts in the Muslim community, Ambedkar sharply articulated the demand for separate electorates for Dalits. Furthermore, he put forward measures that would have not only taken weightage away from the numerical Hindu majority but also redistributed it among those who were numerically small and economically, socially, and educationally disadvantaged.[10] Ambedkar thus sought to mold the electoral system in ways that might serve the cause of marginalized groups like the Dalits. Gandhi, on the other hand, espoused a more wholesale rejection of electoral democracy.

Gandhi, as I noted in the introduction, equated modern democratic rule with the practice of domination and indeed brute force. His ideal polity discards principles and practices that uphold the rule of the majority; in other words, it discards modern representative democracy as we know it for an imagined polity that places minority life and interests at its center. Equality here is absolute and not just abstract equality in the eyes of the law. Minoritization, making less than equal, is denied as a possibility. Gandhi thus envisions a polity not defined as the rule of the majority but marked by the "welfare of all." In Gandhi's scheme, however, this welfare is not ensured through representatives of "the people" but offices of the virtuous and the wise.[11]

Gandhi's solution need not be ours. Gandhi challenges majority rule but does so in a way that upends the possibility of popular sovereignty altogether. Questions can also be raised about the call for separate electorates and a politics that sought to counter Hindu majoritarianism by pitching a number of other communities against it. The need to defeat organizations that perpetuate Hindutva's majoritarianism and repressive policies in India is urgent. I have however questioned the paradigm of democracy, which revolves around competition to win and vanquish.

Juxtaposing India's present with North Kerala's recent past, I have described how competitive democratic politics became the grounds for seeking dominance and capacity to prevail over other groups. Competitive pursuit of ascendance in Kannur produced tight-knit political communities on the left and the right violently ranged against one another. Based on this analysis, I argue that as modern democracies institute competition for popular presence and electoral majorities to obtain state power, they frequently create conditions in which politics marshals care as well as combative forms of hegemonic masculinity. Furthermore, rules of law cloud over the larger causes behind the violence that democracies condition. This book interrogates that violent democratic condition.

Preface

1 Harsh Mander, "Tabrez Ansari's Killing: Land of Blood and Shame," *The Hindu*, August 31, 2019, https://www.thehindu.com/news/national /land-of-blood-and-shame/article29301014.ece.

2 Special Correspondent, "Amnesty Report: Hate Crimes Rose Sharply the First Half of 2019," *The Hindu*, October 4, 2019, https://www .thehindu.com/news/national/amnesty-report-hate-crimes-rose-sharply -the-first-half-of-2019/article29598191.ece.

3 See Gilmartin, "Historiography of India's Partition," for a helpful review of the vast amount of academic literature on the causes underlying the Indian partition. This literature has explored the "high politics" of negotiations that preceded the partition as well as the local, regional, and imperial dynamics that produced divisive religious identities in late colonial North India and Bengal. In my brief discussion of the causes of the partition here I am following Gilmartin's lead and particularly thinking about the role of political structures in facilitating elite rivalries and unities, divisions, and alliances in the 1920–1940s period and the impact that these had on community formation at the local level. See Gilmartin, "Pakistan, Partition" and "Magnificent Gift." See also Chatterji, *Bengal Divided*; Gould, *Hindu Nationalism*; Nair, *Changing*

Homelands; and Talbot, "1946 Punjab Elections," for some important research that supplements our understanding of the relationship between competitive politics of the twentieth century and the formation of antagonistic Hindu–Muslim communities.

4 N. P. Ullekh, "Why India's Politically Most Violent District Continues to Bleed," *The Times of India*, February 25, 2022, https://timesofindia .indiatimes.com/india/why-kannur-remains-one-of-indias-bloodiest -battlegrounds/articleshow/89771004.cms.

5 Chandrakanth Viswanath, "CPM Worker Hacked to Death in Kerala's Kannur, RSS Activist Killed in Retaliatory Attack," News 18, May 8, 2018, https://www.news18.com/news/india/kerala-cpm-worker-hacked -to-death-in-kannur-left-blames-sangh-calls-for-strike-1740903.html.

6 Viswanath, "CPM Worker Hacked to Death."

7 Gilmartin, "Pakistan, Partition," 1086.

8 By translocal I refer to scale beyond a particular neighborhood, town, village, district, or province.

9 Aijaz Ahmad, "India: Liberal Democracy and the Extreme Right," Verso, March 24, 2017, https://www.versobooks.com/blogs/3144-india-liberal -democracy-and-the-extreme-right.

10 V-Dem Institute, "Democracy Report 2022: Autocratization Changing Nature?," Democracy Reports, https://www.v-dem.net/publications /democracy-reports, accessed November 22, 2022; Soutik Biswas, "'Electoral Autocracy': Downgrading of India's Democracy," BBC, March 16, 2021, https://www.bbc.com/news/world-asia-india -56393944.

11 Partha Chatterjee, "Response to Vishnupad and Hansen," Society for Cultural Anthropology, November 1, 2017, https://culanth.org /fieldsights/response-to-vishnupad-and-hansen.

Introduction

1 According to my computations more than four thousand workers of the left and right were tried for acts ranging from criminal intimidation, attempt to murder, and murder of members of the opposing party between the late 1970s and early 2000s. These calculations are based on records of trial court judgments archived at Kannur District Court, Thalassery. Media accounts speak of two thousand "clashes" during the 1980s and 1990s. See John Mary, "Political Murder Tally," *New Indian Express*, October 16, 1999. According to *The Hindu*, 127 political murders took place in Kannur in those two decades. See K. M. Tampi, "A Bleeding District," *The Hindu*, December 9, 1999. The *Mathrubhumi* lists 142 political murders between 1980 and 2000. See P. P. Sasindaran,

"Akramarashtreeyatinte," *Mathrubhumi*, December 8, 2000. A response to a right to information query received from the District Police Office, Kannur, recorded ninety-one political murders between 1983 and 2009. According to police records, in thirty-one cases, RSS-BJP workers were deceased and CPI (M) workers were alleged assailants; in thirty-three cases, CPI (M) workers were deceased and RSS-BJP workers were assailants; and the other cases are spread between Congress (I), Indian Union Muslim League, and the National Democratic Front.

2 The journalist N. P. Ullekh has put together the following figures for the 1990s and 2000s based on police records and crime bureau statistics: since 1991, forty-five CPI (M) workers, forty-four RSS-BJP workers, fifteen Congress workers, four Muslim League activists, and some from the Popular Front of India have been killed in Kannur. Between 2001 and 2016, thirty RSS-BJP workers and thirty-one CPI (M) workers were killed in Kannur. Ullekh, *Kannur*, 11.

3 There are several insightful analyses of the citizenship law in the public domain. Civil society groups linked to the Indian diaspora across the world also protested against it. I am drawing on a public statement that the Cape Town–based organization People Against Apartheid and Fascism put together. The statement summarizes the history of the law and its anticipated effects in the following words: "The Citizenship Amendment Act (CAA) became a law in December 2019. The Act associates Indian citizenship with religious identity attacking the basic tenets of egalitarianism enshrined in the constitution. The legislation, in conjunction with the soon to be implemented National Population Register (NPR) to be followed by the National Registry of Citizens (NRC), will enable the persecution of religious and social minorities, producing a domino effect of statelessness and disintegration of fundamental human rights. While designed to fast-track citizenship for non-Muslim refugees from neighboring countries, the CAA threatens life and livelihood of India's 200 million Muslims as well as other economically and socially marginalized groups in India. The NPR, through its stringent documentation requirements, will isolate and inhibit members of other socioeconomically disadvantaged groups from validating their citizenship. Together, the nature of the CAA-NPR and NRC threatens to dispossess people from oppressed castes, the urban and rural poor, the LGBTQIA+ community and religious minorities of India from their cultural, economic and human rights." "Repeal India's Exclusionary Citizenship Amendment Act," *Mail and Guardian*, August 17, 2020, https://mg.co.za/special-reports/2020-08-17-repeal-indias-exclusionary-citizenship-amendment-act/. Last modified August 17, 2020.

4 Shekhar Tiwari, "Muzaffarnagar Violence: Muslims Forced to Live in Fear," The Wire, December 24, 2019, https://thewire.in/rights/watch

-muzaffarnagar-violence-muslims-forced-to-live-in-fear; Hannah Ellis-Petersen and Shaikh Azizur Rahman, "'I'll Destroy Your Family': India's Activists Tell of False Arrest and Torture in Custody," *The Guardian*, February 1, 2020, https://www.theguardian.com/world/2020/feb/01/uttar-pradesh-india-activists-false-arrest-torture-custody-citizenship-amendment-act; "Gunman Fires at Anti-CAA Rally outside Jamia, Student Injured," *Economic Times*, January 31, 2020, https://economictimes.indiatimes.com/news/politics-and-nation/massive-protests-in-jamia-after-student-injured-by-armed-man/articleshow/73770576.cms; "Indian Diaspora Demand Withdrawal of All Charges against 18 Activists over CAA Protests," *Deccan Herald*, January 26, 2022, https://www.deccanherald.com/international/indian-diaspora-demand-withdrawal-of-all-charges-against-18-activists-over-caa-protests-1074947.html.

5 India is home to almost two hundred million Muslims. Approximately 80 percent belong to subordinated castes. Increasingly these "lower-caste" Muslims have been mobilizing under the banner of Pasmanda Muslims. In Persian, the term *Pasmanda* means "those who have fallen behind." Following the 2006 Sachar committee report on their socio-economic and educational status, Muslims have also been identified as the "new underclass"—marginal in multiple respects and comparable to Dalits—in land ownership, employment, housing, education, experience of discrimination in employment, and political representation. See Bidwai, "Muslims, the New Underclass." See also Ansari, "Pluralism and the Post-Minority Condition," 111.

6 Mufti, *Enlightenment in the Colony.*

7 For a detailed critical discussion of the ways in which electoral majorities became imperfect procedural expressions of the general will, see Rosanvallon, *Democratic Legitimacy,* 1–4, 17–32.

8 Ismail, *Abiding by Sri Lanka.*

9 Scott, *Refashioning Futures,* 162.

10 These include constitutional rights as well as consociational arrangements of different degrees, forms, and shapes. But even as minority rights and consociational arrangements have sought to undo the tyranny of the majority, they struggle with the hegemony that the principle of majority rule has acquired in practical governance matters as well as in public discourse. For an illuminating reflection on consociationalism and its limits and possibilities, see Ismail, *Abiding by Sri Lanka,* 271–93.

11 Kaviraj, *Enchantment of Democracy,* location 67 of 6178, Kindle edition.

12 Kaviraj, *Enchantment of Democracy,* location 161 of 6178, Kindle edition.

13 The corpus of both Chatterjee's and Kaviraj's work is large. While penning this section, I am particularly thinking about Partha Chatterjee's *Politics of the Governed,* his recent collection of lectures *I Am the*

People, and Kaviraj's essays put together in the collection *Enchantment of Democracy*.

14 Here I am paraphrasing Sunder Rajan, *Scandal of the State*, xii.

15 Kaviraj, *Enchantment of Democracy*, location 148 of 6178, Kindle edition.

16 P. Chatterjee, *Politics of the Governed*, 75–76.

17 Kaviraj, *Enchantment of Democracy*, location 364 of 6178, Kindle edition.

18 Kaviraj, *Enchantment of Democracy*, location 360 of 6178, Kindle edition.

19 P. Chatterjee, *I Am the People*.

20 P. Chatterjee, *I Am the People*, 112–14; Tuck, *Sleeping Sovereign*.

21 Ake, *Feasibility of Democracy*, 7–32.

22 Gender-based hierarchies and discrimination against groups deemed as slaves went hand-in-hand with Athenian emphasis on equal participation. On the move from this egalitarian to the more elitist representative democracy, see Dunn, *Democracy*, and Manin, *Principles of Representative Government*, for an instructive history of this aristocratic turn in democracies. See also Mantena, "Political Identity," for insightful reflections on this history and its implications for politicization of identities in Indian and other postcolonial contexts.

23 Ake, *Feasibility of Democracy*, 11.

24 P. Chatterjee, *I Am the People*, 114; emphases in the original.

25 See Manin, *Principles of Representative Government*, for an overview of the role that Madison played in conceptualizing and instituting representative democracy as we now know it.

26 Schumpeter quoted in Ake, *Feasibility of Democracy*, 18.

27 Ake, *Feasibility of Democracy*, 7. See also Dunn, *Democracy*, on the question of how this trivialized form of democracy came to gain tremendous global credence.

28 Scott, *Refashioning Futures*, 162.

29 This is not to say that there have not been endogenous critiques of representative democracy in postcolonial contexts since its institutionalization there. Staying with the African continent for now, Mary Moran describes how in Liberia electoral competition for power to become representatives came to be associated with ritual murders and maiming. She regards this popular association as an expression of profound skepticism about representative democracy, which breaks apart the body politic just as mutilation dismembers the human body. See Moran, *Liberia*, 27–52.

30 Mamdani, "Africa," 2230.

31 Tambiah, *Leveling Crowds*, 261. See also the writings of Thomas Blom Hansen and Jonathan Spencer, who have plotted the ethnicization of particular communities in South Asia: Hansen, *Saffron Wave* and *Wages of Violence*; Spencer, *Anthropology, Politics and the State*. Paul Brass and Steven Wilkinson's comprehensive studies on "Hindu-Muslim riots" describe the role that the search for popular support and electoral legitimacy has played in transforming ethnic communities into cohesive but hostile unities: Brass, *Production of Hindu-Muslim Violence* and *Forms of Collective Violence*; Wilkinson, *Votes and Violence*. Insofar as my analysis is anchored in the emergence of an antagonistic political field over several decades drawing both on historical records as well as interviews and ethnographic research, it is akin to Brass's and Hansen's influential writings. My overall argument about the relationship between political violence and democratic life also has strong affinities with both Brass's as well as Wilkinson's work. But unlike Brass, I do not frame the violence between the party left and the Hindu right in Kannur as a result of self-conscious production of ethnic solidarities and animus to obtain electoral advantage. Instead, I describe the slow formation of a conflictual political field and the ways in which it drew in members of similar caste and class backgrounds pitching them against one another in violent competition for electoral and popular support. Furthermore, unlike Wilkinson, my emphasis is not on electoral conditions that might or might not produce violence but on reckoning with the potential for violence that is contained in modern democracies. The gradual ways in which that potential marks the local-level political field, subjectivities, and communities are at the heart of my analysis.

32 In related work, the sociologist Michael Mann compares histories of genocide and ethnic cleansing in many different parts of the world to posit a close relationship between democracy and violent escalation of ethnonationalist politics. Ranging from Armenia to Indonesia to India, Mann draws on research that other scholars have done on a number of sites of grave ethnic violence to posit an overarching thesis about ethnic cleansing as the "dark side of democracy." This thesis hinges on the notion of the "demos" or the "the people" in whose name a democratic state rules and how, in multiple settings, a particular ethnicized formation or "ethnos" has stepped in to become dominant and coterminous with the demos excluding all others. See Mann, *Dark Side of Democracy*, 3, 13–14, 148, 512–29. Mann is especially perceptive when he describes how ethnic differences entangle with other hierarchies to generate violent hostility. His map of conditions in which societies reach the point of murderous cleansing and enact it is instructive. That said, his book fails to describe the specific democratic drivers that accentuate difference. For an elaboration of this critique, see Richard Bourke's review of Mann's book: Bourke, "Modern Massacres."

33 Mbembe, "On Politics," 317. Mbembe is drawing his insights from Geschiere and Nyamnjoh, "Capitalism and Autochtony."

34 Ossome, *Gender, Ethnicity, and Violence.*

35 See Przeworski, "Divided We Stand?," and Boutros-Ghali, "Democracy," for two influential academic and public endorsements of democracy as a mode of obtaining peace through political participation and electoral competition within and among democratic states.

36 Benjamin Constant cited in Kaviraj, *Enchantment of Democracy,* 26.

37 Mbembe, "On Politics," 313, 317.

38 On this point, see P. Chatterjee, *I Am the People,* ix. I agree with Keane that several contemporary democracies have cultivated considerable monitoring of and calls for accountability of violence against women, migrants, minorities, and others. That said, as his own later writings note, that capacity is contingent and precarious. Historical experience of democracies—from Athens to United States—not as peace builders but empires facilitating and enacting incredible violence against other states raises critical questions about the future of dissent against violence in democracies, and the specter of "[further] militarization of their domestic politics," Keane, "Epilogue," 378. Also see Keane, *Violence and Democracy.*

39 I find Claudio Colaguori's description of the agon as a philosophy and cultural rationality instructive. He describes the agon as "the arena of competition, the scene of contest, and the locus of adversarial conflict." "The philosophy of agonism," Colaguori notes, "affirms the idea that transcendence, truth and growth are generated from the outcome of the contest." Colaguori, *Agon Culture,* vii.

40 Agonism, as Wenman notes, involves two aspects—necessary interdependence and strife: Wenman, "'Agonistic Pluralism,'" 168. This idea, central to Michel Foucault's writings on the subject, has in turn been drawn from Friedrich Nietzsche's *On the Genealogy of Morals.* Drawing from Nietzsche, Foucault describes agonism as "a relationship which is at the same time reciprocal incitation and struggle; less face-to-face confrontation, which paralyzes both sides than a permanent provocation." See Foucault, "Subject and Power," 790. For one of the most cogent descriptions of the idea of agonism as the bases of a "generous ethos of engagement" derived from Foucault, see Connolly, "Beyond Good and Evil," 369.

41 Connolly, "Response"; Connolly, *Pluralism*; Honig, "Politics of Agonism"; Honig, "Agonistic Feminism"; Mouffe, *Democratic Paradox*; Mouffe, *Agonistics.*

42 Mouffe is drawing on Lefort in her work *Return of the Political,* 11.

43 Kalyvas, "Democratic Narcissus," 32; Wenman, "'Agonistic Pluralism.'"

44 David Scott makes this point while commenting on Claude Lefort's conception of power as an empty place in democracies. See Scott, *Refashioning Futures*, 150–52.

45 Foucault, *Society Must Be Defended*, 241.

46 P. Chatterjee, *Politics of the Governed*, 55–57. Also see Michelutti, *Vernacularization of Democracy*, and Narayan, *Making of the Dalit Public*, for important ethnographic and oral history accounts of the ways in which disadvantaged and subaltern communities have emerged as moral communities—held together by a shared sense of solidarity and signifiers in India.

47 L. Gandhi, *Affective Communities*, 25.

48 Cited in L. Gandhi, *Affective Communities*, 25.

49 Breen, "Agonism, Antagonism," 139.

50 Kalyvas, "Democratic Narcissus," 34.

51 This definition draws and expands on Jonathan Spencer's explanation of the political offered in his work on democracy and violence in South Asia. See Spencer, *Anthropology, Politics and the State*, 17.

52 Spencer, *Anthropology, Politics and the State*, 33.

53 Schmitt, *Concept of the Political*.

54 Prathama Banerjee reminds us of intersections between Schmitt and Lefort's conceptualization of the political and the ways in which both of them distinguished it from politics. She also reflects on the ways in which the distinction is sustained in the writings of a number of French theorists ranging from Jean-Luc Nancy to Alain Badiou. Each one, she notes, has a different definition of the political, but each one separates it from the life and work of politics. See P. Banerjee, *Elementary Aspects*, 6–8.

55 P. Banerjee, *Elementary Aspects*, 6–8.

56 P. Banerjee, *Elementary Aspects*, 8.

57 Hansen and Steppput, *Sovereign Bodies*, 11. Here Hansen and Stepputat are especially describing the concept of sovereignty as Georges Bataille elaborated it in works where he described it as the assertive impulse to go beyond instrumentality; an "animality" (14) that, among other things, expresses itself through excess "strength to violate the prohibition against killing" (Bataille, *Accursed Share*, 221–22).

58 I am influenced here by the ways in which Banerjee, Nigam, and Pandey have described the work of theorizing. They consider theory "as a particular mode of working with the world rather than of abstracting from it. The image . . . is then not of a theory being put into action, after the fact of its thinking as it were. Rather it is the image of theory itself as an activity—that of coursing through 'reality,' processing the world so to

speak. That is, theory not as 'shedding' light on the world from above, but as emanating and illuminating it from within, thus transforming the world's visible and apprehensible contours. The transformative potential of a theory then lies not in its successful application to a separate domain called the domain of practice but in its ability to change our sense of the world." P. Banerjee, Nigam, and Pandey, "Work of Theory," 44.

59 P. Banerjee, *Elementary Aspects*, 13.

60 I am alluding to the demand for separate electorates that Ambedkar articulated in 1930, which had the potential to neutralize the numerical, electoral, and political dominance of Hindus as well as proposals he drafted in the 1947 memorandum on behalf of the All India Schedule Castes Federation in a memorandum that the federation presented to the Constituent Assembly. In this document, Ambedkar clearly stated his worries about what majority rule will mean for India and its citizens. He believed that the majority in India would be defined in communal terms and accepting the rule of the majority would not be democratic but equivalent to imperialism. See Ambedkar, *States and Minorities*.

61 Skaria, "Relinquishing Republican Democracy," 204.

62 M. Gandhi, *Hind Swaraj*, 59.

63 M. Gandhi, *Hind Swaraj*, 58–61.

64 See M. Chatterjee, "Bandh Politics," for a recent generative discussion of the role that spectacular violence has played in majoritarian violence of the kind seen in Gujarat in 2002. I believe that in Kannur in the first instance, acts of exceptionally lethal violence served to shock and terrify the broader public as supporters of the opposing party. Over a period of time, they contributed to the formation of vengeful political communities as I document in chapters 2 and 3.

65 See, for instance, Sessions Case (hereafter SC) 4 of 1981 and SC 111 of 1995.

66 See Ginzburg, *Clues, Myths*, and Levi, "On Microhistory."

67 Peltonen, "Clues, Margins, and Monads," 351, 357.

68 Cited in de Vries, "Playing with Scales," 28; Peltonen, "Clues, Margins, and Monads," 359. I would like to thank the late Kavita Datla for drawing attention to the affinities between my approach and Grendi and Peltonen's work vis-à-vis the exceptional typical.

69 Basu and Roy, *Violence and Democracy*, 4.

70 Basu and Roy, *Violence and Democracy*, 4. Contributors in the volume focus on politics of territoriality, marginal communities veering toward majoritarianism, and Islamophobic global discourses among other things. My focus is on a different, albeit intersecting set of drivers of violence.

71 Basu and Roy, *Violence and Democracy*, 4.

72 This view has been expressed in journalistic writings as well as in some commentaries by academics and bureaucrats. For instance, in his piece on political violence in Kannur, the journalist Amrith Lal talked about the sixteenth-century warrior figures of Othenan and Unniarcha, and the ways in which their vengeful warrior ethos still haunts the region. Politics, he wrote, "has acquired the language of medieval feudal rivalries." Lal, "A Fort When under Siege," n.d., Express News Service Collections, Kochi. In the same vein, another journalist, C. Gouridas Nair, while describing the situation in Kannur in his article "A Tenuous Peace," wrote about the "Chekuvar," or militant, warrior culture of North Kerala where a "feudal legacy of blood feuds" lives on in the garb of political violence. Nair, "A Tenuous Peace," n.d., Express News Service Collections, Kochi.

73 The historian Rajan Gurukkal presents a similar but more complicated perspective in his 2008 article "Murder in Malabar" on Kannur violence in the pages of the *Indian Express* (March 12, 2008), http://archive .indianexpress.com/news/murder-in-malabar/283674/0. Gurukkal outlines a range of sociohistorical factors that according to him underlie the political violence in Kannur. Among them he cites a history of "juridico-political instability in the absence of state control," "strong persistence of clan-like ties," "fragmented political control by martial households," and "ideological dominance of heroic rituals and related cultural constructs." In subsequent interventions, however, he retracted this view. A 2012 article quotes Gurukkal as saying, "I . . . once thought that there could be an anthropological explanation to the violence in the north Malabar or northern Kerala, the region of heroic poems called Northern Ballads eulogizing the fighters. If you read these 18th century heroic poems you come across the tradition of using mercenaries just as in cock-fights for resolving individual-level conflicts." But he had now changed his mind; in light of reports of political and other forms of violence from the rest of the area, Gurukkal no longer thought that North Kerala is so peculiar. He noted that in the last few years, murders, attempts to murder, and instances of intimidation between workers of various parties have been reported not only from the nearby Kozhikode district but also from various parts of relatively distinct South Kerala. As Gurukkal stated, Kannur no longer seems so different from Thiruvananthapuram, Alleppey, Kottayam, and Pathanamthitta. In some ways, like the argument I am presenting here, Gurukkal also emphasizes what he calls "party-political fraternity" informed by emotions and sentiments pervasive in kinship networks. Unlike Gurukkal, however, I do not locate such sentiments and fraternities in fragmented political control, martial culture, and the persistence of clan-like ties but in modern political processes and practices. See N. P. Ullekh and Nidhi Sharma, "In CPM Bastion Kannur, Political Violence Takes a Turn for the Worse,"

Economic Times, August 6, 2012, https://economictimes.indiatimes.com
/news/politics-and-nation/in-cpm-bastion-kannur-political-violence
-takes-a-turn-for-the-worse/articleshow/15368442.cms.

74 Racialized accounts of Kannur's martial culture have especially been
offered by the police officer Alexander Jacob, who has, since retirement,
written and lectured on the topic. In the writings that I am familiar with,
he borrows tropes from colonial ethnographers and administrators and
speaks of "martial nature" as that exceptional behavioral strand that
afflicts the denizens of Malabar and generates violence among them. A
proud policeman born and brought up in post-independence politically
vigorous Kerala, Jacob also speaks about that so-called militant nature
of Thalassery's residents with a touch of admiration when he notes that
people from the area have been "rebellious from ancient days" and goes
on to inform his readers that "riots in Tellicherry and its suburbs are
as old as 1500 years." See Jacob, *Study of the Riots*, 73. Fierce resistance
against invading armies in the eighteenth century, the Mappila revolt
in the 1900s, other rebellions against British forces, and the violent
peasant insurrections of the 1930s and 1940s all become testimonies to
the particularly warlike nature that Jacob ascribes to people from North
Kerala. N. P. Ullekh has reproduced Jacob's more racialized explanations
of this "martial nature" where he speaks about waves of miscegenation
between the indigenous inhabitants of current-day Kerala and Kolar-
ians, Assyrians, Kalabhras, and Lankans infusing "martial blood" into
the local populace. See Ullekh, *Kannur*, 150–60. I have outlined some
of the explanatory and ethical problems with this reasoning in this
introduction.

75 See Mamdani, *Citizen and Subject*, 9–11, for a discussion of such reductive explanations of political violence in postcolonial contexts.

76 I discuss this point in the preface. See Partha Chatterjee in *Lineages of
Political Society*, 1–28, for an insightful critique of the "norm-deviation
paradigm" in Western political theory. In its place, Chatterjee calls for a
political theory that has moved from its normative inclinations and is more
attentive to the ways in which realities of power are lived and negotiated
with in actuality. Chatterjee makes this recommendation and suggests
that these lived realities and practices might enable political theorists to
fundamentally redefine their field's normative standards while forsaking
the norm-deviation model.

77 Mamdani, *Citizen and Subject*, 10.

78 Mamdani, *Citizen and Subject*, 10–11. Mamdani is especially invoking
Jean Francis Bayart's *The State in Africa* as he makes this critique.

79 Mbembe, "Banality of Power," 2.

80 Meagher, "Cultural Primordialism," 595.

81 My observations here are also drawing on Kate Meagher's strong critique of Bayart et al.'s *Illusion of Cultural Identity*: Meagher, "Cultural Primordialism."

82 "One Caste, One Religion, One God" is one of the most famous sayings of the reformist leader Sree Narayana Guru, who under the aegis of the Sree Narayana Dharama Paripalan (SNDP) built upon the reformist activities of the late nineteenth-century untouchable Ezhava community leaders. Ezhavas have occupied a structurally similar position in South Kerala as Thiyyas in the North. The SNDP movement emphasized educational, religious, and social reform among members of the Ezhava community while fighting against caste discrimination in temples, schools, and employment. See Lukose, *Liberalization's Children*, 3. For another ethnographically informed discussion of the SNDP's contribution to Ezhava social mobility and its intersections with contemporary political and economic variables, see Ossella and Ossella, *Social Mobility in Kerala*.

83 In the ritual hierarchy, Thiyyas, the largest subgroup of Hindus in North Kerala while placed below the Namboodris, Nayars, and other artisan castes, were placed above Dalit groups such as Cherumas, Pulayas, and Nayadis. See Awaya, "Some Aspects." While the percentage of landowning Thiyyas was relatively small, by the early twentieth century an elite group had emerged among them deriving their position from education, employment as lawyers and civil servants, involvement with trade and commerce, and setting up of factories. What the emergent Thiyya elite brought with them were new ideas and practices of caste equality, which in turn played a significant role in the emergence and consolidation of the Communist movement in north Kerala. See Menon, *Caste, Nationalism, and Communism*. See also Sam, "Place and Caste Identification."

84 Toddy is an alcoholic beverage made from coconut tree sap. Traditionally pursued by members of lower-caste groups such as Thiyyas and Ezhavas, toddy tapping has over the decades become a more protected occupation within the informal sector. In recent years it has also become a site of rivalries between different sections of toddy-tapping ethnicized linguistic communities. See Sportel, "Agency," 47.

85 Foucault, *Security, Territory, Population*, 115–30, 191–226.

86 Devika, "Egalitarian Developmentalism," 809, 815.

87 MacCannell's *Regime of the Brother* has helped me identify and articulate the characteristics of these big brotherly figures. See location 380 of 6205, Kindle edition.

88 Devika and Thampi, "Beyond Feminine Public Altruism." See also Devika and Thampi, "Mobility towards Work," and U. Kumar, "Autobiography as a Way."

89 Devika, "Imagining Women's Social Space," 7.

90 Devika, "Imagining Women's Social Space," 12.

91 Devika and Thampi, "Mobility towards Work," 10–12.

92 Devika and Thampi, "Mobility towards Work," 12.

93 U. Kumar, "Autobiography as a Way."

94 I particularly discuss David Scott's reflections on the topic in chapter 1. See Scott, *Refashioning Futures*, 206. See also Seshadri-Crooks, "I Am a Master," and Tomlinson, "To Fanon, with Love."

95 MacCannell, *Regime of the Brother*, location 504 of 6205.

96 MacCannell, *Regime of the Brother*, location 988 of 6205.

97 Pateman, *Sexual Contract*, 76, 78.

98 SC 252 of 2001, 14.

99 See chapter 5 for references to well-known cases in which capital punishment has been demanded and granted.

1. Containment and Cretinism

1 Media accounts of violence between workers of the Left and Right in Kerala not only became especially prurient in the late 1980s and through the 1990s (after an intense spate of murders and countermurders) but they also began describing local-level party workers allegedly involved in the violence as deeply deviant and almost diabolical persons. These descriptions were supplemented by hyperreal images of the disjuncted and violated bodies of the victims of violence, which filled the pages of newspapers and magazines as well as television screens at various points in the long-running conflict. In my experience, such representations infected the public discourse about the conflict. See chapter 5, note 52 for references and discussion of such notable journalistic accounts, and chapter 5, note 15 for a discussion of the ways in which such representations came alive inside the courts, especially in moments when prosecutors sought the death penalty for accused political workers of one or another group.

2 See the section "Political Violence in Kannur: An Exceptional-Normal Phenomenon" in the introduction.

3 See Connolly, "Response"; Honig, "Politics of Agonism"; Mouffe, *Agonistics*. For further elaboration of their arguments and my disagreement with theorists of agonistic democracy, see the section "Competitive Politics, Majority Rule, and Its Critics" in the introduction.

4 Damodaran, "Memoir." See Marx, *Eighteenth Brumaire*, 91, for Marx's historically situated definition of the phenomenon.

5 See the preface for my reference to the specter of genocide of Muslims that emerged in December 2021 with hate-filled public assemblies led by Sangh sympathizers and affiliates.

6 Ake, *Feasibility of Democracy*, 7. See the section "A Paradoxical Bequest" in the introduction for a lengthier elaboration of this term.

7 I am drawing on privately commissioned translations of two different editions (1985 and 2015) of P. R. Kurup's autobiography, *Ente Nadinte Katha, Enteyum* [Story of my village and me] (hereafter cited as Kurup, *Story of My Village*). I have sought to transliterate notable and controversial phrases. See the acknowledgments for details on translators.

8 Kerala in the 1930s was a region of insecure tenancies, growing depredations by landlords, a rising population, and a shrinking occupant-to-land ratio, all of which contributed to a growing crisis. In both rural and urban sectors there was a growing trend toward proletarianization, which contributed to the conditions favoring Left party ascendancy. See Desai, "Relative Autonomy." Hindu tenants, on the other hand, took to another form of radical politics, the one promulgated by the newly formed CSP. In Kerala, the CSP was a precursor to the formation of the CPI. An important reason for the emergence and consolidation of the CPI itself in the 1930s was its ideological opposition to the INC as a representative of the bourgeois and dominant peasant group interests. This ideological opposition also contained a practical, or one might say methodological, aspect as questions began to be raised about the nature and degree of representation that the Gandhian forms of protest could offer to the "masses" and the people at large. As noted in chapter 1, like the late 1920s, 1933 and 1934 were also years of labor revival, with the number of strikes in the jute and cotton mill sector steadily rising. Socialist groups had emerged within the Congress that sought to push it leftward—leading, in fact, to the formation of the CSP in May 1934. The CSP was composed of young, more radical members of the Congress who espoused the creed of Marxian "scientific socialism" and distinguished it sharply from the mere "social reformism" of the Congress. See S. Sarkar, *Modern India*, 254–348. Several units of the CSP had been infiltrated by members who had converted to communism. By September 1939, provincial branches of the CSP in Punjab, Bengal, and Bihar had covertly renounced the policies of the INC leadership, and CSP members in Kerala were also veering in that direction. See Menon, *Caste, Nationalism, and Communism*, 154.

9 See Panikkar, *Against Lord and State*; Menon, *Caste, Nationalism, and Communism*; Desai, "Relative Autonomy."

10 Desai, "Relative Autonomy," 641.

11 Awaya, "Some Aspects."

12 Zagoria, "Ecology of Peasant Communism."

13 Menon, *Caste, Nationalism, and Communism.*

14 In 2021, on the hundredth anniversary of the Mappilah rebellion, the Indian Council of Historical Relations guided by Sangh informed rendering of history caricatured the rebels as fanatical jihadists and removed the names of 387 rebels from the Dictionary of Indian Martyrs. For a thoughtful analysis of this intervention, see G. Arunima, "Muslims, Hindus and the Malabar Rebellion," *The Federal*, September 7, 2021, https://thefederal.com/opinion/muslims-hindus-and-the-malabar-rebellion-why-1921-matters/.

15 As noted earlier, in Kerala, the CSP was a precursor to the formation of the CPI.

16 As Dilip Menon informs us, several units of the CSP had been infiltrated by members who had converted to communism. By September 1939, provincial branches of the CSP in Punjab, Bengal, and Bihar had covertly renounced the policies of the Indian National Congress leadership, and CSP members in Kerala were also veering in that direction. See Menon, *Caste, Nationalism, and Communism*, 154. Pillai was especially formative in this period and contributed significantly to the spread of an assertive egalitarian ethos and growth of the Communist Party networks among beedi and mill workers as well as peasants. Pillai however died at a relatively young age of a snake bite in 1948, and the responsibility of building on his legacy fell on young leaders such as Gopalan. For a recent compelling summary of Pillai's career and influence as a socialist and a communist in North Kerala, see Ullekh, *Kannur*, 88–97.

17 For a detailed account of the eighteenth-century context in which landownership was conferred on a range of groups with an array of rights to collect revenue, evict, and inherit land—all usually clubbed under the term *zamindar*—see Raychaudhuri, "Land and the People." See D. Kumar, "Caste and Landlessness," for an account of resilient precolonial forms of rural abjectness and persistent landlessness tied to caste status in eighteenth, nineteenth, and early twentieth century South India. See Satyanarayana, "Rise and Growth," for an account of the relationship between agrarian movements and new socialist and incipient communist formations in late-1930s Andhra. And see socialist leader N. G. Ranga's account of parallel developments in Ranga, "Bihar Peasantry."

18 See Oomen, *From Mobilization to Institutionalization*; Radhakrishnan, *Peasant Struggles*; Menon, *Caste, Nationalism, and Communism.*

19 Dhanagare, "Social Origins."

20 Desai, "Relative Autonomy," 642–43.

21 In the princely states of Travancore and Cochin, struggles of coir workers, toddy tappers, agricultural workers, and laborers in the informal sector all came together under the wing of the Travancore Labor Association. The CSP took over its leadership in 1934, and under its leadership struggles against the princely state, colonial capital, and the upper castes all came to be linked to one another. See Jeffrey, "'Destroy Capitalism!'"; Desai, "Relative Autonomy," 643–44.

22 Menon, *Caste, Nationalism, and Communism*, 37.

23 Scholarship on this numerically strong group of North Kerala remains scant. For transformation of household and gender relations among the Thiyya in recent times, see Abraham, "'Matriliny Did Not Become Patriliny!'" See also Abraham, "'Why Did You Send Me Like This?'" For an overview of the ways in which Kerala modernity has been conceptualized and historicized, see Bose and Varughese, *Kerala Modernity*, 3–12.

24 Menon, *Caste, Nationalism, and Communism*, 40–88.

25 Menon, *Caste, Nationalism, and Communism*, 40–88. For crucial intervention on elite appropriation of shrine festivals such as theyyam in the interests of Hindu majoritarianism, see Dasan, *Theyyam*. For detailed discussion of current caste composition and relations with the Communist Party in a typical North Kerala village where CPI (M) cadres are a strong social presence, see Kaul and Kannangara, "Persistence of Political Power."

26 Menon, *Caste, Nationalism, and Communism*, 7.

27 Menon, *Caste, Nationalism, and Communism*, 7. The key instrument of the state's violence in this period was the Malabar Special Police (MSP), which gained considerable notoriety as the peasant activists also became increasingly militant. The failure of official channels to cope with near-famine conditions in the early 1940s led to attacks on granaries held by the government and landlords. Government sale of forest land to landowners from Travancore was also militantly opposed. In turn, the "people committees" formed by peasant unions met with the force of the MSP. The famous "Kayyur incident" (1943), which I discuss later in this chapter, belongs to this period of clashes with the MSP, which continued into the mid- and late 1940s. The "Karivellur incident" (1946) and the "Munayankunnu incident" (1948), when Krashaka Sangham activists clashed with the MSP resulting in the death of two people in 1946 and six activists in 1948, are the other key reference points of this period around which local communist lore has been constructed. See Nayanar, *My Struggles*.

28 Menon, *Caste, Nationalism, and Communism*, 37.

29 Communist Party of India (Marxist), "Remembering Comrade AKG on His 38th Death Anniversary," https://www.facebook.com/cpimcc

/posts/akgbeloved-leader-comakg-red-saluteon-his-38th-death
-anniversaryremembering-comr/411002002404819/, accessed April 16,
2021.

30 Communist Party of India (Marxist), "Remembering Comrade AKG."

31 Arunima, "Glimpses from a Writer's World," 210. More precisely, we
may describe a tharavadu as a matrilineal land and property-owning
group that began taking a consolidated form as the locus of administrative, ritual, and economic power in eighteenth-century Malabar
when it also started emerging as a political force in a largely decentral-
ized political context. See Arunima, "Multiple Meanings," 285–92. She
reminds us of changes that occurred in the first half of the nineteenth
century as the colonial state sought to centralize political and economic
authority through the granting of tenurial rights and recognition of
property rights. In this context, the colonial courts came to describe the
tharavadu as an "impartible and corporate unit with inalienable rights in
land," which it never was in the eighteenth century (293). Furthermore,
the eldest male in the matrilineal household was deemed responsible
for revenue payments, but with that responsibility also came various
kinds of authority, and the mother's brother emerged as the head of
tharavadus. Consequently, the mother–child unit was rendered as a
"purely domestic and apolitical unit," and the mother's brother came to
enjoy greater control over children, women, and other members of the
family (295). As the matrilineal household began taking a more patriarchal character, women were increasingly allowed to move out of the
household only upon marriage. While the colonial period saw greater
restrictions being placed on women's mobility, it afforded more professional and educational opportunities to young men. In keeping with the
patriarchal interpretation of property rights and family structures, more
courts recognized the rights of these young men to live and work away
from the tharavadu while allowing them to retain shares in household
property. Changes in marriage laws and the greater value placed on
monogamous marriage by young educated professional men of matrilineal tharavadus meant that "patri-virilocal" residence also became more
prevalent, and with that came more demands for division of tharavadu
property. These demands became louder in the 1900s, leading to considerable weakening of the tharavadu and matriliny and its transmutation
into a patrilineal nuclear family form especially from the 1930s onward,
when the Tenancy and Matriliny acts were passed (301–5).

32 Menon, *Caste, Nationalism, and Communism*, 119–29.

33 Gopalan, *In the Cause*, 1–3.

34 Devika, "Egalitarian Developmentalism."

35 Foucault, "Subject and Power," 783–75.

36 Devika, "Egalitarian Developmentalism," 806.

37 Arunima, "Glimpses from a Writer's World," 194.

38 Menon discusses the emergence of education as a critical desire and goal for lower caste groups and their associations such as the Adi Dharm movement in Punjab and the Kerala Artisans Association. In this context, Menon cites the declaration made by the Araya Mahajans Sabha in 1920 that "their salvation depends on 'education and education alone.'" Menon, *Caste, Nationalism, and Communism*, 144–45.

39 Menon, *Caste, Nationalism, and Communism*, 144; Lukose, *Liberalization's Children*, 137.

40 Gopalan, *In the Cause*, 7.

41 Gopalan, *In the Cause*, 6.

42 Gopalan, *In the Cause*, 97.

43 Gopalan, *In the Cause*, 76.

44 Gopalan, *In the Cause*, 10.

45 S. Sarkar, *Modern India*, 254.

46 S. Sarkar, *Modern India*, 266.

47 S. Sarkar, *Modern India*, 273–74.

48 Gopalan, *In the Cause*, 11–14.

49 Gopalan, *In the Cause*, 14–15.

50 See Lukose, *Liberalization's Children*, 136–40, on the reformist but also revolutionary singular nature of political agency that became predominant in Kerala's increasingly gendered public sphere in this period. See also Mannathukkaren, "Rise of the National-Popular," on the cultural ethos that emerged with the spread of the communist movement in Kerala.

51 Haridas, "Travancore State Congress"; Jeffrey, *Decline of Nair Dominance*, 236–38.

52 Gopalan, *In the Cause*, 102–3.

53 See MacCannell, *Regime of the Brother*, location 214–27 of 6205, Kindle edition, and the introduction for a more detailed discussion of the ways in which her insights about the gendered nature of the ego that is being privileged in modernity speak to the forms of political masculinity that became hegemonic in Kerala in the early and mid-twentieth century.

54 Scott, *Refashioning Futures*, 194.

55 Scott, *Refashioning Futures*, 206.

56 M. K. Gandhi, *Satyagraha in South Africa*, 110–12.

57 As noted above, CSP and Communist Party leaders like Gopalan were part of mass actions such as the civil disobedience movement, which took their cues from Gandhian politics and were led by Gandhian

leaders such as K. Kelappan. At the same time, at various points in its career, the CPI and Gopalan's colleagues were unequivocal in their critique of Gandhi's call for nonviolent satyagraha. They maintained that that the truth or untruth of democracy and political actions do not depend on their violent or nonviolent character. Indeed, the Party's 1951 "Statement of Policy," where it first announced its program for People's Democracy, dismissed the question of violent vs. nonviolent action as merely a riddle for Gandhian ideology. What was emphasized was the degree of representation political actions that forms of political practice afford. Where Gandhi saw blind frenzy, the Communist Party saw mass participation and the possibility of People's Democracy. That is to say, the Party saw the nature of a political action, and how it is performed, as having a direct bearing on who could participate in it, and who was represented by it. The attempt was to speak and act for "the whole people." The Party committees and stalwarts adjudged certain methods and practices to be more representative, and some others less so. The 1930 "Draft Platform of Action of the Communist Party of India" opened with this passage: "The Communist Party declares that the road to victory (over the colonial government) is not the method of individual terror but the struggle and the revolutionary armed insurrection of the widest possible masses of the working class, the peasantry, the poor of the towns and Indian soldiers, around the banner and under the leadership of the Communist Party of India." (Cited in Ghose, *Socialism and Communism*, 135–36.) In fact, it was the Gandhian method of satyagraha that was being equated here with "the method of individual terror." This phrase comes from Mohit Sen's book *The Mahatma* and is also cited in Ghose, *Socialism and Communism*, 137. Ajoy Ghosh, who was the general secretary of the party in 1930, was more categorical in his retrospective elaboration of the draft platform cited above. Satyagraha, he recounted in 1954, "was a form of struggle, which disrupted mass participation and brought only some pressure upon the enemy. "In fact," he wrote, "it was a counterpart of terrorism that relied on the same principle, by which it were the heroes who led the passive masses, and the people were reduced to the role of mere spectators. While, in some backward areas, satyagraha might have become necessary at the first stage, it should not have been allowed to become a substitute for mass action" (Ghosh cited in Ghose, *Socialism and Communism*, 137). Thus, according to this critique, Gandhian forms of political action not only undo the capacity of the masses to act as political agents, but in fact undo the very existence of individuals as an explosive mass, and political force. The rigorous conditions demanded of a *satyagrahi* make an isolated individual the locus of action and it is up to this individual to generate in himself a force and spirit equivalent to that of the collective.

58   U. Kumar, "Autobiography as a Way."

59 U. Kumar, "Autobiography as a Way," location 8654 of 9555, Kindle edition. Also see Radhakrishnan, "Masculinity," 134–72, on the revolutionary masculinity evidenced in influential communist leaders like P. Krishna Pillai and disseminated in films of popular actors like Sathyan.

60 M. K. Gandhi, *Young India*, August 9, 1920, cited in Prabhu, *Communism and Communists*, 17.

61 S. Sarkar, *Modern India*, 333.

62 Ankit, "Marxist Guru, Socialist *Neta*."

63 Nossiter, *Communism in Kerala*, 72–73.

64 Nossiter, *Communism in Kerala*, 70.

65 Nossiter, *Communism in Kerala*, 76.

66 Gopalan, *In the Cause*, 88.

67 Gopalan, *In the Cause*, 88.

68 Nossiter, *Communism in Kerala*, 77.

69 K. K. N. Kurup, *Peasantry, Nationalism, and Social Change*; K. K. N. Kurup, *Kayyur Riot*; Menon, "Prehistory of Violence?"

70 S. Bhattacharya, "Colonial State"; S. Sarkar, *Modern India*, 384–85, 411.

71 S. Sarkar, *Modern India*, 427. See also Manzer, "Communist Party."

72 Sen Gupta, *Communism in Indian Politics*, 23.

73 S. Sarkar, *Modern India*, 426.

74 Gopalan, *In the Cause*, 159.

75 Gopalan, *In the Cause*, 159.

76 General elections took place between October 1951 and February 1952. In most reports they are referred to as 1951 elections, but occasionally also as 1952 elections. Travancore-Cochin and Madras legislative assembly elections followed soon after. Travancore-Cochin politics impacted Malabar deeply, even though elected representatives from the region belonged to Madras assembly until 1956, when the two regions were merged as single political unit. See note 120 on the *Aikya Keralam* or United Kerala movement.

77 Gopalan, *In the Cause*, 180.

78 Damodaran, "Memoir," 42.

79 Sen Gupta, *Communism in Indian Politics*, 28–30.

80 Damodaran, "Memoir," 43.

81 Damodaran, "Memoir," 44–45.

82 Stalin cited in Ghosh, "Proletarian Leadership," 5–6.

83 Nossiter, *Communism in Kerala*, 106.

84 Gopalan, *In the Cause*, 180.

85 Gopalan, *In the Cause*, 215.

86 Gopalan, *In the Cause*, 159; Sen Gupta, *Communism in Indian Politics*, 23.

87 Damodaran, "Memoir," 47.

88 Damodaran, "Memoir," 44.

89 Damodaran, "Memoir," 44.

90 Gopalan, *In the Cause*, 263.

91 P. R. Kurup, "Kerala Niyamsabha," http://www.stateofkerala.in/niya masabha/p_r_kurup.php, accessed February 23, 2022.

92 Kurup, *Story of My Village* (2015), 9.

93 Kurup, *Story of My Village* (1985), 9.

94 Kurup, *Story of My Village* (1985), 78.

95 Kurup writes, "njan ennum avaril orallaye perumarittilu." *Story of My Village* (2015), 72.

96 A. Nigam, "Secularism, Modernity, Nation," 42–63.

97 Kurup, *Story of My Village* (1985), 78.

98 Kurup, *Story of My Village* (1985), 78.

99 The transliterated Malayalam sentence in Kurup's autobiography is as follows: "thangall adimakalanennu paramparagatavishwasathilninnu thiyyasamudhayakarku mukti labhichatumilla." *Story of My Village* (1985), 100.

100 Kurup, *Story of My Village* (1985), 101.

101 Kurup, *Story of My Village* (1985), 100–103.

102 U. Kumar, "Autobiography as a Way," location 8660 of 9555, Kindle edition.

103 Scott, *Refashioning Futures*, 206.

104 U. Kumar, "Autobiography as a Way," location 8614 of 9555, Kindle edition.

105 Kurup, *Story of My Village* (2015), 32–33.

106 Kurup, *Story of My Village* (2015), 33.

107 Kurup, *Story of My Village* (1985), 110.

108 Kurup, *Story of My Village* (1985), 109–12.

109 Weiner, *Party Politics in India*, 25–65.

110 Kurup, *Story of My Village* (1985), 149–57.

111 Kurup, *Story of My Village* (1985), 160–62.

112 Arunima, "Glimpses from a Writer's World," 190. Autobiographies such as the one by Kurup do not necessarily provide an objective fact sheet of

events but perform a historiographical role. "Snapshot(s) of history" that these autobiographies offer are necessarily fragmentary as well as colored by the vision of the "remembering subject." U. Kumar, "Autobiography as a Way," location 8422 of 9555, Kindle edition. This is important to remember as we read excerpts of Kurup's account.

113 Kurup, *Story of My Village* (2015), 147.

114 Kurup, *Story of My Village* (2015), 147.

115 Kurup, *Story of My Village* (2015), 146–47.

116 See the section "Political Violence in Kannur: An Exceptional-Normal Phenomenon" in the introduction.

117 Arendt, *Human Condition*, 41.

118 Weiner, *Party Politics in India*, 31.

119 Nossiter, *Communism in Kerala*, 116.

120 The CPI's popularity also got a boost in the course of the Aikya Keralam (United Kerala) movement for bringing together Malayalam speaking regions of Travancore, Cochin, and Malabar together as a single political unit. See Devika, "People United," for a detailed discussion of the ways in which CPI leaders like E. M. S. Namboodripad were able to mobilize the cultural history of the region during the Aikya Keralam movement to position the party as an agent of change for a united Malayali community and its development in the future.

121 Nossiter, *Communism in Kerala*, 105–23.

122 Leiten, "Education, Ideology and Politics," 3–18.

123 Leiten, "Education, Ideology and Politics," 15–21.

124 Nossiter, *Communism in Kerala*, 145.

125 Nossiter, *Communism in Kerala*, 147.

126 Ajayan, "Dismissal," 283.

127 Leiten, "Education, Ideology and Politics," 18.

128 Kurup, *Story of My Village* (1985), chap. 29.

129 Interview with Churai Chandran, October 2017; Kurup, *Story of My Village* (1985), 105; Ullekh, *Kannur*, 25, 115–16.

130 Kurup, *Story of My Village* (1985), chap. 25.

131 Kurup, *Story of My Village* (1985), 105.

132 The first time I learned about the conflict was from the late I. V. Das, CPI (M) state committee member and former editor of *Deshabhimani*, the party's long-standing newspaper, in 2000 when I was carrying out predoctoral fieldwork in Kerala. While I was unable to speak to Kurup's contemporaries in the PSP who participated in the conflict, some relatively younger CPI (M) local leaders like Churai Chandran talked at length about it when I interviewed him several years later. References

to this conflictual period abound in conversations among residents of the region and can also be found in journalistic accounts such as Ullekh, *Kannur*, and "Politics of Violence: Kannur Witnessed 186 Murders," *Economic Times*, https://economictimes.indiatimes.com/news/politics-and -nation/politics-of-violence-kannur-witnessed-186-murders/articleshow /57532865.cms?from=mdr, last updated March 8, 2017.

133 Kurup, *Story of My Village* (1985), chap. 28.

134 Interview with Churai Chandran, October 2017; interview with Pattiam Rajan, October 2017.

135 Kurup, *Story of My Village* (1985), chap. 3.

136 Kurup, *Story of My Village* (1985), 300–301.

137 Kurup, *Story of My Village* (1985), chap. 30.

138 In Kurup's words, "pratyakramanangall nadathuvan njangal nirbhandhi- taraitund." *Story of My Village* (2015), 285.

2. The CPI (M) and the Making of an Antagonistic Political Field

1 See Chaturvedi, "Political Violence, Community," where I have analyzed some parts and aspects of these self-narratives.

2 Local Hindu right-wing workers fondly remember Jaykrishnan Master, the slain schoolteacher and BJP youth wing leader. Others speak of him as the mastermind behind attacks on his political opponents. Of the seven CPI (M) workers accused of Jaykrishnan Master's murder, one committed suicide in the course of the district trial. One person was acquitted while five were convicted and sentenced to death. While the High Court upheld the district court judgment and punishment, the Supreme Court acquitted four, finding only one person guilty. The CPI (M)-led government waived his prison sentence in 2011. Ullekh, *Kannur*; 61–65 SC 146 of 2001. In July 2012, seven years after the Supreme Court judgment, Jaykrishnan Master's murder case once again made headlines. News reports described how a CPI (M) member arrested for an altogether different political murder had divulged important information about the old case. Reportedly, this so-called insider who was in the know had told the police that only one of the original seven persons accused of the schoolteacher's murder in 1999 was a real culprit, while the other six had been "made accused." See "Crime Branch to Re-probe Jayakrishnan Murder," *The Times of India*, December 4, 2012, https:// timesofindia.indiatimes.com/city/kozhikode/Crime-branch-to-re -probe-Jayakrishnan-murder/articleshow/17471586.cms. In chapters 4 and 5, I engage with the category of the "made accused" and the nature of criminal trials Kannur has witnessed in political violence cases.

3 I am drawing on unpublished list prepared by the Mathrubhumi Kannur office for numbers and details of those killed from 1980 to 2000.

4 Mamman Vasu was killed on December 12, 1995; five RSS workers were tried at the Kannur District Court and sentenced to rigorous life imprisonment for his murder. See SC 22 of 1999. Pannianur Chandran was said to be "the brain behind Mamman Vasu's murder." See Kerala High Court judgment in the case: Death Sentence Reference no. 1 of 2005, 40. Chandran had risen through the Sangh ranks to become an influential local figure. He was killed outside his house in May 1996; five CPI (M) workers were tried for his murder. The Kannur District Court Judge presiding over the case sentenced the accused workers to capital punishment; High Court judges commuted the death sentence and gave a life sentence to the accused political workers. For a detailed account of the attack on CPI (M) leader P. Jayarajan, the court case, and the accompanying public discourse and string of reprisals, see Ullekh, *Kannur*, 50–60.

5 The RSS filed an appeal on their behalf in the Supreme Court. E. Manoj, one of the accused and a well-known Sangh worker believed to be involved in multiple attacks on CPI (M) members, was killed in 2014. In 2017, the Central Bureau of Investigation charged Jayarajan under the Unlawful Preventive Activities Act (UAPA). See "Six BJP/RSS Men Found Guilty in Attempt to Murder Case," *Hindustan Times*, June 28, 2007, https://www.hindustantimes.com/india/six-bjp-rss-men-found -guilty-in-attempt-to-murder-case/story-ispfF6czebOsjoOkgKRkNP .html; Venkatesan R., "CPI(M) Leader Named 'Principal Conspira- tor' in RSS Worker's Killing," BusinessLine, January 9, 2018, https:// www.thehindubusinessline.com/news/national/cpim-leader-named -principal-conspirator-in-rss-workers-killing/article9838604.ece; Ullekh, *Kannur*, 50–60. I discuss the place of exceptional laws such as UAPA in the adjudication of political violence cases in chapter 5.

6 Two research assistants that I worked with over the years played a cru- cial role in these interviews. Their disposition, social skills, and position- ality facilitated and helped shape the conversations with CPI (M) and RSS-BJP workers that I draw upon in this and the following chapters. This work owes a large debt to these assistants whose names however I have, after a lot of consideration, omitted. I am concerned that their well-being may be adversely affected if their names do appear here in print. The responsibility for the analytical arguments that I make here is entirely mine. On the question of the role of research assistants particularly while carrying out ethnographic study of violent conflicts, see Hoffman and Tarawalley, "Frontline Collaborations," and Jenkins, "Assistants, Guides."

7 Preman mentioned both months while talking about this encounter.

8 The publicly noted reasons for Raghavan's expulsion highlight the ways in which preoccupation with electoral victories affected regional and

national political life. These revolved around the party's decision to distance itself from identitarian organizations like the Muslim League and Kerala Congress and Raghavan's advocacy against that move. Raghavan cited the INC as the real opponent to be vanquished and emphasized the need for building electoral alliances with a range of groups to do the same. See P. Sudhakaran, "Communist Leader M V Raghavan, Who Took on CPM, Dead," *The Times of India*, November 9, 2014, https://timesofindia.indiatimes.com/city/thiruvananthapuram /Communist-leader-M-V-Raghavan-who-took-on-CPM-dead/article show/45086241.cms.

9   Raghavan, *Oru Janmam*, 9–13. I would like to thank Nirmala Nair for reviewing translations of the text with me.

10 Raghavan details the context in the 1960s when as Pappinseri Pancha-yath president he initiated efforts to start various medical facilities in the region. This was also the time when he made important strides in his career as a notable CPI (M) leader in Kannur. See Raghavan, *Oru Jan-mam*, 55–64. Institutions that he came to be associated with closely over the years are the Pappinseri Visha Chikitsa Kendram, A. K. Gopalan Memorial Hospital (AKG Hospital), and Periyaram Medical College. Control over AKG Hospital became a bone of violent contention after Raghavan was expelled from the CPI (M). For an account of this period in Raghavan's political career, his role in the confrontations between CPI (M) and Congress workers in the 1980s, and a recounting (based on interviews and personal reminiscences) of the conflict over control of AKG Hospital, see Ullekh, *Kannur*, 118–25.

11 Ullekh, *Kannur*, 118–25.

12 Ullekh, *Kannur*, 105.

13 As Nossiter tells us, disputes within the coalition arose from corrup-tion allegations and the CPI (M)'s alleged cavalier attitude toward other members of the coalition. See Nossiter, *Communism in Kerala*, 214–19.

14 Nossiter, *Communism in Kerala*, 200–207.

15 Nossiter, *Communism in Kerala*, 215–16.

16 Nossiter, *Communism in Kerala*, 203–16.

17 Nossiter, *Communism in Kerala*, 215–16.

18 Raghavan, *Oru Janmam*, 71. I would like to thank Sunilkumar Karintha for assisting me with translation here.

19 Nossiter, *Communism in Kerala*, 216.

20 Nossiter, *Communism in Kerala*, 239.

21 Raghavan, *Oru Janmam*, 73.

22 Raghavan, *Oru Janmam*, 73–74.

23 Gopalan, *In the Cause*, 286.

24 Raghavan, *Oru Janmam*, 73.

25 S. Banerjee, *In the Wake of Naxalbari*.

26 Haridas, "Varghese Encounter Death Case," 19.

27 Raghavan, *Oru Janmam*, 73–74.

28 Ullekh, *Kannur*, 31.

29 Arafath, "Southern Hindutva," 55.

30 Ullekh, *Kannur*, 32.

31 Ullekh's recent sympathetic profile of Vijayan gives substantial insight into Vijayan's career and regional standing: "The Comrade Who Will Lord over Kerala's Tower of Destiny," Manorama Online, May 2, 2021, https://www.onmanorama.com/news/kerala/2021/05/02/pinarayi -vijayan-profile-kerala-assembly-election-result-ldf-win.html. See also a more critical recent review of Vijayan's leadership style that zeroes in on the question of neutralizing competition within the party as well as the glass ceiling that emerging women leaders face in this masculine field: Sruthisagar Yamunan, "Does Pinarayi Vijayan's New Cabinet in Kerala Mark the Overshadowing of the Party by the Leader?," Scroll.in, May 22, 2021, https://scroll.in/article/995385/does-pinarayi-vijayans-new-cabinet -in-kerala-mark-the-overshadowing-of-the-party-by-the-leader.

32 Haridas, "Varghese Encounter Death Case"; Raghavan, *Oru Janmam*, chap. 6; Steur, *Indigenist Mobilization*, 122–23.

33 Ray, *Naxalites and Their Ideology*.

34 Encounter refers to a skirmish between armed forces or police and a civilian. Human rights groups have provided extensive information about "fake encounters" in different parts of the country where civilians have been killed extrajudicially at the hands of the police or army and the latter has claimed that the person was killed in a gun battle or skirmish. See Duschinski, "Reproducing Regimes of Impunity," for an academic account of fake encounter killings in Kashmir, which she situates in the larger pattern of extrajudicial killings in the rest of the country.

35 Haridas, "Varghese Encounter Death Case"; Steur, *Indigenist Mobilization*, 122–23.

36 Raghavan, *Oru Janmam*, 80.

37 Raghavan, *Oru Janmam*, 9.

38 See the introduction to this book.

39 Alam, "Communist Politics," 192.

40 *The Program of the CPI* 1951, para 10 cited in Alam, "Communist Politics," 192.

41 Joseph Stalin cited in Ghosh, "Proletarian Leadership," 5–6.

42　Communist Party of India, "Statement of Policy."

43　Communist Party of India, "Statement of Policy."

44　Ghosh, "Proletarian Leadership," 6.

45　Jaffrelot, *Hindu Nationalist Movement*, 169–78.

46　Isaac et al., *Democracy at Work*, 43–46.

47　Isaac et al., *Democracy at Work*, 49.

48　Isaac et al., *Democracy at Work*, 51.

49　Isaac et al., *Democracy at Work*, 52.

50　Ullekh, *Kannur*, 29.

51　Gulati et al., "When a Worker's Cooperative Works," 1431; Isaac et al., *Democracy at Work*, 65.

52　Isaac et al., *Democracy at Work*, 65.

53　Isaac et al., *Democracy at Work*, 65–66.

54　Isaac et al., *Democracy at Work*, 66.

55　Isaac et al., *Democracy at Work*, 66.

56　Isaac et al., *Democracy at Work*.

57　Jaffrelot, *Hindu Nationalist Movement*, 240–43.

58　Jaffrelot, *Hindu Nationalist Movement*, 240–45, 255–66.

59　B. Chandra, *In the Name of Democracy*, 76–79. See also Prakash, *Emergency Chronicles*, 185–200, for a detailed contextual and thematic history of this period and the emergency more broadly.

60　Jaffrelot, *Hindu Nationalist Movement*, 272–73.

61　B. Chandra, *In the Name of Democracy*, 157.

62　Jaffrelot, *Hindu Nationalist Movement*, 275.

63　B. Chandra, *In the Name of Democracy*, 246–60.

64　Jaffrelot points out that across the country, the number of shakhas had grown to more than 10,000 in April 1977, rising to 11,500 a year later and to 13,000 in 1979. The expansion also included affiliates such as the Bharatiya Mazdoor Sangh (BMS), which grew from 1.2 million to 1.8 million adherents between 1977 and 1980, while the RSS student organization Akhil Bharatiya Vidyarthi Parishad's (ABVP) strength grew from 170,000 to 250,000 between 1977 and 1982 (*Hindu Nationalist Movement*, 302). The infamous campaign to demolish the fourteenth-century Babri mosque in North India began in the late 1980s and can be seen as the centerpiece of this aggressive phase.

65　Newspapers have frequently quoted RSS leaders who declare that Kerala has the highest number of shakhas in the country. The figure that was cited in 2003 was three thousand. TNN, "Kerala Has 3,000

RSS Shakhas: Adhisji," *The Times of India*, Ahmedabad edition, May 17, 2003. https://timesofindia.indiatimes.com/city/ahmedabad/kerala-has -3000-rss-shakhas-adhisji/articleshow/43605766.cms. More recently too, Sangh leaders maintain that of all the provinces Kerala has the highest number of shakhas. See PTI, "At 4,500, Kerala Has Highest Number of Shakhas Held Daily in the Country: Senior RSS Leader," Financial Express, March 9, 2020, https://www.financialexpress.com /india-news/at-4500-kerala-has-highest-number-of-shakhas-held-daily -in-the-country-senior-rss-leader/1892969/.

66 Personal communication. See also Ullekh, *Kannur*, 114.

67 In North Kerala, as in other parts of the country, RSS workers played an important role in printing and disseminating underground literature during the emergency. These included tracts on theories of personal and political liberty written by everyone from Vivekananda to Lokmanya Tilak, protest essays and poetry against the Indira Gandhi regime, messages of support from leaders of the J. P. movement and the RSS, and news of political activists, journalists, and others arrested elsewhere in the country. Present-day RSS workers I met in the course of my field research spoke of the deep impression that the dissemination of this literature made on them. What they also found impressive was the large number of RSS workers arrested at the time. In recounting those times, RSS workers spoke about their and their colleagues' veritable conversion from the Congress (I), socialist, and even communist parties—to the RSS.

68 See chapter 3 for more details.

69 During one conversation about that period of conflict between the Marxist left and the Hindu right, Ajayan, who had been an RSS worker since the early 1980s, mapped the conflict in a fairly typical fashion. He said, "At one point, the area around Thalassery old bus stand was a Communist center. Porters and head loaders had made a temporary office affiliated with CITU [the CPI (M)-allied Centre of Indian Trade Unions]. They used to attack from behind the office façade, using it as a shield. This was—Chirakkara, PC Mukku, there are Marxist Party offices at these places. They too were in these people's hands [in CPI (M) workers' hands]. Then this goods shed road was also in their hands. Then a small part of Gopal petta and other seacoast areas was in their hands. Then beyond Keernantimukku, Mannodi area, Kollasseri—all of these were their majority areas. Gradually, through consistent clashes we became the majority. Became majority implies that along with the conflict/clashes we started organization work as well. As time changed/ as the era changed people started cooperating with us. In one era, even the 'goondas' who used to work with the Party [CPI (M)] joined us."

70 The RSS-BJP workers I spoke to often referenced Panunda Chandran's murder. See also Ullekh, *Kannur*, 140.

71 Jacob, *RSS-CPM Clashes*, 839.

72 Bateson, *Naven*.

73 Thomassen, "Schismogenesis." See also Colaguori, *Agon Culture*, on the important place that competition occupies in contemporary cultural ideology and its under-studied contribution to ongoing conflicts and war.

74 SC 65 of 1981.

75 I often prefix the word *alleged* before references to the political workers' violence. While many workers have been accused of political violence, and media reports hold the workers responsible as a collective for it, I seek to retain the tension between the charges filed against individuals and the frequency with which they have been cleared of them. At the same time, as I discuss in chapters 4 and 5, by virtue of their membership of certain groups, accusations of violence nevertheless implicate workers in political violence. For instance, the RSS workers accused of the attack on one of the Dinesh Beedi factories and the murder of two CPI (M) sympathizers were acquitted. And while these particular RSS workers had been acquitted of the said attack, it was widely held that RSS–Jan Sangh workers as an organized collective were behind the attack and regarded the attacks as an important turning point in the career of the Hindu right in Kannur. In conversations about it, they also directly or obliquely admitted to it. See SC 60 of 1981.

76 I am particularly referring to Pannianur Chandran who went on to become a member of the BJP district committee and Rajshekharan who became the district president of the Vishwa Hindu Parishad in the early 2000s.

77 See SC 60 of 1981. See also SC 20, 26, and 65 of 1981.

78 Jacob draws on the complaints that were registered in various police stations of the area, computes statistics about the clashes, and summarizes key facts surrounding the attacks by members of the two groups. He mentions names and fathers of the accused, tells us how these workers of either the RSS or the CPI (M) constituted an "unlawful assembly," the place where they met, the place they proceeded to, and the weapons they used as they turned to a solitary member (in majority of incidents that he writes about) of the opposing group and inflicted fatal injuries. He also briefly notes the status of the police investigation related to the event, whether criminal charges have been filed or not, and, if so, the outcome of the case. Jacob, *RSS-CPM Clashes*.

79 Jacob, *RSS-CPM Clashes*, 836, 839.

80 Jacob notes that in 1979, twenty cases of such competitive violence were recorded that included five murder cases, six attempts to murder, and nine cases of rioting. In ten cases, CPI (M) members were complainants while members of the RSS-BJS combine filed a complaint in the other ten. In 1980, twenty-eight such cases were registered and workers of one or the other group filed the initial complaint. This included two murder cases, nine attempts to murder, fourteen cases of rioting, and three cases of what police records describe as "causing hurt with mischief." The following year, the counts were much more and ten cases (six murder and four attempts to murder) were reported in just one month. Jacob, *RSS-CPM Clashes*, 839.

81 Jacob, *RSS-CPM Clashes*, 839.

82 In many of these cases (to use the journalist Ullekh's description), "the accused political parties offered the police a list of perpetrators from their side. The police then arrested those persons." See Ullekh, *Kannur*, 174–75. In chapter 4 I discuss the implications of this practice of offering the police a list of assailants; for now, it is important to note that complaints filed by political parties have strongly colored judicial and other accounts of different violent events.

83 That is the term that is used in court records.

84 See chapter 3 for more details.

85 The Land Reform (Amendment) Act came into force on January 1, 1970. As T. K. Oomen tells us in his study of the agrarian movement in Kerala, the act was designed to distribute excess land under the ownership of the government, public endowment, and private individuals to the landless. Apart from this, ownership rights to 7.5 cents, or 435 square feet, of land around their huts were to be conferred on all hutment dwellers. Encouraged by these provisions, the Kerala Krashaka Sangham and the Kerala State Labor Union initiated the "land grab movement" in December 1969. At the joint convention held by the two groups and attended by 150,000 delegates, it was declared that hutment dwellers should not pay rent to landowners; that landless families should forcibly occupy excess land; that 10 cents, or 580 square feet, of land around their huts should be fenced by hutment dwellers, and they should start harvesting crops from such plots; and that all steps taken by the government, police, courts, and landlords against this movement should be resisted. According to Oomen's estimates, twenty thousand hutment dwellers complied with the "Punnapra Declaration"; most of them were CPI (M) workers or sympathizers. The land-grab agitation was particularly active in South Kerala, especially in the Alleppey district where, between January 1, 1970, and May 31, 1970, 931 encroachments took place and 4,881 CPI (M) and Krashaka Sangham activists were arrested. See Oomen, *From Mobilization to Institutionalization*, 124–42.

86 For a historically informed critique of the Kerala land reform policy—
its focus on land for building houses, rather than as a productive asset
for Dalit agricultural laborers—see Devika, "Contemporary Dalit
Assertions."

87 In many respects, Preman was echoing both the party rhetoric and the
social science literature on Kerala. While the welfare state has a long
history in Kerala, it was considerably strengthened under several communist governments. See Desai, "Indirect British Rule." The Communist Party and social scientists, especially in the 1980s, thus hailed its
developmentalist character and the "Kerala model of development" that
had achieved high points on all the indexes of well-being without the
stimulus of an industrial revolution. An article in the *New York Times*,
for instance, told its readers that Kerala was a place "where births are
kept down but women are not," an area of the "third world" where both
the birth rate and the infant mortality rate were falling, where average
life expectancy was approaching seventy years, where the large majority of men and women could read and write, and where women indeed
outnumbered men. Cited in Jeffrey, *Politics, Women and Well-Being*. See
also Hill, "Kerala Is Different"; Franke and Chasin, *Kerala*; Franke et al.,
"Kerala State"; and Heller, *Labor of Development*. These are just some
works that have exalted Kerala and its development model. In J. Devika's
words, "Within Kerala, communists have claimed the major share of
credit for progressive state policy and politics; the 'Kerala model' literature reiterates the claim in international arenas." Devika, "Egalitarian
Developmentalism," 801. For a historically and theoretically grounded
critique of scholarship that lauds Kerala's social democracy without
attending to its contradictions, see Mannathukkaren, "Conjuncture of
'Late Socialism.'"

88 The party's networks of disbursing care took on a new life with the institution of the People's Planning Campaign in the late 1990s. Launched
and gradually implemented between 1996 and 1998, the campaign revolved around increasing popular participation in establishing and realizing local-level development and welfare goals. Party workers such as
Preman were not members of local village councils, and the campaign
had only just got underway when I first met him in the early 2000s.
Nevertheless, I believe it intensified local-level party workers' identification with their role as agents of people's welfare and well-being attending to popular concerns on the ground, and their attachment to a party
that they saw as doing the same. In this sense, the campaign worked to
reinforce the party's hegemony over its cadres as well as in Kerala
society more broadly. On this point, see Devika, "Participatory
Democracy."

89 L. Gandhi, *Affective Communities*, 30.

90 Frequent references to the party and fellow party workers as family, kith, and kin circulate among CPI (M) workers and local leaders in Kannur and other parts of Kerala.

91 The last set of Preman's words *verukkappedentavare verukkappeduka thanne cheyyanam* might also be translated as "the people who need to be hated should be hated."

92 Hansen, *Wages of Violence*; Michelutti, *Vernacularization of Democracy*.

93 While common ethnic origins are not a key referent of CPI (M) ideology, communist participation in the united Kerala or Aikya Kerala and writings from that time, as well as CPI (M) stalwart E. M. S. Namboodripad's many tracts on communal life in Kerala, are just some instances of the ways in which communists also posit Kerala and Malayalis as a proud coherent and cohesive cultural community.

94 MacCannell, *Regime of the Brother*, 11.

95 L. Gandhi, *Affective Communities*, 28.

96 Women are often absorbed in the protocols of this network of brothers. The nature of this absorption in Kerala is underlined by relatively equal levels of access to livelihood and income, but denial of what (with MacCannell) we can call equal access to identity in families associated with the Communist Party. This is an issue that deserves considerable research on its own terms. See MacCannell, *Regime of the Brother*, 26–27. I was however unable to obtain access to women in "party families" in ways that would do justice to this topic.

97 Between 2010 and 2015, critical accounts came to light about ways in which these masculine fraternities of CPI (M) political workers have also targeted women lower down the socioeconomic and political hierarchy. I am referring to what has come to be known as the "Chitralekha case" in the wake of the harassment that Chitralekha, a Dalit woman auto driver, faced at the hands of members of the CPI (M)-led auto drivers' union for several years. I have briefly discussed this case elsewhere (see Chaturvedi, "Political Violence, Community"). For a more detailed discussion, see the report of the solidarity mission that studied the contexts and facts surrounding the case. The report is reproduced in Nivedita Menon, "'Living Outside the Track': A Woman Worker's Struggle against Caste and Patriarchy in Kerala," Kafila, February 25, 2010, https://kafila.online/2010/02/25/%E2%80%9Cliving-outside-the-track%E2%80%9D-a-woman-worker%E2%80%99s-struggle-against-caste-and-patriarchy-in-kerala/.

98 Martha Minow has offered some of the clearest accounts of the ways in which vengeance carries a certain moral appeal but can also become "maliciously spiteful and dangerously aggressive." Building on Jean Hampton's defense of retributive punishment, she distinguishes between vengeance and retribution. To paraphrase Minow, retribution may be

thought of as vengeance inhibited by outside intervention and carried out by someone other than the hurt person(s) in keeping with norms such as proportionality and individual rights. See Minow, *Between Vengeance and Forgiveness*, 10–14. Also see Hampton, "Correcting Harms." In this chapter I have not followed that distinction but noted the harsh turns that the vengeful spirit can take while sometimes using vengeance and retribution as interchangeable terms. In chapters 4 and 5 I question the primacy given to criminal justice anchored in principles of reciprocal punishment for cases of political violence.

99 Several scholars have critically appraised the CPI (M)'s position with respect to caste and religious identities. While a number of them have foregrounded the ways in which casteism has been masked in CPI (M)'s discourse and practices, others have discussed the tensions between Dalit and class-based politics. See Devika, "Egalitarian Developmentalism"; Ilaiah, "Dalitism versus Brahminism"; Menon, *Being a Brahmin*; and A. Nigam, "Secularism, Modernity, Nation." See also recent debates about the Dalit Marxist figure R. B. More, triggered by the publication of his memoirs with an introduction by Anupama Rao. See Mhaskar and Pol, review of Satyendra More, *The Memoirs of a Dalit Communist*, and see Rao's rejoinder to Mhaskar and Pol in *South Asia Multidisciplinary Academic Journal*. With respect to the CPI (M) in Kerala, it is important to note that electoral cretinism and calculations have often led the party to enter a range of alliances with political parties such as the Muslim League that foreground religious identities. While an argument may be made that this has been in the defense of secular ideals, some commentators see a new turn. They note that in the wake of intensified Hindu majoritarian discourse, the CPI (M) in Kerala has also been partaking in dangerous politics of minoritization against Muslims. They are hence emulating the Hindu right even while maintaining a critical stance against it. See Kuriakose and Prasad-Aleyamma, "Turning Minorities." More locally, in other parts of North Kerala (particularly in nearby Kozhikode district), conflict between Hindu Thiyya affiliates of the CPI (M) and members of the Indian Union Muslim League has taken more recognizable communal forms. See Arafath, "Nadapuram Enigma," for a rich and insightful account of how martial history, political economy, religion, and party politics came to produce violent communal conflagrations there. It is also important to attend to the emergence of organizations such as now-banned Popular Front of India and the National Democratic Front that iterate violently communitarian forms of political Islam to understand that violence.

100 Ahmed, "Muzaffarnagar 2013"; Mander et al., "Wages of Communal Violence"; Youth for Human Rights Documentation, *An Account of Fear and Impunity*, March 8, 2020, https://www.thepolisproject.com/read /an-account-of-fear-impunity-a-preliminary-fact-finding-report-on

-communally-targeted-violence-in-ne-delhi-february-2020/; Teltumbde, *Khairlanji*.

101   See Hannah Ellis-Petersen, "'We Are Not Safe': India's Muslims Tell of Wave of Police Brutality," *The Guardian*, January 3, 2020, https://www.theguardian.com/world/2020/jan/03/we-are-not-safe-indias-muslims-tell-of-wave-of-police-brutality.

3. Care, Connectedness, and Violence in Hindu Right Communities

1   Andersen and Damle, *Brotherhood in Saffron*; Bacchetta, *Gender in the Hindu Nation*; T. Basu et al., *Khaki Shorts and Saffron Flags*; Hansen, *Saffron Wave*; Hansen, "Political Theology of Violence"; Jaffrelot, *Hindu Nationalist Movement*; Jaffrelot, *The Sangh Parivar*; Valiani, *Militant Publics in India*.

2   Pandey, *Construction of Communalism*, 6. In recent years, as members of the Sangh have gained state power at the national level, they have perpetuated this hostile attitude against minorities at the level of legislative policy and executive decision-making as well as sought to influence avenues of judicial redress. The Sangh has also pursued that hostile attitude through judicial and governmental institutions. Also see Anderson and Longkumer, *Neo-Hindutva*; Reddy, "Hindutva as Praxis"; Kanungo, *RSS's Tryst with Politics*; Zavos, *Emergence of Hindu Nationalism*.

3   The 2015 figures from the RSS databank indicate that there are 165,000 welfare units operating in different parts of the country. Cited in Bhattacharjee, *Disaster Relief and the RSS*, 11.

4   The 1971–1972 Thalassery riot occurred when, according to various versions, slippers were flung from a Muslim-owned hotel at a Hindu religious procession. According to members of the Hindu right, this act of alleged desecration provoked members of the procession to react. The violence that followed resulted in considerable damage to Muslim- and Hindu-owned property, but thankfully no deaths or incidents of sexual violence took place. Nevertheless, rumors and accounts that emphasized Muslim misdemeanors and aggression consolidated feelings of Hindu persecution in parts of Thalassery town and even saw some CPI (M) workers joining forces with the RSS and the Jan Sangh.

5   The 1971 riot unfolded on the backs of two agitations led by the RSS– Jan Sangh combine in nearby areas in the late 1960s. The first agitation revolved around the call to restore an ancient Hindu temple allegedly destroyed by the Muslim ruler from Mysore, Tipu Sultan. The second consisted of an especially vociferous stir against the Kerala government's decision to carve out the separate district of Malappuram with a Muslim majority. In 1978–1979 the RSS and its associates organized

long marches from North to South Kerala around the question of idols that had been destroyed in a local Thalassery temple. A few years later, in 1983, RSS activists and sympathizers came together under various banners to successfully oppose the construction of a Church near a Hindu temple. Each instance was a step in generating a more cohesive and sharply articulated Hindu identity among the majority population. See Jayaprasad, RSS and Hindu Nationalism, 189–94; Thachil, Elite Parties, Poor Voters, 208.

6 S. Chandra, "Communal Consciousness"; Lobo and D'Souza, "Images of Violence."

7 The BJP's vote share came down to 5.56 percent in 1991 from 4.76 percent in 1987 according to Thachil, Elite Parties, Poor Voters, 210. The Hindu right wing's ability to make electoral gains through polarizing communal politics in the early 1990s was curbed in Kerala due to the presence of a numerically and socioeconomically strong Muslim minority community, the community's affiliations with different regional ruling blocs, and the readiness of dominant parties like the CPI (M) to mobilize police power in the event of riots. Chiriyankandath, "Changing Muslim Politics."

8 Thachil, Elite Parties, Poor Voters, 208–12.

9 Thachil, Elite Parties, Poor Voters, 212.

10 Bhattacharjee, Disaster Relief and the RSS; Thachil, Elite Parties, Poor Voters.

11 Thachil, Elite Parties, Poor Voters, 46–47.

12 The vote share returned to 5.61 percent in 1996 and grew to 10.38 percent in the 2004 national elections (Election Commission Data). In the 2014 national elections, its vote share in Kerala was 10.8 percent, which grew to 12.93 percent in the 2019 national elections. In legislative assembly elections, the BJP's vote share remained below 6 percent until 2016, when it grew to 10.5 percent. James Chiriyankandath, "The Kerala Election: A Shift to the Left—and a Move to the Right," London School of Economics blogs, May 26, 2016, http://eprints.lse.ac.uk/74736/. These increases in national and provincial elections show that the BJP has been making somewhat slow but fairly steady and significant gains in the popular vote. It might be surmised that its outreach among lower-caste, Dalit, and Adivasi constituents, alliances with Ezhava groups such as the Bharatiya Dharma Jan Sena and Adivasi Gothra Maha Sabha, dense shakha networks, and attempts to create a consolidated Hindu identity in Kerala have begun reaping electoral rewards. Simultaneously, the decline in stature of the Congress and its alliance partners in Kerala has contributed to increases in the BJP's vote share in Kerala.

13 Foucault, Security, Territory, Population, 172, 115–227.

14 Here, I am mobilizing Joan Tronto's definition of care, especially the formulation she offers at the beginning of her 2015 book where she notes "Care is about meeting needs; and it is always relational." See Tronto, *Who Cares?*, 4.

15 I have found Anand Pandian's elaboration of Foucault's genealogy of pastoral power and its iterations in South India helpful here. See Pandian, "Pastoral Power in the Postcolony."

16 See Foucault, *Security, Territory, Population*, 183.

17 Valiani, "Physical Training, Ethical Discipline." Self-conscious cultivation of a free masculine Hindu subject has a long genealogy. See Chakraborty, *Masculinity, Asceticism, Hinduism*; C. Gupta, "Masculine Vernacular Histories."

18 See chapter 2, note 6 for my motivation behind anonymizing my research assistants.

19 OTCs, also known as Sangh Shikhsha Varg or Sangh Training Workshops, are held across the country for three to four weeks in the summer months coinciding with term breaks in schools and higher-educational institutions. Recruits above the age of sixteen looking for greater integration in the Sangh networks and keen to go up its ranks are required to attend three such camps in their careers as RSS workers. The final graduating camp is held in Nagpur. RSS ideologues describe the camps as important rites of passage where recruits are trained in organizational aspects, the nationalist values, and "selfless service" while following a strict physical regimen. See Sharda, *RSS 360*.

20 Chaturvedi, "Somehow It Happened." This article reviews the material presented here with a special focus on questions of individuation and collectivization of responsibility.

21 The suffix "Master" is used across Kerala for respected schoolteachers. As in other parts of the country, in Kerala too, schoolteachers have been extremely active in the work of raising civic and political consciousness as well as mediating state and political party apparatuses and society at large. See Bhattacharya, "'Civic Community' and Its Margins" for an analysis of the role that schoolteachers have played, for instance in Bengal, as the interface between parties (especially the party left) and society.

22 See Ullekh, *Kannur*, 65–69, where the journalist Ullekh also focuses on Sadanandan Master as an important local figure in the regional history of political violence. He sketches Sadanandan Master's political biography with special attention to the RSS-BJP leader's encounters with violent attacks and counterattacks.

23 See chapter 1 for a more detailed discussion about such figures.

24 Ossella and Ossella, *Social Mobility in Kerala*, 37.

25 As Satish Deshpande points out, Hindu nationalist groups have excelled in recruiting everyday experiences and the "sedimented banalities of neighborliness" for their cause. See Deshpande, "Hegemonic Spatial Strategies," 269. The "house contact program" that Sadanandan Master describes is one more instance of it. In a similar vein, while studying the Shiv Sena, Dipankar Gupta showed how such engagement with everyday concerns is not confined to fixing pipes but extends even to managing marital problems in a household. See D. Gupta, *Nativism in a Metropolis*, 75. Tanika Sarkar's work on RSS women (1991) and Atreyee Sen's (2007) work on women in the Shiv Sena bear out those insights about Hindu right-wing groups and their reliance on the intimacy of the everyday to forge a political community. See T. Sarkar, "Woman as Communal Subject"; Sen, *Shiv Sena Women*.

26 Ossella and Ossella, *Social Mobility in Kerala*, 38.

27 Ossella and Ossella, *Social Mobility in Kerala*, 56.

28 Massumi, *Parables of the Virtual*; Stewart, *Ordinary Affects*.

29 Stewart, *Ordinary Affects*, 2.

30 According to local accounts, court records, and journalist Ullekh's description, Sadanandan Master was attacked for his role in the beating of a CPI (M) branch secretary earlier that day. A few hours after the attack on Sadanandan Master, local CPI (M) student leader Sudheesh was murdered on January 25, 1994. One violent encounter had piled atop another. Sessions Case (SC) 125 of 1997. Also see Ullekh, *Kannur*, 65–68.

31 Subject pronouns are often omitted in South Asian and East Asian languages. While the statements cited here and recorded in Malayalam contained many impersonal constructions, I have inserted subject pronouns to make the statements readable in English. It is also important to note that the "utterance context" and gestures personalize "syntactically impersonal constructions." Wilce, *Eloquence in Trouble*, 86.

32 Peircian understanding of relationship between sign, object, and interpretants emphasizes the sensual modes by which the meaning of a sign comes to realize itself in the very physical self of a person. Indeed, for Peirce, every thought is a sign without meaning, until interpreted by a subsequent thought or person. In Peirce's conception, there is no unbridgeable gap between external realities and the thought or act by which they are mediated within us. The meaning of the thought contained in the stop sign would get established in the material reality of the self that stops. The self too emerges at this moment. In this way, elements of the world just never "are" but are—in a constant state of becoming—with each other. See Valentine, *Fluid Signs*, 22; Peirce and Hoopes, *Peirce on Signs*, 49.

33 See Hansen, "Political Theology of Violence."

34 These concepts are especially important for Madhav Sadashiv Gol-walkar, one of the founding members of the RSS and its highest func-tionary from 1940 to 1973. He is remembered among RSS followers as an able organizer and as the Sangh's eminent ideologue. In his *Bunch of Thoughts*, Golwalkar identifies the corporate Hindu nation as a "living God" and refers to its soul, *chiti*, as a kind of higher law that takes pre-cedence over any political institutions or manmade rules. Therefore, performance of dharma, and experiencing the unifying "life force" in all of us are keys to realizing that higher law. For a further elaboration of the concept in Hindu right-wing literature, see Andersen and Damle, *Brotherhood in Saffron*, 71–85.

35 Golwalkar, *Bunch of Thoughts*, 31–32.

36 Golwalkar, *Bunch of Thoughts*, 53–54.

37 Here it is important to note that the term *dharma* has multiple meanings in Hindu, Jain, and Buddhist traditions that range from virtue to law or norm. A comprehensive account of the term is outside my scope and expertise. But see Holdrege, "Dharma," for an instructive review of the category, particularly the relationship between the spiritual and ritual dimensions of dharma on the one hand and as mediating sociocultural practices on the other.

38 "*Avane vetti murichchu*" (cut him up) were words often used to describe violent attacks that made up the conflict between members of the Marx-ist left and the Hindu right in North Kerala. They indicate not just the nature of injuries but also the instruments such as sickles and swords that have been used to inflict the injuries.

39 Wilce, *Eloquence in Trouble*, 44–104; Jayaseelan, *Parametric Studies*.

40 The "pro-drop" (pronoun-dropping) phenomenon in various Western languages such as Italian has been linked to the richness of the subject–verb agreement in these languages so that even if the subject is missing, the person–number–gender features of the subject can be judged from the verb form. However, as Jayaseelan points out, Malayalam has no verb agreement at all. Nevertheless, the subject is frequently omitted in spoken Malayalam, retaining considerable ambiguity about it. See Jayaseelan, *Parametric Studies*, 24.

41 Valentine, *Charred Lullabies*, 104–34.

42 Aijaz Ahmad, "Liberal Democracy and the Extreme Right," *Verso* (blog), March 24, 2017, https://www.versobooks.com/blogs/3144-india-liberal-democracy-and-the-extreme-right.

43 P. S. Gopikrishnan Unnithan and Jeemon Jacob, "Kerala: Jan Raksha Yatra Culminates in Thiruvananthapuram, Here Are the Key Takeaways," *India*

Today, October 18, 2017, https://www.indiatoday.in/india/story/kerala-jan
-raksha-yatra-thiruvananthapuram-bjp-amit-shah-1066772-2017-10-18.

44 I have struggled to find credible reports on the exact number of people
who attended and have hence given an approximate estimate based on
my impressions.

45 Hannah Ellis-Petersen and Shaikh Azizur Rahman, "Coronavirus Conspiracy Theories Targeting Muslims Spread in India," *The Guardian*,
April 13, 2020, https://www.theguardian.com/world/2020/apr/13
/coronavirus-conspiracy-theories-targeting-muslims-spread-in-india;
Rory Sullivan, "Muslims Turned Away from Hospital in India 'Unless
They Can Prove They Are Coronavirus-Free,'" *Independent*, April 20,
2020, https://www.independent.co.uk/news/world/asia/coronavirus
-muslims-rejected-indian-hospital-a9474161.html.

4. Law's Subterfuge

1 In the course of my research, local-level workers of the two groups
especially highlighted three well-known cases of the late 1990s where
trial court judges handed out the death sentence. They included Sessions
Case (hereafter SC) 252 of 2001—the case involving the murder of
RSS members and schoolteacher Jaykrishnan Master; the murder of a
CPI (M) worker killed soon after Jaykrishnan Master's murder allegedly
by RSS-BJP workers; and the case involving the murder of another well-
known RSS-BJP local leader, Pannianur Chandran, in 1997 allegedly by
CPI (M) supporters [SC 151 of 1997].

2 See Foucault, "Political Function."

3 See Mamdani, "Beyond Nuremberg," 63. Here he offers an instructive definition of political violence while reflecting on the ways
in which justice has been apprehended following the Nuremberg
model.

4 M. Chatterjee, "Impunity Effect."

5 Grover, "Elusive Quest for Justice"; Kannabiran, *Wages of Impunity*.

6 Hoenig and Singh, *Landscapes of Fear*.

7 U. Singh, *State, Democracy and Anti-Terror Laws*, 73.

8 Lokaneeta, *Transnational Torture*, 196.

9 Project 39A, *Death Penalty Report India Report*, for instance, tells us that
74.1 percent of people sentenced to death in the country belong to economically and socially marginal groups.

10 See the research done by the Innocence Network, which has particularly
gathered documents related to the 2006 Mumbai blast cases of wrongfully incarcerated persons who were on trial for years before being proven

innocent (https://theinnocent.in/mumbai-train-blast-711/, accessed June 27, 2022). Abdul Wahid Sheikh's case has become particularly well known in recent years. See Sonam Saigal's overview of recent cases, such as "Prisoners of the System," *The Hindu*, February 20, 2017, https://www.thehindu.com/news/cities/mumbai/prisoners-of-the-system/article17333262.ece. It is important to note, however, that long, grueling trials and the experience of languishing in prisons until proven innocent is not peculiar to those charged in terrorism cases. See Amnesty International India's report on the issue, *Justice under Trial*.

11 Kannabiran, *Wages of Impunity*, 10.

12 See Mamdani, "Logic of Nuremberg." See also Mamdani, "Beyond Nuremberg." He has built on these insights in his latest book, *Neither Settler Nor Native*.

13 Mamdani, "Beyond Nuremberg," 63, 81.

14 Mamdani, "Beyond Nuremberg," 81.

15 Mamdani, "Beyond Nuremberg," 81.

16 Mamdani, "Lessons of Nuremberg and CODESA," 4–5; Mamdani, "Beyond Nuremberg," 81.

17 TADA was in force between 1985 and 1997. While legislative justifications for its promulgation and enactment emphasized violent events in Punjab, TADA was enforced in many other parts of the country too at various junctures. Its provisions, which expanded police powers, relaxed evidentiary requirements for convictions, and made confessions submitted to police officials without the presence of a judicial authority admissible as legal evidence, have survived in different forms in similar enactments. For a comprehensive history up to the mid-2000s, see U. Singh, *State, Democracy, and Anti-Terror Laws*.

18 U. Singh, *State, Democracy, and Anti-Terror Laws*, 49–54.

19 Mamdani, "Beyond Nuremberg," 67–68, 79.

20 Accords between representatives of various subnationalist movements in North-East India and Punjab, for instance, have abated the violence of these movements and a counterinsurgent state. The extent to which these accords have addressed core issues driving these violent movements and led to comprehensive institutional change is, however, debatable. While the literature on these movements and efforts to obtain peace is large, see Rajagopalan, *Peace Accords*, for an evaluation of resolutions obtained in the North-East, and see Singh, *Ethnic Conflict in India*, and Jodhka, "Review," for a review of the critical questions that the Khalistan movement in Punjab and its containment raise. In places such as Kashmir and Central India, counterinsurgency operations and state violence continues to be mounted against marginal populations and dissenting movements. Simultaneously, meaningful reform of a

sociopolitical system that perpetuates majoritarian and communal violence remains elusive.

21 I draw the term from Baxi's important account of rape trials involving upper-caste men and Dalit and Adivasi victims under the aegis of the Prevention of Atrocity Act of 1989 (POA). Her analysis helps us grasp the ways in which legal frameworks and associated technicalities can disjunct acts of violence from their contexts and the larger circuit of relations and actions that they belong to. See Baxi, *Public Secrets of Law*, 283–339.

22 Goffman's theorization of the front- and backstage of everyday life has been formative in the formulation of these concepts. See Goffman, *Presentation of Self*, 111–21.

23 This case was tried in Kannur District Sessions Court as SC 4 of 1981.

24 While the information I share about case no. 1 is in the public domain, narratives I gathered around case no. 2 call for maintaining anonymity.

25 M. Chatterjee, "Impunity Effect"; Grover, "Elusive Quest for Justice."

26 Grover, "Elusive Quest for Justice," 374.

27 See M. Chatterjee, "Against the Witness." See also Hoenig and Singh, *Landscapes of Fear*. Essays and case studies collected here relate to state violence in places such as Jammu, Kashmir, Punjab, and North-East India.

28 See Ullekh, *Kannur*, 174, on some of the structural problems affecting Kannur police. Their sheer paucity, he writes, hinders investigative processes. His observations echo scholarship on the institutional challenges that have historically faced police in India. These range from lack of decent pay to being subjected to multiple political pressures. See Baxi, *Crisis*, 86. Beatrice Jauregui's recent ethnographic work on police in North India is especially illuminating in this regard. See Jauregui, *Provisional Authority*. Related insights have also emerged in Lokaneeta's study of the relationship between custodial violence and use of scientific techniques in the investigative process. Torture and custodial deaths in India, as she notes, need to be situated in organizational aspects that push members of the police force to shortchange the investigative process. Lokaneeta, *Truth Machines*, 39–44.

29 In this case, seven CPI (M) workers were accused of murdering the local Hindu right-wing leader, Jaykrishnan Master. The CPI (M) has been at the helm of the Kerala state government several times and has controlled the workings of the police and appointment of prosecutors. This might suggest collusion between the party, state, and police, but such lines of collusion are not easy to establish. Furthermore, opposition groups have also led the state governments seven times from the late 1970s to the early 2000s sometimes albeit for short durations. And like

the CPI (M) workers charged with different violent crimes in this period, RSS-BJP workers have also had considerable success in obtaining acquittals. Thus, while overt influence over the police is difficult to determine, we know that like the workers of the two groups and their supporters and sympathizers, police personnel have inhabited a competitive, strife-ridden political space. Degrees of police laxity and absence of adequate corroboratory material evidence have played an important role in trials of the workers of the two groups.

30 SC 146 of 2001, 79–80.

31 Ullekh, *Kannur*, 183.

32 A kathival or a knife-sword, as the court translates it, may be described as a dagger that curves like a sword.

33 AIR (*All India Reporter*) SC 807 of 1950, cited in Ahmad and Ansari, *Law Relating to Burden of Proof*, viii.

34 See SC 146 of 2001. The judge in this case was quoting Supreme Court judgment 1998 AIR SC 192 of 1998, *Surendra Narain alias Munna Pandey v/s State of U. P.*

35 AIR SC 807 of 1950.

36 See section 149 of the Indian Penal Code.

37 In the judge's words, "The prosecution relies much on the testimony of PW 3 and 4 (Nambiar and the electrician) to bring home the guilt of the accused." See SC 4 of 1981, 7.

38 SC 4 of 1981.

39 SC 4 of 1981, p. 11.

40 SC 4 of 1981, p. 11.

41 SC 4 of 1981, p. 11.

42 Monir, *Textbook*, 20.

43 SC 4 of 1981, 7. To cut or *vayttuka*, as noted elsewhere, is often used to imply to attack with a sword or chopper. I understand it to mean the act of slashing with a sword or a kathival.

44 Lokaneeta, "Sovereignty, Violence and Resistance," 78.

45 U. Singh, *State, Democracy, and Anti-Terror Laws*, 69–70.

46 Cited in U. Singh, *State, Democracy, and Anti-Terror Laws*, 69.

47 U. Singh, *State, Democracy, and Anti-Terror Laws*, 69.

48 "Correctly" here implies that it corresponded to the prosecution's case and the experts' interpretation of the events.

5. Individuating Responsibility

1　As I noted in the introduction, according to my computations more than four thousand individuals often belonging to lower castes and economic classes have been prosecuted for the political violence between various parties in Kannur. See Chaturvedi, "Political Violence, Criminal Law," for an earlier version of this chapter.

2　Kolsky, "Codification and the Rule"; Wright, "Macaulay's Indian Penal Code."

3　Kannabiran, "Contexts of Criminology," 462–69. Kannabiran's 2008 essay offers an eye-opening summary of police complicity in the persecution of political dissenters as well as marginalized communities from the earliest decades of Indian democracy until the early 2000s. See also Lokaneeta, *Truth Machines*, 30, for a discussion about the ways in which the poor as well as members of other minority groups have been especially vulnerable to custodial violence.

4　The word *draconian* recurs in several descriptions of the UAPA. As a 2019 news report indicates, the word has also been used in parliamentary speeches about the act. See "Opposition Slams Amendment to UAPA, Call It Draconian," *Deccan Herald*, August 2, 2019, https:// www.deccanherald.com/national/national-politics/opposition-slams -amendment-to-uapa-call-it-draconian-751479.html. For a statistical overview of recent arrests under the act, see "3,005 Cases Registered, 3,974 Arrested under UAPA from 2016–18," *The Tribune*, September 16, 2020, https://www.tribuneindia.com/news/nation/3-005-cases-registered -3-974-arrested-under-uapa-from-2016-18-142049. For a report on discharge rates until 2018, see Chaitanya Mallapur and Devyani Chhetri, "Arrested Activists: 67% Ended in Acquittal or Discharge under UAPA Act," *Business Standard*, September 14, 2018, https://www.business -standard.com/article/current-affairs/arrested-activists-67-ended-in -acquittal-or-discharge-under-uapa-act-118090800801_1.html. Numbers have been rising. I am focusing mostly on well-known arrests of intellectuals and activists such as the Bhima Koregaon case and the East Delhi case, but I am also thinking about ongoing arrests in Andhra.

5　See this analysis of the National Crime Records Bureau reports from 2010 to 2018: "Analysis of Use of UAPA from NCRB Data," Centre for Law and Policy Research, July 1, 2020, https://clpr.org.in/blog/use-of-the-uapa-from -the-national-crime-reports-bureau/. In this chapter I invoke some well-known instances where the UAPA has been used against intellectuals and activists opposed to the dominant dispensation. However, it is important to note that the numbers of people so charged are steadily increasing.

6　U. Singh, *State, Democracy and Anti-Terror Laws*, 69. I also drew on that category in the previous chapter.

7 Sessions Case (hereafter SC) 34 of 1982, 10. As I explain later, will and intention are closely related in the IPC and the writings on criminal law that it deems authoritative. In various judicial commentaries, will and intention are also used interchangeably. A popular commentary on the IPC, whose exegesis I discuss later in this chapter opens its discussion on *mens rea* with these words: "It is the combination of act and intent which makes a crime. The intent and the act must both concur to constitute a crime. An act by itself is not wrong. But an act, if prohibited, done with a particular intent makes it criminal.... The responsibility in crimes must depend on the doing of a 'willed' or 'voluntary' act and particular intent behind the act." Misra, *Indian Penal Code*, 11.

8 Section 300 of the IPC lists the conditions grave and sudden provocation, private defense, exercise of legal power, sudden fight, or act done without premeditation and consent in cases of passive euthanasia as exceptions where culpable homicide does not amount to murder.

9 I am paraphrasing the insights that William Connolly puts forward in his important history of the concept of the will and its evocation in capital punishment cases in contemporary American courts. See Connolly, *Why I Am Not a Secularist*, 120.

10 One of the most candid statements about their inability to grasp the nature of violence that district court judges were being called on to adjudicate came from Judge R. Basant in a case involving the murder of a Muslim League worker, Saduli. No witnesses appeared to back the prosecution's account of the murder, and the four CPI (M) workers accused of it were acquitted. Judge Basant noted that he did not have even "a faint legal idea" about what transpired. The lack of empirical information compounded his sense of helplessness; for it seemed that there was no way he could really understand the heinous crime or its context. See SC 90 of 1993.

11 SC 34 of 1982, 11.

12 SC 34 of 1982.

13 SC 151 of 1997, 44.

14 SC 252 of 2001, 110.

15 I have written elsewhere about the judicial history of terms such as "depraved" and "diabolical." See Chaturvedi, "Down by Law," 202–40. A key moment in that history is the well-known *Bachan Singh v. State of Punjab* case. See AIR SC 898 of 1980, which became an important turning point in penal jurisprudence in India. Equating the nature of an act with the character of the actor, the constitution bench set up to examine the case, and the constitutional legitimacy of capital punishment in India regarded "the style" in which the murder was committed an index of the depraved character of the perpetrator. The bench argued that the

manner in which the act was committed and its facts and circumstances could not be treated separately. According to the bench, "extreme depravity" was legitimate grounds for imposing capital punishment. See *Bachan Singh*, AIR SC 898 of 1980, 902.

16 See Gaur, *Commentaries on the Indian Penal Code*.

17 See Pillai and Aqil, *Essays on the Indian Penal Code*.

18 Misra, *Indian Penal Code*, 10.

19 Misra, *Indian Penal Code*, 14.

20 Cited in Misra, *Indian Penal Code*, 12.

21 Misra, *Indian Penal Code*, 10.

22 Fassin writes, "In sum, the idea that a crime, and perhaps even the worst one, calls for a punishment cannot be regarded as a general and universal truth. This assertion signifies more than the banal relativist affirmation that punishment takes distinct forms in different societies. It is a statement on what we consider to be self-evident about the necessary moral and legal link between crime and punishment, namely the principle that any violation of the rule should be punished." See Fassin, *Will to Punish*, 55.

23 I am especially drawing on insights that Talal Asad has developed in his genealogical account of agency and pain in Western philosophical discourse. See Asad, *Formations of the Secular*, 73–74.

24 Connolly's essay on the will and capital punishment that I mentioned earlier in this chapter is especially instructive here. Here Connolly discusses the "constitutive uncertainty" and anxiety about the relationship between individual will, criminal responsibility, and punishment found in the works of one of the founders of *mens rea*, Augustine; in the writings of Cesare Beccarai; and even in the works of a supporter of capital punishment like Kant. See Connolly, *Why I Am Not a Secularist*.

25 Lacey, "Responsibility and Modernity," 261.

26 Lacey, "Responsibility and Modernity," 268.

27 Lacey, "Responsibility and Modernity," 258.

28 Carceral demographics reveal the ways in which both social factors that give rise to crime as well as racial, caste, and religious prejudice affect prosecution, conviction, and punishment in these different contexts. As multiple studies show, foreign and working-class migrants are over-represented in European prisons, and Black and Latino men in American ones. See Fassin, *Will to Punish*, 30. In India, as I have discussed previously, members of lower-caste groups, LGBTQ persons, adivasis, and religious minorities are especially vulnerable to police power.

29 Lacey, "Responsibility and Modernity," 266–67.

30 See Wright, "Macaulay's Indian Penal Code," as well as the formative text on the topic, Stokes, *English Utilitarians and India*. As Stokes has argued, Macaulay was ambivalent about utilitarianism as a moral and political theory but eager to embrace its legal philosophy.

31 Mantena, *Alibis of Empire*, 91–92.

32 Singha, *Despotism of Law*.

33 Kugle, "Framed, Blamed and Renamed," 271.

34 Kugle, "Framed, Blamed and Renamed," 271–282.

35 Kugle, "Framed, Blamed and Renamed"; Singha, *Despotism of Law*, vii–ix, 1–35.

36 Singha, *Despotism of Law*, 51–82.

37 Kugle, "Framed, Blamed and Renamed," 54.

38 See Gandee and Gould, "Introduction," for a recent comprehensive overview of scholarship on the two laws and the ways in which they continue to haunt the present judicial and social landscape.

39 Social antecedents and reputation also became the basis for assessing "vagrancy" and "bad livelihood" in sections of the CrPC that sanctioned detentions and granted discretion to the executive and judiciary in the interests of preventive policing. See S. Nigam, "Disciplining and Policing," 139–40. See also Piliavsky, "'Criminal Tribe' in India," and Singha, "Punished by Surveillance."

40 In the last few years, scholars such as Piliavsky, Gandee, and Gould have mounted a sharp critique of histories of the so-called criminal tribe that focused on colonial agency in their formation. In my view, the longue-durée approach that Piliavsky takes and the material she mobilizes does not take away from the productive force of the colonial interventions that for instance Sanjay Nigam has emphasized. I agree that the category was not necessarily an invention in a categorical sense of the word, but effects of its ascription in law and penal processes cannot be underestimated just as precolonial realities of groups so designated cannot be ignored.

41 Singha, "'Providential' Circumstances."

42 Singha, "Criminal Communities," 64.

43 Piliavsky, "'Criminal Tribe' in India," 326–27.

44 Piliavsky, "'Criminal Tribe' in India," 327.

45 Piliavsky, "'Criminal Tribe' in India," 327.

46 The research magazine *Article 14* has carried a series of reports by lawyers and legal researchers on the everyday impact of these acts on marginal groups in present-day India. See, for example, Nikita Sona-

vane and Ameya Bokil, "How Poverty-Struck Tribals Become 'Habitual Offenders,'" May 28, 2020, https://www.article-14.com/post/born -a-criminal-how-poverty-struck-tribals-become-habitual-offenders; Ameya Bokil and Nikita Sonavane, "Why Charan Singh Bolts His House from Inside and Out," May 29, 2020, https://www.article-14.com /post/why-charan-singh-bolts-his-house-from-inside-and-out-before -he-sleeps. See also Sarah Gandee, "Why India's Persecuted Tribes Are Marking Their Alternative Independence Day," *The Conversation*, August 30, 2016, https://theconversation.com/why-indias-persecuted -tribes-are-marking-their-alternative-independence-day-63465.

47 See two incisive pieces by the legal historian Anandaroop Sen in South African news magazines: "India: The Conspiracy of Law," *Mail and Guardian*, August 14, 2020, https://thoughtleader.co.za/anandaroopsen /2020/08/14/the-conspiracy-of-law; "Compliance and Complicity: The Role of India's Judiciary in the Advancement of 'Democratic Totalitarianism,'" *Daily Maverick*, October 25, 2020, https://www.dailymaverick .co.za/article/2020-10-25-compliance-and-complicity-the-role-of-in dias-judiciary-in-the-advancement-of-democratic-totalitarianism. See also Suresh, "Slow Erosion of Fundamental Rights."

48 These charges were particularly filed against Arun Fereira, Sagar Gorkhe, and Ramesh Gaichor, who are among the sixteen lawyers, academics, and activists arrested for what has come to be known as the Bhima Koregaon case. See the following news reports on the reasonings offered for charging them: Charul Shah, "Bhima Koregaon Case: Arrested Accused Wanted to Mobilise Youth through Photo Exhibitions on Mob Lynchings," *Hindustan Times*, October 25, 2020, https://www .hindustantimes.com/mumbai-news/bhima-koregaon-case-arrested -accused-wanted-to-mobilise-youth-through-photo-exhibitions-on -mob-lynchings/story-TFdW59jap6BmT7PXoCvNhI.html; Sukanya Shantha, "NIA Cites Kabir Kala Manch's Songs That Parody Modi, BJP to Justify Arrest of Singers," The Wire, December 14, 2020, https:// thewire.in/rights/nia-kabir-kala-mach-song-parody-modi-bjp-sagar -gorkhe-ramesh-gaichor-arrest. For a comprehensive description of the case, see Apoorva Mandhani, "2 Years, 3 Charge Sheets and 16 Arrests— Why Bhima Koregaon Accused Are Still in Jail," *The Print*, October 31, 2020, https://theprint.in/india/2-years-3-charge-sheets-16-arrests-why -bhima-koregaon-accused-are-still-in-jail/533945/.

49 The Bombay High Court allowed Varavara Rao, arrested in August 2018, to be granted bail on March 1, 2021, due to grave ill health. Previous bail applications had been denied. See "Bhima Koregaon Case: Varavara Rao Granted Bail on Medical Grounds for Six Months," *Mumbai Mirror*, February 22, 2021, https://mumbaimirror.indiatimes.com/mumbai/other /bhima-koregaon-case-varavara-rao-granted-bail-on-medical-grounds

-for-six-months/articleshow/81148069.cms; "Stan Swamy: India Outrage over Death of Jailed Activist," BBC News, July 7, 2021, https://www
.bbc.com/news/world-asia-india-57718361. Father Stan Swamy was
arrested on similar grounds as Varavara Rao. Haider and Fatima were
arrested in April 2020 along with other student activists; Khalid was arrested in May 2020. They remain in prison without trial as I write this
in March 2022. For brief profiles of these and other activists arrested
between 2018 and 2020, see Ismat Ara and Sukanya Shantha, "A List of
Activists, Scholars and Scribes Whose Personal Liberty Remains at Judiciary's Mercy," The Wire, November 13, 2020, https://thewire.in/rights
/jail-bail-hearings-court-delhi-riots-elgar-parishad.

50 Pheroze L. Vincent, "Elgaar Case: Pegasus Exposé Raises Unjust Detention Cry," The Telegraph, July 20, 2021, https://www.telegraphindia.com
/india/2017-elgaar-parishad-case-leaked-pegasus-database-raise-unjust
-imprisonment-cry/cid/1823153; Andy Greenberg, "Police Linked to
Hacking Campaign to Frame Indian Activists," Wired, June 16, 2022,
https://www.wired.com/story/modified-elephant-planted-evidence
-hacking-police/.

51 See chapter 4.

52 My research assistant and I found some of the starkest examples of
English-language journalistic accounts that pathologized workers of
the two groups in the Express News Service archives among their own
publications. A 1998 article described party workers of the two groups
as forging "Frankenstein like gangs": see Express News Service, "And
Now an 'LTTE' to Fight RSS," November 5, 1998. The same news service
described the workers as "bloodhounds" ("Forced to Accept Samurai
Culture," n.d.) and "blood thirsty hit squads" (K. A. Antony, "Hit
Squads Target Kannur Campuses," New Indian Express, October 25,
1999). When these events were not represented through the alleged
actions of the nameless "hounds," readers and viewers were positioned
as voyeurs who were taken on a tour of North Kerala, "the land of widows."
See Leela Menon, "Women and Children—The Ultimate Victims of
Kannur Violence," New Indian Express, December 9, 1999. The reference
to Kerala's achievements in the field of literacy was made repeatedly in
these reports to contrast its educational achievements with the terrible
violence that Kannur has witnessed. See for instance K. M. Tampi, "A
Bleeding District in Kerala," The Hindu, December 9, 1999.

53 In the course of my research I came across rumors about the hardened
and cruel character of several members of the party left and the Hindu
right. These rumors contained allusions to conspiracies to attack and
murder workers of the opposing group, as well as descriptions of actual
acts of physical violence and dismemberment. Drawing on analytical
categories that Veena Das has mobilized in her writings about rumors in

the time of grave violence, I suggest that the anecdotes about CPI (M) and RSS-BJP workers that have circulated in Kannur (particularly in periods of intensified attacks and counterattacks such as the late 1990s and early 2000s) carried a perlocutionary force that (in the minds of many) transformed these men into heinous individuals. They became embodiments of anxieties and reprehensions that circulated among sympathizers of both groups and the public at large. To paraphrase Das, fears projected on these persons also made them appear as fearful. I got to know some workers of the two groups so feared. In order to maintain anonymity, I do not mention their names here. However, from my conversations with these workers about the rumors that circulated about them, I gathered how they grasped the perlocutionary force of these accounts. More than once they alerted me to the ways in which the rumors about them set them up as deserving candidates for retribution and vengeful punishment. See Das, "Specificities"; Austin, *How to Do Things with Words*.

54 Legislations such as the Kerala Anti-Social Activities (Prevention) Act 2007 (KAAPA) take recourse to previous convictions and charge-sheets filed to determine habituality to crime and describe a "known goonda" or a "known rowdy." Middle-class residents of Kannur, members of the media, and police personnel often describe the CPI (M) and RSS-BJP workers who appear in these pages as "anti-socials" or "goondas." While I have been unable to learn exactly how many local-level political workers have been detained over the years in Kannur for preemptive purposes, anecdotal evidence as well as various official accounts sketch several aspects of the practice. The former police commissioner Alexander Jacob's report on the violence between the two groups and the "riot plan" he outlines there gives us some sense of the role that preemptive detention has played in policing of political violence in Kannur. Copies of official communiques (for instance, between the police superintendent and divisional magistrate and between the divisional magistrate and the public prosecutor's office) contained in Jacob's report acquaint us with the anxious measures that these authorities tried to put in place in the wake of attacks and counterattacks between CPI (M) and RSS-BJP workers over the years. Recorded here is the official call to undertake large-scale preventive arrests as well as advice on legal arguments and clauses that might be evoked to deny bail to the people arrested and charged under section 151 of the CrPC. See Note 849 Ref. ___/81 from Sub Divisional Magistrate to Government Pleader cited in Jacob, *Study of the Riots*. Detention orders that mobilize the 2007 KAAPA act also allow us to glimpse the forms of judicial reasoning and preemptive incarceration practices that it has made possible in Kannur. For instance, an order of detention passed against a BJP worker in 2009 in Kannur evoked the provisions of this act, listed the three grievous attacks

against CPI (M) members he had been charged with, and described him as a "hard core criminal" and a "known rowdy" who if allowed to "remain at large" was likely to "indulge in antisocial activities . . . which would directly or indirectly cause harm, danger and a feeling of insecurity or cause harm to the general public." On these bases, the magistrate ordered six months' detention for the twenty-year-old BJP worker (Preventive Detention Order No. SS1 2009/16339/13).

55 I believe that the 1980 Constitution Bench judgment, established to determine the constitutional validity of capital punishment, played an influential role in activating an aesthetic benchmark to distinguish those who deserve capital punishment. It helped to distinguish those "rarest of rare," "bestial" individuals who deserve capital punishment from those whose humanness was evident. See Law Commission of India, *Thirty-Fifth Report*. See also Saikumar, "'To Shock the Conscience.'"

56 Sudha Bharadwaj was granted bail in December 2021 after three years in prison and previous failed attempts to obtain bail. See Soutik Biswas, "Sudha Bharadwaj: The Prison Life of India's Best-Known Woman Activist," BBC News, January 11, 2022, https://www.bbc.com/news/world-asia-india-59933451. On November 18, 2022, Gautam Navlakha's prison term was converted to house arrest, and Anand Teltumbe received bail on November 25, 2022, after thirty-one months in prison.

57 I am drawing on Connolly's reflections on what he calls, following Nietzsche, "visceral modes of appraisal." See Connolly, *Why I Am Not a Secularist*, 26–27.

58 See chapter 2.

Conclusion

1 Rajmohan Gandhi, "India Divided: An Imperialist Spirit within a Nation State," *Daily Maverick*, January 11, 2021, https://www.dailymaverick.co.za/article/2021-01-11-india-divided-an-imperialist-spirit-within-a-nation-state/.

2 Sriram Lakshman, "India Should Be a 'Country of Particular Concern' for Religious Freedom: U.S. Commission," *The Hindu*, April 22, 2021, https://www.thehindu.com/news/international/india-should-be-a-country-of-particular-concern-for-religious-freedom-us-commission/article34379418.ece.

3 Pratap Bhanu Mehta, "The Real Darkness on Horizon Is the Turn Indian Democracy Is Taking," *Indian Express*, January 30, 2021, https://indianexpress.com/article/opinion/columns/farmers-protest-republic-day-agriculture-bill-7167055/.

4 Mukul Kesavan, "False Citizens: What Does a Nation Do with a Minority That It Cannot Purge?," *The Telegraph*, April 28, 2019, https://www.telegraphindia.com/opinion/false-citizens-what-does-a-nation-do-with-a-minority-that-it-cannot-purge-the-case-of-rohingyas-uighurs-and-indian-muslims/cid/1689523; Rana Ayyub, "India's Degraded and Downgraded Democracy," *Washington Post*, March 11, 2021, https://www.washingtonpost.com/opinions/2021/03/11/india-democracy-freedom-house-narendra-modi-rana-ayyub/; Daniela Bezzi, "Arundhati Roy: Indian Muslims Facing 'Genocidal Climate' amid Pandemic," OpenDemocracy, June 11, 2020, https://www.opendemocracy.net/en/arundhati-roy-indian-muslims-facing-genocidal-climate-amid-pandemic/.

5 See the introduction to this book.

6 "Jair Bolsonaro: Far-Right Candidate Wins Brazil Poll," BBC News, October 29, 2018, https://www.bbc.com/news/world-latin-america-46013408; Umut Uras, "Erdogan Wins Re-Election in Historic Turkish Polls," *Al Jazeera*, June 25, 2018, https://www.aljazeera.com/news/2018/6/25/erdogan-wins-re-election-in-historic-turkish-polls.

7 Devji, *Muslim Zion*, 53.

8 Cited in Devji, *Muslim Zion*, 53.

9 Ambedkar, *States and Minorities*.

10 Ambedkar, *States and Minorities*.

11 Skaria, "Relinquishing Republican Democracy," 204–6.

Bibliography

Published Primary Sources

All India Reporter. 1914–. Nagpur: All India Reporter.

Communist Party of India. "Statement of Policy of the Communist Party of India 1951." In *Documents of the History of the Communist Party of India,* vol. 8, *1951–1956,* edited by Mohit Sen, 42–54. New Delhi: People's Publishing House, 1977. https://www.revolutionarydemocracy.org/archive/1951policy.htm.

Deshabhimani Collections. 1978–2002. Accessed at A. K. Gopalan Center for Research and Studies, Thiruvananthapuram.

Express News Service Collections. 1978–2002. Accessed at Indian Express, Kochi.

Jacob, Alexander. *The RSS-CPM Clashes (1979–1982): The History and Post-Mortem Operation.* Accessed at the Police Training College Library, Thiruvananthapuram.

Jacob, Alexander. *A Study of the Riots of the Tellicherry.* Kannur: Presented to the Police Training College Library, Trivandrum, 1989.

Law Commission of India. *Thirty-Fifth Report (Capital Punishment).* Delhi: Government of India, Ministry of Law, 1967.

Mathrubhumi. Kannur edition, select news reports, 1978–2010. Personal files.

Court Documents and Judgments

Criminal Appeal 1280 and 1281 of 2005, Supreme Court of India.

Death Sentence Reference no. 1 of 2005, Supreme Court of India.

Preventive Detention Order No. SS1 2009/16339/13.

Sessions Case 4 of 1981, Kannur District Sessions Court.

Sessions Case 20 of 1981, Kannur District Sessions Court.

Sessions Case 22 of 1999, Kannur District Sessions Court.

Sessions Case 26 of 1981, Kannur District Sessions Court.

Sessions Case 34 of 1982, Kannur District Sessions Court.

Sessions Case 60 of 1981, Kannur District Sessions Court.

Sessions Case 65 of 1981, Kannur District Sessions Court.

Sessions Case 90 of 1993, Kannur District Sessions Court.

Sessions Case 111 of 1995, Kannur District Sessions Court.

Sessions Case 125 of 1997, Kannur District Sessions Court.

Sessions Case 146 of 2001, Kannur District Sessions Court.

Sessions Case 151 of 1997, Kannur District Sessions Court.

Sessions Case 252 of 2001, Kannur District Sessions Court.

Sessions Case 807 of 1950, *All-India Reporter*.

Sessions Case 898 of 1980, *All-India Reporter*.

Sessions Court Judgments 1978–2003. Accessed at Kannur District Sessions Court Records Room and the Prosecutors Office, Kannur District Sessions Court.

Secondary Sources

Abraham, Janaki. "'Matriliny Did Not Become Patriliny!' The Transformation of Thiyya 'Tharavad' Houses in 20th-Century Kerala." *Contributions to Indian Sociology* 51, no. 3 (October 2017): 287–312. https://doi.org/10.1177/0069966717720514.

Abraham, Janaki. "'Why Did You Send Me Like This?' Marriage, Matriliny and the 'Providing Husband' in North Kerala, India." *Asian Journal of Women's Studies* 17, no. 2 (2011): 32–65. https://doi.org/10.1080/12259276.2011.

Ahmad, Ejaz, and Mohammad Shafi Ansari. *Law Relating to Burden of Proof.* Jodhpur: Rajasthan Law House, 1986.

Ahmed, Hilal. "Muzaffarnagar 2013: Meanings of Violence." *Economic and Political Weekly* 48, no. 40 (2013): 10–13. http://www.jstor.org/stable/23528396.

Ajayan, T. A. "Dismissal of the First Communist Ministry in Kerala and the Role of Extraneous Agencies." *The South Asianist Journal* 5, no. 1 (2017): 282–303. http://www.southasianist.ed.ac.uk/article/view/1652.

Ake, Claude. *The Feasibility of Democracy in Africa.* Dakar, Senegal: Council for the Development of Social Science Research in Africa, 2000.

Alam, Javed. "Communist Politics in Search of Hegemony." In *Wages of Freedom: Fifty Years of the Indian State*, edited by Partha Chatterjee, 179–206. Delhi: Oxford University Press, 1998.

Ambedkar, B. R. *States and Minorities: What Are Their Rights and How to Secure Them in the Constitution of Free India.* Chennai: Maven Books, 2018.

Amnesty International India. *Justice under Trial: A Study of Pre-trial Detention in India.* Karnataka: Amnesty International India, 2017. https://www.amnesty.nl/content/uploads/2017/07/UT_Final.pdf?x79902.

Andersen, Walter K., and Shridhar D. Damle. *The Brotherhood in Saffron: The Rashtriya Swayamsevak Sangh and Hindu Revivalism.* Boulder, CO: Westview Press, 1987.

Anderson, Edward, and Arkotong Longkumer, eds. *Neo-Hindutva: Evolving Forms, Spaces, and Expressions of Hindu Nationalism.* London: Routledge, 2020.

Ankit, Rakesh. "Marxist Guru, Socialist *Neta*, Buddhist *Acharya*, Gandhi's *Shishya*: The Many Narendra Deva(s) (1889–1956)." *Global Intellectual History* 2, no. 3 (2017): 350–69. https://doi.org/10.1080/23801883.2017.1370241.

Ansari, Khalid Anis. "Pluralism and the Post-Minority Condition: Reflections on the 'Pasmanda Muslim' Discourse in North India." In *The Pluriverse of Human Rights: The Diversity of Struggles for Dignity*, edited by Boaventura de Sousa Santos and Bruno Sena Martins, 106–27. New York: Routledge, 2021.

Appadurai, Arjun. *Fear of Small Numbers: An Essay on the Geography of Anger.* Durham, NC: Duke University Press, 2006.

Arafath, P. K. Yasser. "The Nadapuram Enigma: A History of Violence and Communalism in North Malabar (1957–2015)." *Economic and Political Weekly* 51, no. 15 (2016): 47–55.

Arafath, P. K. Yasser. "Southern Hindutva: Rhetoric, Parivar Kinship and Performative Politics in Kerala, 1925–2015." *Economic and Political Weekly* 56, no. 2 (2021): 51–60. https://www.epw.in/journal/2021/2/special-articles/southern-hindutva.html.

Arendt, Hannah. *Crises of the Republic.* New York: Harcourt Brace Jovanovich, 1972.

Arendt, Hannah. *The Human Condition.* Chicago: University of Chicago Press, 1958.

Arias, Enrique D., and Daniel M. Goldstein, eds. *Violent Democracies in Latin America.* Durham, NC: Duke University Press, 2010.

Arunima, G. "Friends and Lovers: Towards a Social History of Emotions in 19th and 20th Century Kerala." In *Women of India: Colonial and Post-Colonial Periods*, edited by Bharati Ray, 139–58. New Delhi: Sage, 2005.

Arunima, G. "Glimpses from a Writer's World: O. Chandu Menon, His Contemporaries, and Their Times." *Studies in History* 20, no. 2 (2004): 189–214. https://doi.org/10.1177/025764300402000202.

Arunima, G. "Multiple Meanings: Changing Conceptions of Matrilineal Kinship in Nineteenth and Twentieth Century Malabar." *Indian Economic and Social History Review* 33, no. 3 (September 1996): 283–307. https://doi.org/10.1177/001946469603300303.

Asad, Talal. *Formations of the Secular: Christianity, Islam, Modernity.* Stanford, CA: Stanford University Press, 2003.

Austin, J. L. *How to Do Things with Words.* Edited by J. O. Urmson and M. Sbisa. Cambridge, MA: Harvard University Press, 1975.

Austin, J. L. *Philosophical Papers*. Oxford: Oxford University Press, 1979.

Awaya, Toshie. "Some Aspects of the Thiyyas' Caste Movement." In *Caste System, Untouchability and the Depressed*, edited by Kotani Hiroyuki, 139–66. New Delhi: Manohar, 1998.

Bacchetta, P. *Gender in the Hindu Nation: RSS Women as Ideologues*. New Delhi: Women Unlimited, 2004.

Balibar, Etienne. *Masses, Classes, Ideas: Studies on Politics and Philosophy before and after Marx*. Translated by James Swenson. New York: Routledge, 1994.

Banerjee, Prathama. *Elementary Aspects of the Political: Histories from the Global South*. Durham, NC: Duke University Press, 2020.

Banerjee, Prathama, Aditya Nigam, and Rakesh Pandey. "The Work of Theory: Thinking across Traditions." *Economic and Political Weekly* 51, no. 37 (2016): 42–50. http://www.jstor.org/stable/44003709.

Banerjee, Sumanta. *In the Wake of Naxalbari: A History of the Naxalite Movement in India*. Calcutta: Subarnarekha, 1980.

Basu, Amrita. *Violent Conjunctures in Democratic India*. New York: Cambridge University Press, 2015.

Basu, Amrita, and Srirupa Roy, eds. *Violence and Democracy in India*. Calcutta: Seagull Books, 2007.

Basu, Tapan, Pradip Datta, Tanika Sarkar, Sumit Sarkar, and Sambuddha Sen. *Khaki Shorts and Saffron Flags: A Critique of the Hindu Right*. New Delhi: Orient Longman, 1993.

Bataille, Georges. *The Accursed Share*. Vols. 2 and 3, *The History of Eroticism and Sovereignty*. New York: Zone Books, 1991.

Bateson, Gregory. "Culture Contact and Schismogenesis." *Man* 35 (1935): 178–83. https://doi.org/10.2307/2789408.

Bateson, Gregory. *Naven: A Survey of the Problems Suggested by a Composite Picture of the Culture of a New Guinea Tribe Drawn from Three Points of View*. Palo Alto, CA: Stanford University Press, 1936.

Bateson, Gregory. *Steps to an Ecology of Mind: Collected Essays in Anthropology, Psychology, Evolution and Epistemology*. San Francisco: Chandler Publishing, 1972.

Baxi, Pratiksha. *Public Secrets of Law: Rape Trials in India*. New Delhi: Oxford University Press, 2014.

Baxi, Upendra. *The Crisis of the Indian Legal System*. New Delhi: Vikas, 1982.

Bayart, Jean-François. *The State in Africa: The Politics of the Belly*. 2nd ed. London: Longman, 1993.

Bhattacharjee, Malini. *Disaster Relief and the RSS: Resurrecting "Religion" through Humanitarianism*. New Delhi: Sage, 2019.

Bhattacharya, Dwaipayan. "'Civic Community' and Its Margins: School Teachers in Rural West Bengal." *Economic and Political Weekly* 36, no. 8 (2001): 673–83. https://www.jstor.org/stable/4410324.

Bhattacharya, S. "The Colonial State and the Communist Party of India, 1942–45: A Reappraisal." *South Asia Research* 15, no. 1 (1995): 48–77. https://doi.org/10.1177/026272809501500103.

Bidwai, Praful. "Muslims, The New Underclass." The Transnational Institute, November 15, 2006. https://www.tni.org/my/node/8559.

Biju, M. R. "Local Body Polls 2010 in Kerala: UDF Smashes LDF Fortresses." *Mainstream Weekly* 48, no. 48 (November 2010): 1–15.

Bokil, Ameya, and Nikita Sonavane. "Why Charan Singh Bolts His House from Inside and Out." *Article 14*, May 29, 2020. https://www.article-14.com/post/why-charan-singh-bolts-his-house-from-inside-and-out-before-he-sleeps.

Bose, Satheese Chandra, and Shiju Sam Varughese, eds. *Kerala Modernity: Ideas, Spaces and Practices in Transition.* New Delhi: Orient Blackswan, 2015.

Bourdieu, Pierre. "The Force of Law: Toward a Sociology of the Juridical Field." *Hastings Law Journal*, no. 38 (1987): 814–53.

Bourke, Richard. "Modern Massacres." *The Political Quarterly* 78, no. 1 (2007): 182–85.

Boutros-Ghali, Boutros. "Democracy: A Newly Recognized Imperative." *Global Governance* 1, no. 1 (Winter 1995): 3–11. http://www.jstor.org/stable/27800098.

Brass, Paul R. *Forms of Collective Violence: Riots, Pogroms and Genocide in Modern India.* New Delhi: Three Essays Collective, 2006.

Brass, Paul R. *The Production of Hindu-Muslim Violence in Contemporary India.* Seattle: University of Washington Press, 2003.

Breen, Keith. "Agonism, Antagonism and the Necessity of Care." In *Law and Agonistic Politics*, edited by Andrew Schaap, 133–46. London: Ashgate, 2009.

Chakraborty, Chandrima. *Masculinity, Asceticism, Hinduism: Past and Present Imaginings of India.* Ranikhet: Permanent Black, 2011.

Chandra, Bipan. *In the Name of Democracy: JP Movement and the Emergency.* New Delhi: Penguin Books, 2003.

Chandra, Sudhir. "Of Communal Consciousness and Communal Violence: Impressions from Post-Riot Surat." *South Asia: Journal of South Asian Studies*, no. 17 (1994): 49–61. https://doi.org/10.1080/00856409408723215.

Chatterjee, Moyukh. "Against the Witness: Hindu Nationalism and the Law in India." *Law, Culture and the Humanities* 15, no. 1 (2019): 172–89. https://doi.org/10.1177/1743872116643693.

Chatterjee, Moyukh. "Bandh Politics: Crowds, Spectacular Violence, and Sovereignty in India." *Distinktion: Journal of Social Theory* 17, no. 3 (2016): 294–307. https://doi.org/10.1080/1600910X.2016.1258586.

Chatterjee, Moyukh. "The Impunity Effect: Majoritarian Rule, Everyday Legality, and State Formation in India." *American Ethnologist* 44 (2017): 118–30. https://doi.org/10.1111/amet.12430.

Chatterjee, Partha. *I Am the People: Reflections on Popular Sovereignty Today.* New York: Columbia University Press, 2020.

Chatterjee, Partha. *Lineages of Political Society: Studies in Postcolonial Democracy.* New York: Columbia University Press, 2011.

Chatterjee, Partha. *Politics of the Governed: Reflections on Popular Politics in Most of the World.* New York: Columbia University Press, 2004.

Chatterji, Joya. *Bengal Divided: Hindu Communalism and Partition, 1932–1947.* Cambridge: Cambridge University Press, 1995.

Chaturvedi, Ruchi. "Down by Law: Violence and the Work of Politics in Kerala, South India." PhD diss., University of Columbia, 2007.

Chaturvedi, Ruchi. "Political Violence, Community and Its Limits in Kannur, Kerala." *Contributions to Indian Sociology* 49, no. 2 (2015): 162–87.

Chaturvedi, Ruchi. "Political Violence, Criminal Law and Shifting Scales of Justice." In *The Tumultuous Politics of Scale: Unsettled States, Migrants, Movements in Flux,* edited by Don Nonini and Ida Susser, 69–92. New York: Routledge, 2020.

Chaturvedi, Ruchi. "Somehow It Happened: Violence, Culpability and the Hindu Nationalist Community." *Cultural Anthropology* 26, no. 3 (2011): 340–62.

Chiriyankandath, James. "Bounded Nationalism: Kerala and the Social and Regional Limits of Hindutva." In *The BJP and the Compulsions of Politics,* edited by Thomas Blom Hansen and Christoph Jaffrelot, 202–27. Delhi: Oxford University Press, 1998.

Chiriyankandath, James. "Changing Muslim Politics in Kerala: Identity, Interests and Political Strategies." *Journal of Muslim Minority Affairs* 16, no. 2 (1996): 257–71. https://doi.org/10.1080/13602009608716342.

Chiriyankandath, James. "The Kerala Election: A Shift to the Left—and a Move to the Right." *London School of Economics blogs,* May 26, 2016. http://eprints .lse.ac.uk/74736/.

Colaguori, Claudio. *Agon Culture: Competition, Conflict and the Problem of Domination.* Whitby, ON: de Sitter Publications, 2012.

Connolly, William. "Beyond Good and Evil: The Ethical Sensibility of Michel Foucault." *Political Theory* 21, no. 3 (1993): 365–89. https://doi.org/10.1177 /0090591793021030.

Connolly, William. *The Ethos of Pluralization.* Minneapolis: University of Minnesota Press, 1995.

Connolly, William. *Pluralism.* Durham, NC: Duke University Press, 2005.

Connolly, William. "Response: Realizing Agonistic Respect." *American Academy of Religion* 72, no. 2 (2004): 507–11. https://www.jstor.org/stable/40005815.

Connolly, William. *Why I Am Not a Secularist.* Minneapolis: University of Minnesota Press, 1999.

Damodaran, K. "Memoir of an Indian Communist." *New Left Review* 1, no. 93 (September–October 1975): 35–58.

Das, Veena. "Specificities: Official Narratives, Rumour, and the Social Production of Hate." *Social Identities* 4, no. 1 (1998): 109–30. https://doi.org/10 .1080/13504639851915.

Dasan, M. *Theyyam: Patronage, Appropriation and Interpolation.* Kannur: Kannur University, 2012.

Desai, Manali. "Indirect British Rule, State Formation, and Welfarism in Kerala, India, 1860–1957." *Social Science History* 29, no. 3 (2005): 457–88. doi:10.1215/01455532-29-3-457.

Desai, Manali. "The Relative Autonomy of Party Practices: A Counterfactual Analysis of Left Party Ascendancy in Kerala, India, 1934–1940." *American Journal of Sociology* 108, no. 3 (2002): 616–57. https://doi.org/10.1086/367919.

Deshpande, Satish. "Hegemonic Spatial Strategies: The Nation-Space and Hindu Communalism in Twentieth-Century India." *Public Culture* 10, no. 2 (1998): 249–83. https://doi.org/10.1215/08992363-10-2-249.

Devika, Jayakumari. "Contemporary Dalit Assertions in Kerala: Governmental Categories vs. Identity Politics." *History and Sociology of South Asia* 7, no. 1 (2013): 1–17. https://doi.org/10.1177/2230807512459400.

Devika, Jayakumari. "Egalitarian Developmentalism, Communist Mobilization, and the Question of Caste in Kerala State, India." *Journal of Asian Studies* 69, no. 3 (2010): 799–820. https://www.jstor.org/stable/40929193.

Devika, Jayakumari. "Imagining Women's Social Space in Early Modern Keralam." CDS Working Paper 329, Centre for Development Studies, Trivandrum, 2002. https://opendocs.ids.ac.uk/opendocs/handle/20.500.12413/2932.

Devika, Jayakumari. "Participatory Democracy or 'Transformative Appropriation'? The People's Planning Campaign in Kerala." *History and Sociology of South Asia* 10, no. 2 (2016): 115–37.

Devika, Jayakumari. "A People United in Development: Developmentalism in Modern Malayalee Identity." CDS Working Paper 386, Centre for Development Studies, Trivandrum, 2007. https://opendocs.ids.ac.uk/opendocs/handle/20.500.12413/3111.

Devika, Jayakumari, and Praveena Kodoth. "Sexual Violence and the Predicament of Feminist Politics in Kerala." *Economic and Political Weekly* 36, no. 33 (2001): 3170–77. https://www.jstor.org/stable/4410999.

Devika, Jayakumari, and Binitha V. Thampi. "Beyond Feminine Public Altruism: Women Leaders in Kerala's Urban Bodies." *Economic and Political Weekly* 47, no. 17 (2012): 76–83. http://www.jstor.org/stable/23214844.

Devika, Jayakumari, and Binitha V. Thampi. "Mobility towards Work and Politics for Women in Kerala State, India: A View from the Histories of Gender and Space." *Modern Asian Studies* 45, no. 5 (September 2011): 1147–75. doi:10.1017/S0026749X09000080.

Devji, Faisal. *Muslim Zion: Pakistan as a Political Idea*. London: Hurst and Company, 2013.

de Vries, Jan. "Playing with Scales: The Global and the Micro, the Macro and the Nano." *Past and Present* 242, no. 14 (November 2019): 23–36. https://doi.org/10.1093/pastj/gtz043.

Dhanagare, D. N. "Social Origins of the Peasant Insurrection in Telangana (1946–51)." *Contributions to Indian Sociology* 8, no. 1 (1974): 109–34. https://doi.org/10.1177/006996677400800107.

Dunn, John. *Democracy: A History*. Toronto: Penguin, 2006.

Duschinski, Haley. "Reproducing Regimes of Impunity." *Cultural Studies* 24, no. 1 (2010): 110–32. doi:10.1080/09502380903221117.

Fassin, Didier. *The Will to Punish: The Berkeley Tanner Lectures*. Edited by Christopher Kutz. New York: Oxford University Press, 2018.

Feldman, Allen. *Formations of Violence: The Narrative of the Body and Political Terror in Northern Ireland*. Chicago: University of Chicago Press, 1991.

Foucault, Michel. "Nietzsche, Genealogy, History." In *The Foucault Reader*, edited by Paul Rabinow, 76–100. London: Penguin, 1986.

Foucault, Michel. "The Political Function of the Intellectual." *Radical Philosophy* (Summer 1977): 12–14.

Foucault, Michel. *Security, Territory, Population: Lectures at the Collège de France 1977–78*. Translated by Graham Burchell. New York: Picador, 2009.

Foucault, Michel. *Society Must Be Defended: Lectures at the Collège de France, 1975–1976*. Translated by David Macy. New York: Picador, 2003.

Foucault, Michel. "The Subject and Power." *Critical Inquiry* 8, no. 4 (1982): 777–95. https://www.jstor.org/stable/1343197.

Franke, Richard W., and Barbara H. Chasin. *Kerala: Radical Reform as Development in an Indian State*. San Francisco: Institute for Food and Development Policy, 1989.

Franke, Richard W., Barbara H. Chasin, Maria Helena Moreira Alves, Samir Amin, Prabhat Patnaik, and Carlos M. Vilas. "Kerala State, India: Radical Reform as Development." *Monthly Review*, January 1991. Gale Academic OneFile, accessed January 5, 2023. https://link.gale.com/apps/doc/A9334180/AONE?u=anon~945dd6ff&sid=googleScholar&xid=369a53e2.

Freitag, Sandria B. *Collective Action and Community: Public Arenas and the Emergence of Communalism in North India*. Berkeley: University of California Press, 1989.

Fukuyama, Francis. "The End of History?" *The National Interest*, no. 16 (1989): 3–18. https://www.jstor.org/stable/24027184.

Gandee, Sarah, and William Gould. "Introduction: Margins and the State—Caste, 'Tribe' and Criminality in South Asia." *Studies in History* 36, no. 1 (2020): 7–19. doi:10.1177/0257643020907318.

Gandhi, Leela. *Affective Communities: Anticolonial Thought, Fin de Siècle Radicalism and the Politics of Friendship*. Durham, NC: Duke University Press, 2006.

Gandhi, Mohandas Karamchand. *Hind Swaraj and Other Writings*. Edited by Anthony J. Parel. Cambridge: Cambridge University Press, 1997.

Gandhi, Mohandas Karamchand. *Satyagraha in South Africa*. Translated by Valji Govindji Desai. Ahmedabad: Navajivan Publishing House, 1968.

Gaur, K. D. *Commentaries on the Indian Penal Code*. Delhi: Universal Law Publishing, 2013.

Geschiere, Peter, and Francis Nyamnjoh. "Capitalism and Autochthony: The Seesaw of Mobility and Belonging." *Public Culture* 12, no. 2 (2000): 423–52. https://doi.org/10.1215/08992363-12-2-423.

Ghose, Sankar. *Socialism and Communism in India*. Bombay: Allied Publishers, 1971.

Ghosh, Ajoy. "Proletarian Leadership and the Democratic Movement." *New Age Monthly*, 1954.

Gilmartin, David. "The Historiography of India's Partition: Between Civilization and Modernity." *Journal of Asian Studies* 74, no. 1 (2015): 23–41. http://www.jstor.org/stable/43553642.

Gilmartin, David. "A Magnificent Gift: Muslim Nationalism and the Election Process in Colonial Punjab." *Comparative Studies in Society and History* 40, no. 3 (1998): 415–36. doi:10.1017/S0010417598001352.

Gilmartin, David. "Pakistan, Partition, and South Asian History: In Search of a Narrative." *Journal of Asian Studies* 57, no. 4 (1998): 1068–95. https://doi.org/10.2307/2659304.

Ginzburg, Carlo. "Checking the Evidence: The Judge and the Historian." *Critical Inquiry* 18, no. 1 (1991): 79–92. https://www.jstor.org/stable/1343716.

Ginzburg, Carlo. *Clues, Myths and the Historical Method*. Translated by John and Anne C. Tedeschi. Baltimore: Johns Hopkins University Press, 1989.

Goffman, Erving. *The Presentation of Self in Everyday Life*. Garden City, NY: Doubleday, 1959.

Golwalkar, Madhav Sadashiv. *Bunch of Thoughts*. Bangalore: Vikrama Prakashan, Rashtrotthana Sahitya, 1966.

Golwalkar, Madhav Sadashiv. *Justice on Trial*. Karnataka: Rashtriya Swayamsevak Sangh, Prakashan Vibhag, 1958.

Gopalan, A. K. *In the Cause of the People*. Bombay: Orient Longman, 1979.

Gould, William. *Hindu Nationalism and the Language of Politics in Late Colonial India*. Cambridge: Cambridge University Press, 2004.

Gramsci, Antonio. *Selections from the Prison Notebooks of Antonio Gramsci*. Edited by Quentin Hoare and Geoffrey Nowell-Smith. New York: International Publishers, 1972.

Grover, Vrinda. "The Elusive Quest for Justice: Delhi 1984 to Gujarat 2002." In *Gujarat: The Making of a Tragedy*, edited by Siddharth Varadarajan, 355–87. Delhi: Penguin India, 2002.

Guha, Ranajit. *Rule of Property in Bengal: An Essay on the Idea of Permanent Settlement*. Durham, NC: Duke University Press, 1996.

Gulati, G., T. Isaac, and W. Klein. "When a Worker's Cooperative Works: The Case of Kerala Dinesh Beedi." *UCLA Law Review*, no. 49 (2002): 1417–54.

Gupta, Charu. "Masculine Vernacular Histories of Travel in Colonial India: The Writings of Satyadev 'Parivrajak.'" *South Asia: Journal of South Asian Studies* 43, no. 5 (2020): 836–59. https://doi.org/10.1080/00856401.2020.1789314.

Gupta, Dipankar. *Nativism in a Metropolis: Shiv Sena in Bombay*. Delhi: Manohar, 1982.

Hacking, Ian. *The Taming of Chance*. Cambridge: Cambridge University Press, 1990.

Hampton, Jean. "Correcting Harms versus Righting Wrongs: The Goal of Retribution." *UCLA Law Review* 39, no. 6 (1992): 1659–702.

Hampton, Jean. "Forgiveness, Resentment and Hatred." In *Forgiveness and Mercy*, edited by Jean Hampton and Jeffrie G. Murphy, 35–88. Cambridge: Cambridge University Press, 1988.

Hansen, Thomas B. "Inside the Romanticist Episteme." *Social Scientist* 25, no. 3 (1996): 59–79. https://doi.org/10.2307/3520119.

Hansen, Thomas B. "The Political Theology of Violence in Contemporary India." *South Asia Multidisciplinary Academic Journal*, no. 2 (2008): 1–15. https://doi.org/10.4000/samaj.1872.

Hansen, Thomas B. *The Saffron Wave: Democracy and Hindu Nationalism in Modern India*. Princeton, NJ: Princeton University Press, 1999.

Hansen, Thomas B. *Wages of Violence: Naming and Identity in Postcolonial Bombay*. Princeton, NJ: Princeton University Press, 2001.

Hansen, Thomas B., and Finn Stepputat, eds. *Sovereign Bodies: Citizens, Migrants, and States in the Postcolonial World*. Princeton, NJ: Princeton University Press, 2005.

Haridas, K. "Varghese Encounter Death Case." *Economic and Political Weekly* 46, no. 1 (2011): 19–21. http://www.jstor.org/stable/27917982.

Haridas, P. T. "Genesis of the Travancore State Congress." *Proceedings of the Indian History Congress* 38 (1977): 398–404. http://www.jstor.org/stable /44139095.

Hart, H. L. A. *Punishment and Responsibility: Essays in the Philosophy of Law*. Oxford: Clarendon Press, 1968.

Heller, Patrick. *The Labor of Development: Workers and the Transformation of Capitalism in Kerala, India*. Ithaca, NY: Cornell University Press, 1999.

Hill, Poly. "Kerala Is Different." *Modern Asian Studies* 20, no. 4 (1986): 779–92. https://www.jstor.org/stable/312633.

Hoenig, Patrick, and Navsharan Singh, eds. *Landscapes of Fear: Understanding Impunity in India*. New Delhi: Zubaan Books, 2014.

Hoffman, Danny, and Mohammed Tarawalley Jr. "Frontline Collaborations: The Research Relationship in Unstable Places." *Ethnography* 15, no. 3 (2014): 291–310. doi:10.1177/1466138114533463.

Holdrege, Barbara. "Dharma." In *The Hindu World*, edited by Sushil Mittal and Gene Thursby, 213–48. New York: Routledge, 2004.

Honig, Bonnie. *Political Theory and the Displacement of Politics*. Ithaca, NY: Cornell University Press, 1993.

Honig, Bonnie. "The Politics of Agonism: A Critical Response to 'Beyond Good and Evil: Arendt, Nietzsche and Aestheticization of Political Action.'" *Political Theory* 21, no. 3 (1993): 528–33. https://doi.org/10.1177 /0090591793021003010.

Honig, Bonnie. "Towards an Agonistic Feminism: Hannah Arendt and the Politics of Identity." In *Feminist Interpretations of Hannah Arendt*, edited by Bonnie Honig, 135–66. Philadelphia: University of Pennsylvania Press, 1995.

Hoopes, James, ed. *Peirce on Signs: Writings on Semiotic by Charles Sanders Peirce*. Chapel Hill: University of North Carolina Press, 1991.

Ilaiah, Kancha. "Dalitism versus Brahminism: The Epistemological Conflict in History." In *Dalit Identity and Politics: Cultural Subordination and the Dalit Challenge*, vol. 2, edited by Ghanshyam Shah, 108–28. New Delhi: Sage Publications, 2001.

Isaac, T. M. Thomas, Richard W. Franke, and Pyaralal Raghavan. *Democracy at Work in an Indian Industrial Cooperative: The Story of Kerala Dinesh Beedi*. Ithaca, NY: ILR Press, 1998.

Islam, Shamsul. *Golwalkar's We or Our Nationhood Defined: A Critique*. New Delhi: Pharos Media and Publishing, 2006.

Ismail, Qadri. *Abiding by Sri Lanka: On Peace, Place, and Postcoloniality*. Minneapolis: University of Minnesota Press, 2005.

Jaffrelot, Christophe. *The Hindu Nationalist Movement in India*. New York: Columbia University Press, 1998.

Jaffrelot, Christophe. *The Sangh Parivar: A Reader*. Delhi: Oxford University Press, 2007.

Jauregui, Beatrice. *Provisional Authority: Police, Order, and Security in India*. Chicago: University of Chicago Press, 2017.

Jayaprasad, K. *RSS and Hindu Nationalism: Inroads in a Leftist Stronghold*. New Delhi: Deep and Deep Publications, 1991.

Jayaseelan, K. A. *Parametric Studies in Malayalam Syntax*. Hyderabad: Allied Publishers, 1999.

Jeffrey, Robin. *The Decline of Nair Dominance: Society and Politics in Travancore, 1847–1908*. New Delhi: Manohar, 1994.

Jeffrey, Robin. "'Destroy Capitalism!' Growing Solidarity of Alleppey's Coir Workers, 1930–40." *Economic and Political Weekly* 19, no. 29 (1984): 1159–65.

Jeffrey, Robin. *Politics, Women and Well-Being: How Kerala Became a Model*. Hampshire, UK: Macmillan, 1992.

Jenkins, Sarah Ann. "Assistants, Guides, Collaborators, Friends: The Concealed Figures of Conflict Research." *Journal of Contemporary Ethnography* 47, no. 2 (April 2018): 143–70. https://doi.org/10.1177/0891241615619993.

Jodhka, Surinder S. "Review: Looking Back at the Khalistan Movement: Some Recent Researches on Its Rise and Decline." *Economic and Political Weekly* 36, no. 16 (April 2001): 1311–18. https://www.jstor.org/stable/4410511.

Jullien, François. *The Propensity of Things: Toward a History of Efficacy in China*. Translated by Janet Lloyd. New York: Zone Books, 1999.

Kadish, Sanford, Stephen J. Schulhofer, and Carol S. Steiker. *Criminal Law and Its Processes: Cases and Materials*. New York: Aspen Publishers, 2007.

Kalyvas, Andreas. "The Democratic Narcissus: The Agonism of the Ancients Compared to That of the (Post) Moderns." In *Law and Agonistic Politics*, edited by Andrew Schaap, 15–42. London: Ashgate, 2009.

Kannabiran, Kalpana. "The Contexts of Criminology: A Brief Restatement." In *Challenging the Rules of Law: Colonialism, Criminology and Human Rights in India*, edited by Kalpana Kannabiran and Ranbir Singh, 451–76. New Delhi: Sage, 2008.

Kannabiran, Kalpana. *The Wages of Impunity: Power, Justice and Human Rights.* New Delhi: Orient Longman, 2004.

Kant, Immanuel. *The Philosophy of Law: An Exposition of the Fundamental Principles of Jurisprudence as the Science of Right.* Edinburgh: T. T. Clark, 1887.

Kanungo, Pralay. RSS's *Tryst with Politics: From Hedgewar to Sudarshan.* New Delhi: Manohar Publishers, 2017.

Kaul, Nitasha, and Nisar Kannangara. "The Persistence of Political Power: A Communist 'Party Village' in Kerala and the Paradox of Egalitarian Hierarchies." *International Journal of Politics, Culture, and Society* (2021). https://doi.org/10.1007/s10767-021-09411-w.

Kaviraj, Sudipta. "The Culture of Representative Democracy." In *Wages of Freedom: Fifty Years of the Indian State,* edited by Partha Chatterjee, 147–78. Delhi: Oxford University Press, 1998.

Kaviraj, Sudipta. "Democracy and Social Inequality." In *Transforming India: Social and Political Dynamics of Democracy,* edited by Francine R. Frankel, Zoya Hasan, Rajeev Bhargava, and Balveer Arora, 89–119. New Delhi: Oxford University Press, 2000.

Kaviraj, Sudipta. *Enchantment of Democracy and India: Politics and Ideas.* Ranikhet: Permanent Black in Association with Ashoka University, 2018.

Kaviraj, Sudipta. *The Imaginary Institution of India: Politics and Ideas.* New York: Columbia University Press, 2010.

Keane, John. "Epilogue: Does Democracy Have a Violent Heart?" In *War, Democracy and Culture in Classical Athens,* edited by David Pritchard, 378–408. Cambridge: Cambridge University Press, 2010.

Keane, John. *Violence and Democracy.* Cambridge: Cambridge University Press, 2004.

Kolsky, Elizabeth. "Codification and the Rule of Colonial Difference: Criminal Procedure in British India." *Law and History Review* 23, no. 3 (2005): 631–83. doi:10.1017/S0738248000000596.

Kugle, Scott Alan. "Framed, Blamed and Renamed: The Recasting of Islamic Jurisprudence in Colonial South Asia." *Modern Asian Studies* 35, no. 2 (2001): 257–313. https://www.jstor.org/stable/313119.

Kumar, Dharma. "Caste and Landlessness in South India." *Comparative Studies in Society and History* 4, no. 3 (1962): 337–63. http://www.jstor.org/stable/177526.

Kumar, Udaya. "Autobiography as a Way of Writing History: Personal Narratives from Kerala and the Inhabitation of Modernity." In *History in the Vernacular,* edited by Raziuddin Aquil and Partha Chatterjee. Delhi: Permanent Black, 2012. Kindle edition.

Kuriakose, Mathew, and Mythri Prasad-Aleyamma. "Turning Minorities against Each Other: Leftist Hindu Politics in Kerala." Counter Currents, February 2, 2021. https://countercurrents.org/2021/02/turning-minorities-against-each-other-leftist-hindu-politics-in-kerala/.

Kurup, K. K. N. *The Kayyur Riot: A Terrorist Episode in the Nationalist Movement in Kerala.* Cannanore: Sandhya Publications, 1978.

Kurup, K. K. N. *Peasantry, Nationalism, and Social Change in India*. Allahabad: Chugh Publications, 1991.

Kurup, P. R. *Ente Nadinte Katha, Enteyum* [Story of my village and me]. Kottayam, Kerala: Sahithya Pravarthaka Cooperative Society, 1985. Reprinted in 2015.

Lacey, Nicola. "Responsibility and Modernity in Criminal Law." *Journal of Political Philosophy* 9, no. 3 (2001): 249–76. https://doi.org/10.1111/1467-9760.00127.

Laclau, Ernesto. *On Populist Reason*. New York: Verso, 2005.

Lefort, Claude. *Democracy and Political Theory*. Translated by David Macey. Minneapolis: University of Minnesota Press, 1988.

Legassick, Martin, and Gary Minkley. "'Not Telling': Secrecy, Lies and History." *History and Theory* 39, no. 4 (2000): 1–10. https://www.jstor.org/stable/2678046.

Leiten, Georges Kristoffel. "Education, Ideology and Politics in Kerala 1957–59." *Social Scientist* 6, no. 2 (September 1977): 3–21. http://www.jstor.org/stable/3516681.

Levi, Giovanni. "On Microhistory." In *New Perspectives on Historical Writing*, edited by Peter Burke, 97–119. 2nd ed. Cambridge: Polity Press, 1991.

Lindberg, Anna. *Modernization and Effeminization in India: Kerala Cashew Workers since 1930*. Copenhagen: NIAS Press, 2005.

Lobo, Lancy, and Paul D'Souza. "Images of Violence." *Economic and Political Weekly* 28, no. 5 (1993): 152–54.

Lokaneeta, Jinee. "Sovereignty, Violence and Resistance in North-East India: Mapping Political Theory Today." *Theory and Event* 20, no. 1 (2017): 76–86. https://www.muse.jhu.edu/article/646844.

Lokaneeta, Jinee. *Transnational Torture: Law, Violence and State Power in the United States and India*. New York: New York University Press, 2011.

Lokaneeta, Jinee. *The Truth Machines: Policing, Violence, and Scientific Interrogations in India*. Ann Arbor: University of Michigan Press, 2020.

Lukose, Ritty. "Empty Citizenship: Protesting Politics in the Era of Globalization." *Current Anthropology* 20, no. 4 (2005): 506–33. https://www.jstor.org/stable/3651541.

Lukose, Ritty. *Liberalization's Children: Gender, Youth and Consumer Citizenship in Globalizing India*. Durham, NC: Duke University Press, 2009.

MacCannell, Juliet F. *The Regime of the Brother: After the Patriarchy*. London: Routledge, 1991.

Machiavelli, Niccolò. *The Prince and the Discourses*. Translated by Luigi Ricci. New York: Modern Library, 1959.

Macpherson, C. B. *The Life and Times of Liberal Democracy*. Don Mills, ON: Oxford University Press, 1977.

Mamdani, Mahmood. "Africa: Democratic Theory and Democratic Struggles." *Economic and Political Weekly* 27, no. 1 (1992): 2228–32. https://www.jstor.org/stable/4398993.

Mamdani, Mahmood. "Amnesty or Impunity: A Preliminary Critique of the Report of the Truth and Reconciliation Commission of South Africa." *Diacritics* 32, no. 4 (2002): 32–59. https://www.jstor.org/stable/1566444.

Mamdani, Mahmood. "Beyond Nuremberg: The Historical Significance of the Post-Apartheid Transition in South Africa." *Politics and Society* 43, no. 1 (2015): 61–88.

Mamdani, Mahmood. *Citizen and Subject: Contemporary Africa and the Legacy of Late Colonialism*. Princeton, NJ: Princeton University Press, 1996.

Mamdani, Mahmood. "Lessons of Nuremberg and CODESA: Where Do We Go from Here?" Lecture, Africa Memorial Day, University of the Free State, Bloemfontein, July 2010.

Mamdani, Mahmood. "The Logic of Nuremberg." *London Review of Books* 35, no. 21 (2013).

Mamdani, Mahmood. *Neither Settler Nor Native: The Making and Unmaking of Permanent Minorities*. Cambridge, MA: Belknap Press of Harvard University Press, 2020.

Mander, Harsh, Akram Akhtar Chaudhary, Zafar Eqbal, and Rajanya Bose. "Wages of Communal Violence in Muzaffarnagar and Shamli." *Economic and Political Weekly* 51, no. 43 (October 2016): 39–45.

Manin, Bernard. *The Principles of Representative Government*. Cambridge: Cambridge University Press, 1997.

Mann, Michael. *The Dark Side of Democracy: Explaining Ethnic Cleansing*. Cambridge: University of Cambridge Press, 2005.

Mannathukkaren, Nissim. "The Conjuncture of 'Late Socialism' in Kerala: A Critique of the Narrative of Social Democracy." In *Development, Democracy and the State: Critiquing the Kerala Model of Development*, edited by K. Ravi Raman, 157–75. London: Routledge, 2010.

Mannathukkaren, Nissim. "The Rise of the National-Popular and Its Limits: Communism and the Cultural in Kerala." *Inter-Asia Cultural Studies* 14, no. 4 (2013): 494–518. doi:10.1080/14649373.2013.831160.

Mantena, Karuna. *Alibis of Empire: Henry Maine and the Ends of Liberal Imperialism*. Princeton, NJ: Princeton University Press, 2011.

Mantena, Karuna. "Political Identity and Postcolonial Democracy." Paper presented at On the Subject of Citizenship, Center for Humanities Research at the University of the Western Cape, Cape Town, August 2016.

Manzer, Habib. "The Communist Party and the Communal Question." *Proceedings of the Indian History Congress* 63 (2002): 768–77. http://www.jstor.org/stable/44158146.

Marx, Karl. *The Eighteenth Brumaire of Louis Bonaparte*. Rockville, MD: Serenity Publishers, 2009. First published in 1852 by Die Revolution.

Massumi, Brian. *Parables of the Virtual: Movement, Affect, Sensation*. Durham, NC: Duke University Press, 2002.

Mbembe, Achille. "The Banality of Power and the Aesthetics of Vulgarity in the Postcolony." *Public Culture* 4, no. 2 (1992): 1–30. https://doi.org/10.1215/08992363-4-2-1.

Mbembe, Achille. "On Politics as a Form of Expenditure." In *Law and Disorder in the Postcolony*, edited by Jean Comaroff and John L. Comaroff, 299–336. Chicago: University of Chicago Press, 2006.

Meagher, Kate. "Cultural Primordialism and the Post-Structuralist Imaginaire: Plus Ça Change." Review of *Culture Troubles: Politics and the Interpretation of Meaning* by Patrick Chabal and Jean-Pascal Daloz and *The Illusion of Cultural Identity* by Jean-François Bayart, Steven Rendall, Janet Roitman, and Jonathan Derrick. *Africa: Journal of the International African Institute* 76, no. 4 (2006): 590–97. doi:10.3366/afr.2006.0071.

Menon, Dilip. *Being a Brahmin the Marxist Way: E.M.S. Nambudiripad and the Pasts of Kerala.* New Delhi: Centre for Contemporary Studies, Nehru Memorial Museum and Library, 1998.

Menon, Dilip. *The Blindness of Insight: Essays on Caste in Modern India.* Pondicherry: Navayana Press, 2006.

Menon, Dilip. *Caste, Nationalism, and Communism in South India: Malabar, 1900–1948.* Cambridge: Cambridge University Press, 1994.

Menon, Dilip. "Lost Visions: Imagining a National Culture in the 1950s." 10th Daniel Thorner Memorial Lecture, Hyderabad, 2001.

Menon, Dilip. "A Prehistory of Violence? Revolution and Martyrs in the Making of a Political Tradition in Kerala." *South Asia: Journal of South Asian Studies* 39, no. 3 (2016): 662–77. doi:10.1080/00856401.2016.1195452.

Menon, Nivedita, and Aditya Nigam. *Power and Contestation: India since 1989.* London: Zed Books, 2007.

Mhaskar, Sumeet, and Prabodhan Pol. Review of Satyendra More, *The Memoirs of a Dalit Communist: The Many Worlds of R.B. More. South Asia Multidisciplinary Academic Journal,* no. 26 (2021). https://journals.openedition.org/samaj/7111#toctoin4.

Michelutti, Lucia. *The Vernacularization of Democracy: Politics, Caste, and Religion in India.* New Delhi: Routledge, 2008.

Minow, Martha. *Between Vengeance and Forgiveness: Facing History after Genocide and Mass Violence.* Boston: Beacon Press, 1999.

Misra, S. N. *Indian Penal Code.* Delhi: Central Law Publications, 2004.

Monir, Muhammad, Manjula Batra, and Hemant Kumar Pandey. *Textbook on the Law of Evidence.* New Delhi: Universal Law Publishing Co., 2013.

Moran, Mary H. *Liberia: The Violence of Democracy.* Philadelphia: University of Pennsylvania Press, 2006.

Mouffe, Chantal. *Agonistics: Thinking the World Politically.* London: Verso, 2013.

Mouffe, Chantal. *The Democratic Paradox.* London: Verso, 2000.

Mouffe, Chantal. *The Return of the Political.* London: Verso, 1993.

Mouffe, Chantal. *Thinking in Action.* New York: Routledge, 2005.

Mufti, Aamir. *Enlightenment in the Colony: The Jewish Question and the Crisis of Postcolonial Culture.* Princeton, NJ: Princeton University Press, 2007.

Nair, Neeti. *Changing Homelands: Hindu Politics and the Partition of India.* Cambridge, MA: Harvard University Press, 2011.

Nancy, Jean-Luc. *The Inoperative Community.* Translated by Peter Connor, Lisa Garbus, Michael Holland, and Simona Sawhney. Minneapolis: University of Minnesota Press, 1991.

Narayan, Badri. *The Making of the Dalit Public in North India Uttar Pradesh, 1950–Present*. New Delhi: Oxford University Press, 2011.

Nayanar, E. K. *My Struggles: An Autobiography*. New Delhi: Vikas Publication House, 1982.

Neoclaus, Mark. *The Fabrication of Social Order: A Critical Theory of Police Power*. London: Pluto Press, 2000.

Nietzsche, Friedrich. *On the Genealogy of Morality*. Edited by Keith Ansell Pearson. Cambridge: Cambridge University Press, 1994.

Nietzsche, Friedrich. *On the Genealogy of Morals and Ecce Homo*. Edited by Walter Kaufmann. Translated by Walter Kaufmann and R. J. Hollingdale. New York: Vintage Books, 1967.

Nigam, Aditya. "Democracy, State and Capital: The 'Unthought' of 20th Century Marxism." *Economic and Political Weekly* 44, no. 51 (2009): 35–39. https://www.jstor.org/stable/25663912.

Nigam, Aditya. "Secularism, Modernity, Nation: Epistemology of the Dalit Critique." *Economic and Political Weekly* (November 2000): 4256–68. https://www.jstor.org/stable/4410008.

Nigam, Sanjay. "Disciplining and Policing the 'Criminals by Birth,' Part 1: The Making of a Colonial Stereotype—The Criminal Tribes and Castes of North India." *Indian Economic and Social History Review* 27, no. 2 (1990): 131–64. doi:10.1177/001946469002700201.

Niranjana. *Stars Shine Brightly (Chirasmarana)*. New Delhi: People's Publishing House, 1977.

Nossiter, Thomas Johnson. *Communism in Kerala: A Study in Political Adaptation*. Berkeley: University of California Press, 1982.

Oomen, T. K. *From Mobilization to Institutionalization: The Dynamics of Agrarian Movement in Twentieth Century Kerala*. Bombay: Popular Prakashan, 1985.

Ossella, Fillipo, and Caroline Ossella. *Social Mobility in Kerala: Modernity and Identity in Conflict*. London: Pluto Press, 2000.

Ossome, Lyn. *Gender, Ethnicity, and Violence in Kenya's Transitions to Democracy: States of Violence*. Lanham, MD: Lexington Books, 2018.

Pandey, Gyanendra. *The Construction of Communalism in Colonial North India*. New Delhi: Oxford University Press, 2012.

Pandian, Anand. "Pastoral Power in the Postcolony: On the Biopolitics of the Criminal Animal in South India." *Cultural Anthropology* 23 (2008): 85–117. https://doi.org/10.1111/j.1548-1360.2008.00004.x.

Panikkar, K. N. *Against Lord and State: Religion and Peasant Uprisings in Malabar, 1836–1921*. Delhi: Oxford University Press, 1989.

Pateman, Carole. *The Sexual Contract*. Stanford, CA: Stanford University Press, 1988.

Peirce, Charles S., and James Hoopes. *Peirce on Signs: Writings on Semiotic*. Chapel Hill: University of North Carolina Press, 1991.

Peltonen, Matti. "Clues, Margins, and Monads: The Micro-Macro Link in Historical Research." *History and Theory* 40, no. 3 (2001): 347–59. https://www.jstor.org/stable/2677970.

Piliavsky, Anastasia. "The 'Criminal Tribe' in India before the British." *Comparative Studies in Society and History* 57, no. 2 (2015): 323–54. doi:10.1017/S0010417515000055.

Pillai, K. N. Chandrashekharan, and Shabistan Aqil. *Essays on the Indian Penal Code*. Delhi: Universal Publishing, 2005.

Prabhu, R. K. *Communism and Communists*. Ahmedabad: Navajivan Publishing House, 1959.

Prakash, Gyan. *Emergency Chronicles: Indira Gandhi and Democracy's Turning Point*. Princeton, NJ: Princeton University Press, 2019.

Project 39A. *Death Penalty India Report*. Delhi: National Law University, 2016. https://www.project39a.com/dpir.

Przeworski, Adam. "Divided We Stand? Democracy as a Method of Processing Conflicts." *Scandinavian Political Studies* 34, no. 2 (2011): 168–82. https://doi.org/10.1111/j.1467-9477.2011.00265.x.

Radhakrishnan, P. *Peasant Struggles, Land Reforms, and Social Change: Malabar, 1836–1982*. New Delhi: Sage Publications, 1989.

Radhakrishnan, Ratheesh. "Masculinity and the Structuring of the Public Domain in Kerala: A History of the Contemporary." PhD diss., Manipal Academy of Higher Education, 2006.

Raghavan, M. V. *Oru Janmam*. Thiruvananthapuram: D.C. Books, 2010.

Rajagopalan, Swarna. *Peace Accords in Northeast India: Journey over Milestones*. Washington, DC: East-West Center Washington, 2008.

Rammohan, K. T. "Caste and Landlessness in Kerala: Signals from Chengara." *Economic and Political Weekly* 43, no. 37 (2008): 14–16. https://www.jstor.org/stable/40277941.

Ram-Prasad, C. "Hindutva Ideology: Extracting the Fundamentals." *Contemporary South Asia* 2, no. 3 (1993): 285–309. doi:10.1080/09584939308719718.

Rancière, Jacques. *Disagreement: Politics and Philosophy*. Minneapolis: University of Minnesota Press, 1999.

Rancière, Jacques. *Dissensus: On Politics and Aesthetics*. London: Continuum, 2010.

Rancière, Jacques. "Politics, Identification, Subjectification." *October* 61 (1992): 58–64.

Ranga, N. G. "The Bihar Peasantry and the Kisan Sabha." *International Studies* 23, no. 1 (1986): 75–87. https://doi.org/10.1177/002088178602300100 5.

Rao, Anupama. *The Caste Question: Dalits and the Politics of Modern India*. Berkeley: University of California Press, 2009.

Rao, Anupama. Rejoinder to the book review by Sumeet Mhaskar and Prabodhan Pol of Satyendra More, *The Memoirs of a Dalit Communist: The Many Worlds of R.B. More*, edited and introduced by Anupama Rao. *South Asia Multidisciplinary Academic Journal*, no. 26 (2021). https://journals.openedition.org/samaj/7166.

Ray, Rabindra. *The Naxalites and Their Ideology*. Oxford: Oxford University Press, 2012.

Raychaudhuri, Tapan. "The Land and the People: The Mid-Eighteenth Century Background." In *The Cambridge Economic History of India*, vol. 2, c. *1757–*

c. 1970, edited by Dharma Kumar and Meghnad Desai, 3–35. Cambridge: Cambridge University Press, 1983.

Reddy, Deepa. "Hindutva as Praxis." *Religion Compass* 5 (2011): 412–26. https://doi.org/10.1111/j.1749-8171.2011.00288.x.

Ricoeur, Paul, and Lewis S. Mudge, eds. *Essays on Biblical Interpretation*. Philadelphia: Fortress Press, 1981.

Rosanvallon, Pierre. *Democratic Legitimacy: Impartiality, Reflexivity and Proximity*. Translated by Arthur Goldhammer. Princeton, NJ: Princeton University Press, 2011.

Rose, Nikolas. "Governing by Numbers: Figuring out Democracy." *Accounting, Organizations and Society* 16, no. 7 (1991): 673–92. https://doi.org/10.1016/0361-3682(91)90019-B.

Saikumar, Rajgopal. "'To Shock the Conscience': Rhetoric in Death Penalty Judgements of the Supreme Court of India." *South Asia: Journal of South Asian Studies* 42, no. 4 (2019): 694–710. doi:10.1080/00856401.2019.1616246.

Sam, Jillet Sarah. "Place and Caste Identification: Distanciation and Spatial Imaginaries on a Caste-Based Social Network." PhD diss., University of Maryland, 2014.

Sarkar, Sumit. *Modern India, 1885–1947*. Delhi: Macmillan, 1983.

Sarkar, Tanika. "Woman as Communal Subject: Rashtrasevika Samiti and Ram Janmabhoomi Movement." *Economic and Political Weekly* 26, no. 35 (1991): 2057–62. https://www.jstor.org/stable/41498633.

Satyanarayana, A. "Rise and Growth of the Left Movement in Andhra, 1934–1939." *Social Scientist* 14, no. 1 (1986): 34–47. https://doi.org/10.2307/3520420.

Schmitt, Carl. *The Concept of the Political*. Chicago: University of Chicago Press, 2007.

Scott, David. *Refashioning Futures: Criticism after Postcoloniality*. Princeton, NJ: Princeton University Press, 1999.

Sen, Atreyee. *Shiv Sena Women: Violence and Communalism in a Bombay Slum*. London: Hurst and Company, 2007.

Sen Gupta, Bhabhani. *Communism in Indian Politics*. New York: Columbia University Press, 1972.

Seshadri-Crooks, Kalpana. "I Am a Master: Terrorism, Masculinity, and Political Violence in Frantz Fanon." *Parallax* 8, no. 2 (2002): 84–98. https://doi.org/10.1080/13534640210130430.

Sharda, Ratan. *RSS 360: Demystifying Rashtriya Swayamsevak Sangh*. New Delhi: Bloomsbury, 2018.

Singh, Gurharpal. *Ethnic Conflict in India: A Case-Study of Punjab*. New York: St. Martin's Press, 2000.

Singh, Ujjwal K. *The State, Democracy and Anti-Terror Laws in India*. New Delhi: Sage, 2007.

Singha, Radhika. "Criminal Communities." In *Crime through Time*, edited by Anupama Rao and Saurabh Dube, 58–79. New Delhi: Oxford University Press, 2013.

Singha, Radhika. *A Despotism of Law: Crime and Justice in Early Colonial India.* New York: Oxford University Press, 1998.

Singha, Radhika. "'Providential' Circumstances: The Thuggee Campaign of the 1830s and Legal Innovation." *Modern Asian Studies* 27, no. 1 (1993): 83–146. doi:10.1017/S0026749X00016085.

Singha, Radhika. "Punished by Surveillance: Policing 'Dangerousness' in Colonial India, 1872–1918." *Modern Asian Studies* 49, no. 2 (2015): 241–69. doi:10.1017/S0026749X13000462.

Skaria, Ajay. "Relinquishing Republican Democracy: Gandhi's *Ramarajya.*" *Postcolonial Studies* 14, no. 2 (2011): 203–29. https://doi.org/10.1080 /13688790.2011.563459.

Sonavane, Nikita, and Ameya Bokil. "How Poverty-Struck Tribals Become 'Habitual Offenders.'" *Article 14*, May 28, 2020. https://www.article-14.com/post /born-a-criminal-how-poverty-struck-tribals-become-habitual-offenders.

Spencer, Jonathan. *Anthropology, Politics and the State: Democracy and Violence in South Asia.* Cambridge: Cambridge University Press, 2007.

Sportel, Terah. "Agency within a Socially Regulated Labour Market: A Study of 'Unorganised' Agricultural Labour in Kerala." *Geoforum* 47 (2013): 42–52. https://doi.org/10.1016/j.geoforum.2013.02.007.

Sreerekha, M. S. "Challenges before Kerala's Landless: The Story of Aralam Farm." *Economic and Political Weekly* 45, no. 21 (2010): 55–62. https://www .jstor.org/stable/27807051.

Steur, Luisa. *Indigenist Mobilization: Confronting Electoral Communism and Precarious Livelihoods in Post-Reform Kerala.* Hyderabad: Orient Black Swan, 2017.

Stewart, Kathleen. *Ordinary Affects.* Durham, NC: Duke University Press, 2007.

Stokes, Eric. *The English Utilitarians and India.* Oxford: Clarendon Press, 1959.

Sunder Rajan, Rajeshwari. *The Scandal of the State: Women, Law and Citizenship in Postcolonial India.* Durham, NC: Duke University Press, 2003.

Suresh, Mayur. "The Slow Erosion of Fundamental Rights: How Romila Thapar v. Union of India Highlights What Is Wrong with the UAPA." *Indian Law Review* 3, no. 2 (2019): 212–23. doi:10.1080/24730580.2019.1640593.

Talbot, I. A. "The 1946 Punjab Elections." *Modern Asian Studies* 14, no. 1 (1980): 65–91. http://www.jstor.org/stable/312214.

Tambiah, Stanley J. *Leveling Crowds: Ethnonationalist Conflicts and Collective Violence in South Asia.* Berkeley: University of California Press, 1997.

Teltumbde, Anand. *Khairlanji: A Strange and Bitter Crop.* New Delhi: Navayana, 2008.

Thachil, Tariq. *Elite Parties, Poor Voters: How Social Services Win Votes in India.* Cambridge: Cambridge University Press, 2016.

Thomassen, Bjorn. "Schismogenesis and Schismogenetic Processes: Gregory Bateson Reconsidered." Paper presented at the Social Pathologies of Contemporary Civilization Conference organized by the Danish Center of Philosophy and Science Studies, Aalborg, October 2010. https://forskning

.ruc.dk/en/publications/schismogenesis-and-schismogenetic-processes
-gregory-bateson-recon.

Tomlinson, Yolande. "To Fanon, with Love: Women Writers of the African Diaspora Interrupting Violence, Masculinity, and Nation-Formation." PhD diss., Emory University, 2010.

Trivellato, F. "Is There a Future for Italian Microhistory in the Age of Global History?" *California Italian Studies* 2, no. 1 (2011). https://escholarship.org /uc/item/0z94n9hq.

Tronto, Joan C. *Who Cares? How to Reshape a Democratic Politics.* Ithaca, NY: Cornell Selects, 2015.

Tuck, Richard. *The Sleeping Sovereign: The Invention of Modern Democracy.* Cambridge: Cambridge University Press, 2016.

Ullekh, N. P. *Kannur: Inside India's Bloodiest Revenge Politics.* New Delhi: Penguin, 2018.

Valentine, Daniel E. *Charred Lullabies: Chapters in an Anthropography of Violence.* Princeton, NJ: Princeton University Press, 1996.

Valentine, Daniel E. *Fluid Signs: Being a Person the Tamil Way.* Berkeley: University of California Press, 1984.

Valiani, Arafaat A. *Militant Publics in India: Physical Culture and Violence in the Making of a Modern Polity.* New York: Palgrave Macmillan, 2011.

Valiani, Arafaat A. "Physical Training, Ethical Discipline, and Creative Violence: Zones of Self-Mastery in the Hindu Nationalist Movement." *Cultural Anthropology* 25 (2010): 73–99. https://doi.org/10.1111/j.1548-1360.2009.01052.x.

Weiner, Myron. *Party Politics in India: The Development of a Multi-Party System.* Princeton, NJ: Princeton University Press, 1957.

Wenman, Mark. "'Agonistic Pluralism' and Three Archetypal Forms of Politics." *Contemporary Political Theory* 2 (2003): 165–86. https://doi.org/10.1057 /palgrave.cpt.9300091.

White, Luise. "Telling More: Lies, Secrets and History." *History and Theory* 39, no. 4 (2000): 11–22. https://www.jstor.org/stable/2678047.

Wilce, James M. *Eloquence in Trouble: The Poetics and Politics of Complaint in Rural Bangladesh.* New York: Oxford University Press, 1998.

Wilkinson, Steven I. *Votes and Violence: Electoral Competition and Ethnic Riots in India.* Cambridge: Cambridge University Press, 2009.

Wright, Barry. "Macaulay's Indian Penal Code: Historical Context and Originating Principles." In *Codification, Macaulay and the Indian Penal Code: The Legacies and Modern Challenges of Criminal Law Reform,* edited by Wing-Cheong Chan, Barry Wright, and Stanley Yeo, 19–58. London: Routledge, 2016.

Zagoria, Donald S. "The Ecology of Peasant Communism in India." *American Political Science Review* 65, no. 1 (March 1971): 144–60. https://doi.org/10 .2307/1955050.

Zavos, John. *The Emergence of Hindu Nationalism in India.* New Delhi: Oxford University Press, 2000.

judicial responsibility, 21, 113; cognition and, 148, 150, 152, 153, 155–57, 161; criminal responsibility, 62, 128, 132; individuation, 22, 94, 144, 145; individuation and collectivization of responsibility, 22, 23, 144; K. G. Kannabiran, 120, 215; methodological individualism, 22, 117. *See also* Lacey, Nicola

jurisprudence of suspicion, 138, 147, 152, 157

justice, 20, 21, 23, 140, 142, 147, 153, 161, 165; definition of, 21; injustice, 5, 47, 48, 145, 146, 157. *See also* criminal justice system

Kannur, x–xv, 1–5, 8, 12–19, 21–23, 27–29, 46, 47, 51, 57–59, 60, 63–73, 76–80, 84–86, 89, 94, 101, 106, 109–11, 116–18, 122, 124, 127–29, 131, 132, 136, 143, 145, 148, 157, 159–63, 166, 171, 174n1, 175n2, 181n64, 183nn73–74; Hindu right in, x, xi, xiii, xv, 2, 14, 27, 59, 62, 93, 117, 122, 137, 138, 169; political violence in, xiii, 13, 15, 23, 27, 57, 60, 62, 93, 139, 147, 148, 182n72

Kaviraj, Sudipta, 5, 176n13

Kerala Congress, 30, 31

Kerala Dinesh Beedi, 75, 79, 81

Khan, Syed Ahmed, 12, 170

Kumar, Udaya, 20, 40

Kurup, P. R., 30, 33, 41, 46–53, 57, 65, 66, 70, 77, 81–85; *Ente Nadinte Katha, Enteyum*, 29, 186n7

Lacey, Nicola, 152, 153

land redistribution, 11, 18, 32, 82; *Tebhaga* agitations, 32

land reform, 33, 81, 203n86; Land Reform (Amendment) Act, 202n85

Lefort, Claude, 9, 11, 180n44

local-level workers, xv, 2, 13, 16, 21, 22, 28, 34, 58, 64, 67, 79, 81, 84, 86, 89, 92, 96, 110, 112, 118, 121, 122, 129, 144, 145, 160, 161, 169; definition of, 2

Lokaneeta, Jinee, 119, 137, 138, 213n28

love, 20, 59, 85, 90, 96–98, 108, 162, 169; *sneha bandham* (bonds of love), 94, 96; *sneham*, 85, 96, 97, 108

lower castes, 10, 13, 17, 22, 23, 30, 32, 35, 36, 62, 122, 152, 161, 165, 185n1, 207n12, 215n1, 217n28

MacCannell, Juliet, 20, 85, 184n87, 204n96

majoritarian agenda, 3, 168

majoritarian aspirations, 4, 88, 90, 94, 97

majoritarian assertions, 22, 122

majoritarianism, xv, 3, 12, 20, 86, 87, 112, 169, 170, 171; definition of, 3

majoritarian violence, 15, 119, 123, 127, 181n64

majority, xi–xv, 1, 3, 13, 21, 22, 28, 29, 42, 44, 45, 50, 51, 77, 87, 90, 91, 122, 127, 128, 146, 168, 176n10; majority principle, 7, 12, 166

majority rule, 4, 8, 11, 170, 171, 181n60; Qadri Ismail, 4; numerical majority, 10, 23, 57, 112. *See also* Ambedkar, B. R.; Gandhi, Mahatma; Khan, Syed Ahmed; Scott, David

Malabar, 30, 36, 40–45, 51, 182n73, 183n74, 187n14, 189n31, 192n76, 194n120; Malabar Special Police (MSP), 31, 188n27; North Malabar, 35, 37, 182n73

Mamdani, Mahmood, 120, 183n75, 211n3

marginal communities, 119, 181n70

martial culture, 15, 16, 52, 182n73, 183n74; martial history, 15, 205n99

masculinity, 18, 25, 40, 65, 92, 112, 163. *See also* political masculinity

mass action, 30, 37–39, 43, 53, 73, 190–91n57

Menon, Dilip, 32, 33, 190n38

mens rea, 117, 150, 151, 157, 216n7, 217n24

micro-sequences, 21, 130, 131, 143

minoritization, xiv, xv, 3, 109, 112, 119, 142, 159, 171; definition of, 3; minoritized communities, 22; minoritizing the opposition, 97, 116; Aamir Mufti, 4